Maladies of the Indian Banking Sector

The global financial crisis of 2007–09 highlighted the importance of capital structure for the economy as a whole and for individual firms as well. The ensuing credit and profitability crunch due to the contraction of the global economy made it vitally imperative to understand how the capital structure choices of the firms are affected and what impact these choices have on the functioning of the markets. Since, like in most emerging countries, the capital structure of Indian firms is dominated by bank borrowing, it has become important to understand the role of bank borrowing in a larger context.

Maladies of the Indian Banking Sector provides an in-depth analysis of bank credit allocation to non-financial companies in the Indian corporate sector over a long period of 28 years. The authors also conduct a micro-level analysis in the backdrop of recent banking scams in the country which exposed the fragility and quality of the banks' governance in reducing misappropriation of bank credit. The book brings a broader perspective to assess whether weak banks are rolling over their loans to less-deserving firms and tending to avoid declaring them as non-performing assets (NPAs). It contributes to understanding the nature of the maladies beyond the conventional approach of studying the trends in NPAs and provides a deeper insight into the structural challenges that determine the allocation of bank credit in the economy and of capital formation at large.

Saumitra N. Bhaduri is Professor at the Madras School of Economics, Chennai. His research interests include economic policy analysis, quantitative research, and corporate finance.

Ekta Selarka is Associate Professor at the Madras School of Economics, Chennai. Her research interests include corporate governance, ownership structure, capital market development, and corporate performance.

Maladies of the Indian Banking Sector

A Critical Perspective beyond NPAs

Saumitra N. Bhaduri

Ekta Selarka

CAMBRIDGE
UNIVERSITY PRESS

University Printing House, Cambridge CB2 8BS, United Kingdom

One Liberty Plaza, 20th Floor, New York, NY 10006, USA

477 Williamstown Road, Port Melbourne, vic 3207, Australia

314 to 321, 3rd Floor, Plot No.3, Splendor Forum, Jasola District Centre, New Delhi 110025, India

103 Penang Road, #05–06/07, Visioncrest Commercial, Singapore 238467

Cambridge University Press is part of the University of Cambridge.

It furthers the University's mission by disseminating knowledge in the pursuit of education, learning and research at the highest international levels of excellence.

www.cambridge.org
Information on this title: www.cambridge.org/9781009225465

First published 2022

Printed in India by Avantika Printers Pvt. Ltd.

A catalogue record for this publication is available from the British Library

ISBN 978-1-009-22546-5 Hardback

In loving memory of my father
—Saumitra N. Bhaduri

Contents

Figures

Tables

Foreword

Dr Saumitra N. Bhaduri and Dr Ekta Selarka have written an extremely valuable book on the performance of Indian banking. The Indian banking system is currently passing through an extremely difficult phase. The non-performing asset (NPA) ratio has reached a very high level. This has its own impact not only on profitability of banks but on their entire functioning. What has led to this situation? Bhaduri and Selarka go beyond NPAs and analyse one key question of how well the banks have performed their major responsibility of allocating resources efficiently. The book is an eye-opener for understanding the NPA malady haunting Indian banks.

In any economy, the financial sector plays a major role in the mobilization and allocation of savings. Financial institutions, instruments, and markets which constitute the financial sector act as a conduit for the transfer of financial resources from net savers to net borrowers – that is, from those who spend less than they earn to those who earn less than they spend. The financial sector performs this basic economic function of intermediation essentially through four transformation mechanisms: liability–asset transformation, size transformation, maturity transformation, and risk transformation. The process of financial intermediation supports increasing capital accumulation through the institutionalization of savings and investment and, as such, fosters economic growth. The gains to the real sector of the economy, therefore, depend on how efficiently the financial sector performs this basic function of financial intermediation. Thus, a critical function of banks is one of allocating the resources raised through deposits efficiently – that is, loans being given to those borrowers who rank higher in terms of productivity of capital.

The period from 2005–06 to 2010–11 was marked by an extraordinary increase in the provision of credit by the banking system. This also coincided with a boom in real economy. The Indian economy grew at an average annual rate of 8 per cent during this period. What started as a 'rational' exuberance became an 'irrational' exuberance of lending. To study whether there has been a misallocation of resources, the authors compute what we call an 'index of credit allocative efficiency'. Their conclusions are staggering. They find a high degree of misallocation of resources. They show that non-deserving borrowers gained more credit than the deserving ones. Extension of credit to low-quality firms indicates, according to them, 'a lack of judgement and negligence'. The study also provides a decomposition of the index to explore size-wise and industry-wise misallocation of resources. They also report that the average share of 'zombie' firms in long-term bank lending increased three times in the post-2010 period. According to them, nearly 45 per cent of total borrowing during the credit-boom period was captured by firms that turned 'zombies' later. They conclude: 'It is noteworthy to mention here, that absence of proper legal framework, low recovery rate, and substantial involvement of the public sector banks have escalated the problem of zombie lending and has given rise to India's NPA crisis in the Indian banking sector.' The authors actually studied the misallocation associated with project lending. Perhaps what they have concluded may apply to short-term credit as well. Of course, the experience of banks in providing long-term credit began only in the post-liberalization period.

Recapitalizing public sector banks in the wake of the NPA crisis is only a partial solution. It only takes care of the damage already done. To avoid falling into the same trap, we need to understand the factors that have contributed to the rise in the NPA ratio. Misallocation of resources, which essentially means preferring 'weak' borrowers over 'strong' borrowers, cuts at the very root of good banking. Bhaduri and Selarka have written a scholarly book which should be of great help to banks and policy makers. I commend this book to everybody interested in the strengthening of the banking system in our country.

C. Rangarajan
Former Chairman, Economic Advisory Council to the Prime Minister
Former Governor, Reserve Bank of India

Chairman, Madras School of Economics
Gandhi Mandapam Road, Kottur
Chennai 600025

Acknowledgements

This book is an outcome of a research project funded by the Indian Council of Social Science Research (ICSSR), New Delhi (F. No. Gen-39/2017-18/ICSSR/RPS). We sincerely thank the ICSSR for the project grant and, specifically, Revathy Vishwanath for her support throughout the project. We thank the anonymous referee for the detailed comments that helped us to significantly improve the presentation of our work. We gratefully acknowledge the insightful discussions and constructive feedback from the members of ICSSR Advisory Committee: M. H. Surynarayana, M. R. Murthy, and Satish Verma.

We also thank Bipin Sony, Anindita Chakraborty, and Aishwarya K. for providing excellent research assistance.

We extend our sincere gratitude to honourable C. Rangarajan for his appreciation and for penning a foreword for our book.

Comments from the participants of seminar series at the Madras School of Economics, Chennai, and the International Conference on Macroeconomics and Finance at the Indira Gandhi Institute of Development Research (IGIDR), Mumbai, are gratefully acknowledged.

Our sincere thanks to Anwesha Rana at Cambridge University Press for taking interest in our research, for her patience and guidance throughout the completion of this book, and to Priyanka Das for guiding us through the publication process.

Last but not the least, Ekta Selarka gratefully acknowledges the unending patience and support from Reva and Devang over the course of this project.

1

Prologue

The nexus between financial development and economic growth has been the subject of considerable debate. There are two important competing views on the relationship between finance and growth. According to the first view, prevalent in the early 19th century, enterprise leads and finance follows, implying that the financial system does not have a leading role in growth. In contrast, the other view stresses on the complementarities between development and capital formation, particularly the role of banks in financing investment in physical capital and growth. An early study by Schumpeter (1911) highlighted the importance of financial intermediaries in mobilizing savings, evaluating projects, diversifying risks, monitoring the management of firms in debt, and facilitating transactions which are essential for innovation and economic growth. Since Schumpeter put forward his view, a considerable amount of theoretical and empirical literature has emerged. The notable early works on finance and development along the Schumpeterian lines include Gurley and Shaw (1955), Goldsmith (1969), and Hicks (1969). These studies argue that the development of a financial system is crucially important in stimulating economic growth and underdeveloped financial systems retard economic growth.

In contrast to Schumpeter's view, the prevalent view held by many economists in the 19th century endorsed Robinson's (1952) famous proposition that 'where enterprise leads, finance follows', suggesting a passive view that as opportunities arise in an economy that needs financing, the economy develops the necessary markets and institutions to finance these opportunities. In a different approach, Tobin (1965), based on the theoretical works of Keynes (1936), argued for financial repression by keeping the interest rate artificially low through government interventions. However, McKinnon (1974) and Shaw (1974) eventually challenged the paradigm of financial repression, emphasizing the complementarities between financial development and capital accumulation, and highlighted the distorting effects of financial repression in developing economies. They further argued that financial repression due to widespread government intervention in credit markets is often growth-reducing. Their approach, however, found only mixed empirical support and failed to explain the sustained increases in the growth rate of many economies.

Further, in the early 1980s, neo-structuralists (Taylor, 1983; Van Wijnbergen, 1982, 1983a, 1983b) criticized the McKinnon-Shaw school and predicted that financial liberalization slows down growth. Stiglitz (1989) criticized financial liberalization on the ground of market failures in financial markets.

However, the literature of the 1980s witnessed a return to Schumpeter's view and emphasized the role of financial development in generating sustained economic growth through an external effect on aggregate investment efficiency. Following Schumpeter's line of reasoning, King and Levine (1993) proposed an endogenous growth model that emphasized the role of innovation. They argued that financial markets direct savings to their most productive uses and diversify the risks associated with these activities, enhancing the probability of successful innovation and the speed of technological progress. Levine (1997) argues that by facilitating the allocation of resources, monitoring managers, exerting corporate control, and mobilizing savings, the financial system fosters capital accumulation. Further, it enhances productivity growth through trading, hedging, diversifying, and pooling of risk.

Finally, the empirical evidence, by and large, finds positive associations between financial development and economic growth and has become a stylized fact. However, the evidence suggests enormous heterogeneity across countries, regions, financial factors, and directions of causality.[1] The Indian experience with financial reforms primarily indicates increased financial fragility as the stock market saw an unprecedented boom and credit squeeze for commodity-producing sectors and the small-scale industry. Despite the financial deepening that resulted from liberalization, these effects have adversely affected the economic growth of the country (Chandrasekhar and Pal, 2006). Studies revealed that an initial spurt in industrial growth immediately after liberalization led to a significant reduction in capacity expansion as a proportion of usage of funds (Bhaduri and Bhattacharya, 2018). In a more recent study, Bhaduri and Bhattacharya (2018) argued that liberalization increased the disassociation between capital formation and value-added by industry. These observations raise concerns about the efficient allocation of capital by the industry in the liberalized regime.

Role of Banks in Financial Intermediation

The banking sector, particularly in emerging economies, plays an essential role in financial intermediation by efficiently allocating funds from savers to borrowers, reducing the cost of obtaining information about both savings and borrowing opportunities, thus leading to economic growth and improvement in the overall efficiency. Despite the waves of capital market reforms witnessed by many economies in the last few decades, the banks provided a significantly large proportion of external financing. Especially in most emerging markets, the share of bank assets in the aggregate financial sector comprises well over 80 per cent of total financial sector assets, which is much lower (around 40 per cent) in the developed economies. Deposits as a share of total bank liabilities have declined since 1990 in many developed countries, while in developing countries public deposits continue to be dominant in banks. In India, the share of banking assets in total financial sector assets is around 75 per cent. Another critical aspect of the Indian banking sector has been the significant participation of the government through public sector banks (PSBs). The total asset share of India's banking market was INR 150 trillion in 2020 out of which PSBs had the largest share – that is, INR 107 trillion (around 70 per cent). However, this sector constitutes the smallest share in terms of number – 12 as of 2021. According to the latest data released by the Reserve Bank of India (RBI), only in recent years, the market share of PSBs in loans has dipped to 59.8 per cent in 2020 from 74.28 per cent in 2015, while private banks' share has surged to 36.04 per cent from 21.26 per cent during this period.

On the supply side, the banking sector also dominates in terms of mobilizing resources from the household sector and channelizing them to various sectors in the economy. As shown by recent estimates, 52.7 per cent of household savings are parked with commercial banks. On the demand side, 75.2 per cent of household sector liabilities are held in commercial banks (Reserve Bank of India, 2020). In addition, the banking sector contributes heavily to the corporate sector as about 90 per cent of commercial credit is channelized by scheduled commercial banks. As shown in Figure 1.1, post-financial liberalization bank borrowings as a proportion of total assets for non-financial and non-utility firms increased sharply. Despite the capital market development since liberalization, the capital structure of Indian firms remains dominated by bank borrowing, and, therefore, it becomes imperative to understand the role of bank borrowing in a larger context.

A similar trend also emerges for the proportion of bank borrowing to these companies' total borrowings (Figure 1.2).

The theoretical literature widely recognizes the role of bank credit in influencing corporate strategy and firm performance through several facets that include

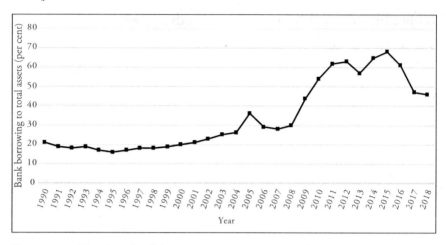

Figure 1.1   Trends in bank borrowing as a proportion of total assets of non-financial companies

Source: Authors' calculations using Centre for Monitoring Indian Economy (CMIE) Prowess.

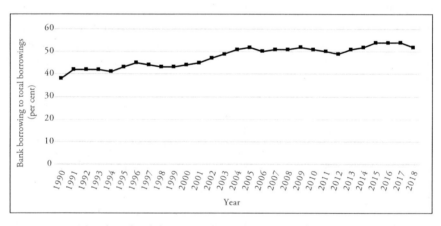

Figure 1.2   Trends in bank borrowing as a proportion of total borrowings of non-financial companies

Source: Authors' calculations using Centre for Monitoring Indian Economy (CMIE) Prowess.

monitoring, screening of creditworthy firms, and reducing information costs incurred by firms. Proposing the theory of delegated monitoring, Diamond (1984) argued that delegated monitoring is cheaper and yields better results than individuals independently monitoring a borrower by minimizing the various costs involved in the process of monitoring. Specifically, bank monitoring reduces the risk by mitigating moral hazards and adverse selection problems due to informational asymmetries between the firm and lenders. Banks screen the loan applications of prospective clients to assess the creditworthiness of the firms (Diamond, 1989), which also facilitates reputation-building for the firms that acquire bank loans. This reputation of creditworthiness further helps the firms raise funds from public markets in the future (Diamond, 1991).

Further, the problem of moral hazard is minimized as banks direct investment decisions using forceful tools of intervention such as the threat not to renew credit (Stiglitz and Weiss, 1983). Such a threat can lead to a reduction of opportunistic incentives, which compels managers to be productive and ensures that they align their incentives with those of the shareholders and positively impact the firm's market value (Grossman and Hart, 1982). Highlighting the cost of information, Fama (1985) argued that public debt financing involves incurring information costs, and these costs can be avoided by bank loan financing as firms would not have to disclose information to the public, thereby reducing the risk of private information being revealed to rival firms (Yosha, 1995). The reduction in such disclosure costs is likely to enhance firm performance. Finally, as Sharpe (1990) suggests, a bank's (own) reputation reduces inefficient resource allocation. When banks efficiently mobilize and allocate funds, this lowers the cost of capital to firms, boosts capital formation, and stimulates productivity growth (Levine, 2005).[2]

However, it is also important to note that empirical evidence of the role of bank credit in firm performance remains mixed, suggesting a significant heterogeneity in findings across the institutional and regulatory environment (Laeven and Levine, 2009). Therefore, the impact of bank credit on firm performance remains an empirical question and could be resolved only through country-specific studies.

In this research, we provide a comprehensive analysis of bank credit allocation to non-financial listed companies in the Indian corporate sector over a long period of 28 years. India serves as a natural choice to conduct our research as it is among the world's largest emerging economies with a bank-dominated financial intermediation system. Financial liberalization in the early 1990s and the subsequent reforms have created an extensive banking system in India. Despite a vibrant equity market and various debt instruments to raise capital, banks remain the preferred avenue for sourcing funds. The banking sector accounts for 63 per cent of household savings and contributes close to 50 per cent of the total flow of resources to the Indian corporate sector as of March 2018. In addition, 80 per cent of the money supply is handled by the banking sector.

The Indian economy witnessed rapid progress during the post-reform period, with the average growth rate of real gross domestic product (GDP) remaining high at 6.4 per cent and 8.8 per cent during the 1990s and 2003–08, reflecting the success of financial sector reforms.[3] Table 1.1 presents the performance of the banking sector until the effects of the global financial crisis (GFC) started appearing in the Indian economy in 2009. As shown in the table, average credit–deposit ratio of banks increased from slightly less than 50 per cent in the second half of the 1990s to 71 per cent by March 2009, reflecting the impact of financial sector reforms and the changes in monetary policy, such as the reduction of statutory liquidity requirement and cash reserve ratio (CRR) and softening of interest rates. However, the growth of credit did not show the deterioration in asset quality as the management of non-performing assets (NPAs) showed significant improvement. The gross NPAs as a percentage of advances declined from about 18 per cent in 1995–96 to 1.7 per cent in 2008–09. As shown in Table 1.1, financial indicators of the banking sector witnessed a significant improvement as the net interest

Table 1.1   Performance indicators of the Indian banking sector in 1996–2009

Year	GNPA ratio	ROA	NIM	Credit deposit rate	CRAR
1996	18.12	−0.43	4.76	50.72	8.76
1997	18.53	0.47	5.79	47.54	9.21
1998	17.04	0.71	4.28	47.25	11.13
1999	16.35	0.43	3.87	46.35	11.24
2000	14.2	0.54	3.33	47.3	11.42
2001	12.72	0.38	3.37	48.45	11.38
2002	11.39	0.73	2.72	50.57	11.45
2003	9.87	1.01	2.97	51.41	12.47
2004	7.58	1.22	2.92	51.87	13.13
2005	5.38	0.85	2.78	56.83	12.54
2006	3.87	0.77	2.57	64.88	12.11
2007	2.55	0.84	2.79	69.15	12.21
2008	1.93	0.86	2.66	71.04	11.93
2009	1.74	0.89	3.04	71.29	13.34

Source: Reserve Bank of India, *Handbook of Statistics on Indian Economy*, various editions.

margins (NIM) hovered around 3 per cent with capital to risk (weighted) assets ratio (CRAR) above 12 per cent in 2003–04.

Therefore, until 2010, particularly immediately before the unprecedented credit bubble of 2003–04, the optimism about Indian economic growth portends well for the Indian banking sector. A spectacular growth rate, coupled with an increase in profitability, had led to an impressive performance of the Indian banking sector. On the supply side, the banks also witnessed a significant increase in deposits during the same period. Due to multiple scams[4] in the capital market and the collapse of the Unit Trust of India's (UTI's) US-64 scheme, a significant part of the household savings moved towards the banking sector as the share of bank deposits in the household savings increased from 31.9 per cent in 1990–91 to 44 per cent during 2003–04 to 2006–07. This is consistent with many studies focusing on country-level financial reforms, which show that the financial liberalization process is positively associated with increased bank credit (McKinnon, 1974; Shaw, 1974; Beck, Levine, and Loayza, 2000; Ueda, 2006).

However, the situation changed significantly after the GFC of 2008, particularly after 2010. Over the last decade (2010–20), the Indian banking sector faced significant challenges in terms of the mounting burden of the NPAs (Figure 1.2). The severity of this problem is alarming because the ratio of NPAs to total advances increased from 2.5 per cent in 2010 to 11.5 per cent in March 2018, thereby eroding the banks' capital base and drying up the credit availability in the market.

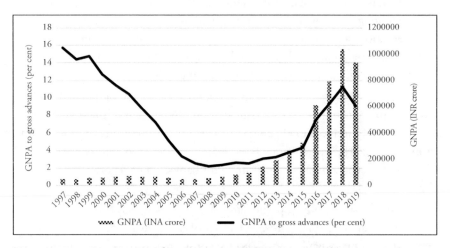

Figure 1.3   Gross non-performing assets (GNPAs) across all banks in India – amount and ratio

Source: Reserve Bank of India, *Handbook of Statistics on the Indian Economy*, 2020.

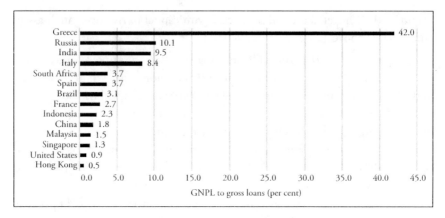

Figure 1.4   Proportion of non-performing loans to gross loans among selected countries in 2018

Source: World Bank, https://data.worldbank.org.

As shown in Figure 1.2, the bad loans on the books of Indian banks surged to INR 10 trillion from INR 0.56 trillion in 2007–08.

Figure 1.3 presents a proportion of non-performing loans to gross loans across selected countries to capture the global context of bad loans. It shows that during 2018 non-performing loans in India translated to approximately 9.5 per cent of all loans disbursed. It is evident from Figure 1.3 that India's NPA ratio is one of the highest among the comparable countries, with only Greece and Russia reporting a higher ratio. More recently, concerns over India's high stock of bad loans gained the International Monetary Fund's (IMF) attention, which ranked India 33 among 137 nations with a bad NPA ratio in descending order.

Moreover, while the PSBs account for around 70 per cent of the total banking assets, their contribution to bad loans is about 86 per cent of the total NPAs in India's banking sector. Table 1.2 presents the NPA ratios for major Indian banks as of March 2018. As seen from Table 1.2, most PSBs had a gross NPA ratio of above 10 per cent compared to private sector banks, which reported a ratio below 5 per cent.

The steady rise in NPAs, particularly after 2015–16, was because of the RBI undertaking an asset quality review (AQR) of banks in 2015, which led to the recognition of many bank loans as NPAs, considered by banks as standard assets till then. Further, according to a financial stability report by the RBI, the Covid-19 pandemic's impact has pushed up the ratio of gross NPAs in the Indian banking system to at least 12.5 per cent in March 2021, from 8.5 per cent in March 2020.

Table 1.2 Gross non-performing assets (NPAs) across all banks in India (INR crore)

S. No.	Name of the bank	NPA ratio	S. No.	Name of the bank	NPA ratio
1	IndusInd Bank Ltd.	1.17	14	State Bank of India	10.91
2	Yes Bank Ltd.	1.28	15	Punjab & Sind Bank	11.19
3	HDFC Bank Ltd.	1.30	16	Syndicate Bank	11.53
4	RBL Bank Ltd.	1.40	17	Canara Bank	11.84
5	DCB Bank Ltd.	1.79	18	Union Bank of India	15.73
6	Kotak	2.22	19	Allahabad Bank	15.96
7	Federal Bank Ltd.	3.00	20	Oriental Bank	17.63
8	IDFC Bank Ltd.	3.31	21	Punjab National Bank	18.38
9	South Indian Bank	3.59	22	Bank Of Maharashtra	19.48
10	Karnataka Bank	4.92	23	Central Bank of India	21.48
11	Vijaya Bank	6.34	24	Dena Bank	22.04
12	Axis Bank Ltd.	6.77	25	UCO Bank	24.64
13	Indian Bank	7.37	26	ICICI Bank Ltd.	8.84

Source: CARE Ratings, 'Report on NPAs of Banks', 15 May 2018, https://www.careratings.com/uploads/newsfiles/NPA%20Update%20March%202018.pdf. Accessed on 8 March 2021.

Since most of the NPAs were contributed by the PSBs, the crisis deteriorated even further as the government continued trying to bolster the books of the PSBs through equity capital infusion and other measures. The government has progressively stepped up its capital infusion in state-owned banks, with INR 3.8 lakh crores infused between 2011 and 2020. To put this number in perspective, the bank recapitalization bill from 2018 to 2020 stands around INR 2.56 lakh crores, double the amount invested in the first 45 years (estimated to be around INR 1.5 lakh crores) since the country's banks were nationalized.[5] In addition, the government sought parliamentary approval to infuse a further INR 200 billion (USD 2.72 billion) in state-run banks in the 2020–21 period to help lenders mitigate the expected surge in bad loans due to the pandemic.

While in any normal business, higher profits are expected to accrue from greater allocation of capital, PSBs continued to report losses as the government was persistent in its capital infusion in state-owned banks, mainly due to rising NPAs requiring banks to set aside a portion of their profits towards provisions and write-offs. As a result, state-owned banks reported a steady decline in profit from a high of INR 45,849 crores in 2012–13 to a collective loss of over INR 66,000 crores in 2019, nearly double the nation's budgetary allocation for education. Further, total provisions made during 2018 increased to a staggering 141 per cent, from INR 43,611 crores to INR 105,150 crores (CARE Ratings, 2018).

Notably, there are two disquieting aspects of India's recent NPA crisis: first, around three-fourths of the overall default originated in the industry (that is, corporate defaults). Second, the concentration of defaulted loans was in the hands of a few large corporations operating in the energy, steel, and infrastructure sectors. Table 1.3 presents the stressed debt by the top 12 loan defaulters filed with the National Company Law Tribunal (NCLT) for the restructuring in 2017. The cumulative outstanding claim filed by banks was 3.45 lakh crores, which accounts for nearly 44 per cent of gross NPAs. These sectors typically have projects with long timelines and significantly large capital expenditures, and therefore the accumulation of bad loans by these corporations indicates the lack of governance and monitoring of stressed assets.

Table 1.3   Concentration of stressed assets in large defaulters of corporate India

Name of the corporation	Stressed debt admitted for recovery (INR crore)
Electrosteel Steels	13,175
Bhushan Steel	56,022
Monnet Ispat & Energy	11,015
Essar Steel India	49,473
Alok Industries	29,523
Jaypee Infratech	23,176
Jyoti Structures	7,365
Bhushan Power & Steel	47,158
Amtek Auto	12,641
Era Infra Engineering	Under Corporate Insolvency Resolution Process (CIRP)
Lanco Infratech	Under Liquidation
ABG Shipyard	Under Liquidation

Source: CARE Ratings, 'Analysis of Movement in Stressed Advances', 13 February 2021, https://www.careratings.com/uploads/newsfiles/13022021110239_Analysis_of_Movement_in_Stressed_Advances.pdf. Accessed on 8 March 2021.

Finally, the Indian capital market has also recognized this substantial destruction of PSB values over the last six years. Compared to December 2014, the Nifty Public Sector Undertaking (PSU) Bank Index has fallen from 4,312 to 1,340 in June 2021, indicating erosion of nearly three-fourths of its value. As a stark contrast, during the same period, the broader market index, Nifty 50, has risen to 15,690 from the level of 8,200, registering a nearly 91 per cent gain. The Economic Survey, 2019–20, also highlighted:

> [T]he foregone return on the taxpayer's investment in PSBs must rank as one of the largest subsidies as the foregone amount of over Rs 1.4 lakh crores compares similarly to the amount provided for the food subsidy…. Over Rs, 4,30,000 crores of taxpayer money are invested as government's equity in PSBs. In 2019, every rupee of taxpayer money invested in PSBs, on average, lost 23 paise. (Government of India, 2020)

The Survey further added:

> [U]sing the ratio of stock market-to-book value of PSBs on average vis-à-vis that of new private sector banks (NPBs). As of 20th January 2020, we note that every rupee of this taxpayer money fetches a market value of 71 paise. In stark contrast, every rupee invested in NPBs fetches a market value of Rs 3.70, i.e., more than five times as much value as that of a rupee invested in PSBs. (Government of India, 2020)

This highlights the fact that NPBs are rapidly catching up with PSBs, particularly during the last five years. According to the RBI's *Report on Trends and Progress of Banking in India, 2018–19*, PSBs' share of banking assets has steadily declined from a high of 74 per cent in 2010 to 61 per cent in 2019 (Reserve Bank of India, 2019b).

Therefore, at the beginning of the 2000s, though it becomes more palpable only after 2015, both the Indian banks and the corporates were under significant stress – corporates have over-borrowed, and banks have over-lent. As such, it is imperative to ask a pertinent question: why has the Indian banking sector (mainly PSBs), which was performing reasonably well in the 2000s, particularly before 2003–04, become so overburdened with NPAs by the end of this decade?

There have been many evidence-based conjectures that try to address the question. For example, according to a recent *Financial Stability Report* by the RBI, the core reasons behind the upsurge of NPAs in India are inadequate restructuring and recovery strategies, disproportionate levels of NPA share by PSBs compared to private banks, a large volume of loan disbursement without proper vigilance, and lack of post-loan monitoring over the decade (Reserve Bank of India, 2019a). In addition to the structural reasons, the borrowing exuberance of corporates during the period of credit growth between 2006 and 2008 further contributed to India's NPA crisis.

Therefore, despite a plethora of anecdotal evidence pointing towards borrowing exuberance and crony capitalism, there has not been much study that analytically addresses the recent maladies of the Indian banking sector. We aim to fill this gap in the extant literature by providing a few insights into the current banking crisis in the Indian economy by decomposing the maladies into three different stages of prognosis: origination of the loan, servicing of loans, and recoveries of bad loans. It is worth noting that our approach shifts the focus from the other contemporary discourse based on an outcome-based measure such as NPA (and its conventional determinants) to a more dynamic approach, by critically examining the process underlying the life cycle of the credit decision and identifying the inefficiencies at different stages of this cycle.

Credit Bubble and Misallocation

It is also interesting to note that the recent crisis in the Indian banking sector precedes a credit bubble period witnessing unprecedented growth, which is the highest in a quarter-century. Therefore, it provides us with a unique natural opportunity to examine whether misallocation of credit during the pro-cyclic credit bubble in the pre-crisis period and the economic slowdown following the GFC led to a rise of NPAs in India. Specifically, we hypothesize that the substantial proportion of NPAs in India is an outcome of a process originating at the point of disbursement of the loan, which gets aggravated during the servicing cycles through practices like evergreening.

While conventional wisdom suggests that a well-developed financial system's fundamental job is to allocate capital efficiently, and the capital would flow from underperforming sectors to high-growth sectors for better returns, there has been limited evidence corroborating it for India. Therefore, the study aims to contribute to the literature by providing a comprehensive analysis of credit misallocation in general and borrowing exuberance, particularly its linkages with economic growth, and with behaviour and performance of the corporate sector. It is worthwhile to note a few pertinent points about our hypotheses.

First, while there is a body of literature that establishes that financial liberalization leads to a positive 'quantity effect' with higher levels of investment (McKinnon, 1974; Shaw, 1974; Beck, Levine, and Loayza, 2000; Ueda, 2006), it remains uncertain whether it also improves the efficacy of the consequent investment decisions based on these allocated funds. Second, a strand of literature argues that banks often overstretch both the quantum and the quality of their credit over the expansionary phase of the economy, leading to misallocation and non-performing credit (Mendoza and Terrones, 2008, 2012; Arena and Julio, 2015). Corroborating this view, Bhaduri and Kumar (2014) observed that a substantial increase in the quantum of funds during the post-liberalization period did not translate into a more efficient allocation in India. Further, in a recent study, Bhaduri and Bhattacharya (2018) examined whether the credit is allocated to firms with higher marginal returns to capital and did not find the presence of any positive association between liberalization and higher allocation efficiency. Therefore, the study contributes to this sparely researched aspect of liberalization ('quality effect') by carefully examining if the financial reforms and consequent growth of bank credit in India have improved the allocation of resources.

Third, the origin of prodigal loans during the credit boom has gained much media attention in recent years. This further rose to prominence in June 2017 when the RBI published a report that included some leading names among India's energy, steel, and other infrastructure companies. These companies alone had an outstanding debt of over INR 2.66 trillion, or a third of the stressed loans, on banks' books. The banker exuberance during 2006–08 further gained credence as a source of the NPA crisis in India when Dr Raghuram Rajan highlighted the following in his detailed reply to the estimates committee of parliament under the chairmanship of Dr Murli Manohar Joshi:[6]

> A larger number of bad loans were originated in the period 2006–2008 when economic growth was strong, and previous infrastructure projects such as power plants had been completed on time and within budget. It is at such times that banks make mistakes. They extrapolate past growth and performance to the future. So they are willing to accept higher leverage in projects and less promoter equity. Indeed, sometimes banks signed up to lend based on project reports by the promoter's investment bank, without doing their due diligence. One promoter told me about how he was pursued then by banks waving chequebooks, asking him to name the amount he wanted. This is the historic phenomenon of irrational exuberance, common across countries at such a phase in the cycle.

Therefore, our hypothesis is consistent with a plethora of anecdotal evidence pointing towards borrowing exuberance. However, there has not been much study that systematically establishes the nexus between the pro-cyclic credit bubble and the downstream consequence of credit misallocation.

Using micro-data of a large number of non-financial corporations from India, we propose a novel measure of misallocation of bank credit at the point of disbursement and explore three main facets of the current banking crisis: first, we trace the trend and patterns of misallocation over a long period of 28 years across multiple credit cycles. Specifically, we examine pro-cyclicality in the lending behaviour and misallocation of resources, particularly during the unprecedented credit boom in the early 2000s. While decomposing the source of misallocation, we explore the extent to which the pro-cyclic credit bubble in the early 2000s has led to 'borrowing exuberance' by channelling bank credit towards firms that are less likely to use it for productive purposes. Using a long time-series data spanning multiple business cycles, we try to trace the 'borrowing exuberance' episodes in India. Notably, we ask the question, can the recent spurt in the 'borrowing exuberance' (after 2004) be attributed to significant credit booms, or do they mirror a more general business cycle trend? Second, using heterogeneous firm-specific micro-data cutting across many industries, we further explore what types of firms are prone to misallocation in general and 'borrowing exuberance' in particular compared to others.

Finally, our approach of decomposing the maladies of the banking sector into three different stages of prognosis – origination of the loan, servicing of loans, and recoveries of bad loans – is consistent with the 'financial instability hypothesis' of Hyman Minsky (1992), which was largely ignored by mainstream economics until recently. Minsky (1992) argued that the credit life cycle goes through three distinct steps: hedge, speculative, and Ponzi.

Banks and borrowers exercise caution, and borrowers make enough profit to repay both the initial principal and the interest in the first stage. The speculative phase is usually associated with borrowing exuberance, suggesting that a period of high growth encourages borrowers and lenders to be progressively reckless – banks are willing to issue riskier loans, and corporates are willing to invest aggressively in their business expansion. As pointed out by Minsky, '... this occurs because the acceptable and desired liability structures of business firms and the organizations acting as middlemen in finance change in response to the economy's success'. In the speculative stage, the firm's expected profit is sufficient to pay the interest but not the principal. During this stage, banks continue to lend or restructure the existing loan under the expectation that the economy will continue to grow and eventually make these loans viable. Then, it reaches the final stage – Ponzi – at which banks issue loans to firms that can afford to pay neither the interest nor the principal.

In our scheme of hypotheses, the line of reasoning evolves closely with Minsky's financial instability hypothesis. As we argued earlier and will see in later chapters, we can decompose the evolution of the banking crisis into similar stages of progression: 1990–91 to 2003–04, the period of hyper-growth akin to the hedge phase of Minsky. The period 2004–10 is one of unprecedented credit bubble leading to the speculative stage. As pointed out by Minsky (1992), 'a period of a relative tranquil growth is transformed into a speculative boom'. The post-2010 period witnessed the Ponzi stage with explosive zombie lending to keep the non-viable loan to remain afloat. Finally, the AQR in 2015 is the 'Minsky moment' for the Indian economy when the banking sector was forced to recognize bad loans and aggressively undertake provisioning for such loans, leading to significant losses.[7]

Organization of Chapters

As a necessary backdrop to our research, Chapter 2 provides a brief history of the Indian banking sector. Specifically, the chapter describes the regulations and reforms implemented by the RBI towards shaping the present banking sector. A review of the effects of the early reforms on the banking sector's health is presented to understand the accumulation of bad assets due to a lack of substantial creditor rights despite instituting the structural measures. Further, by focusing on recent regulations on prudential norms implemented to strengthen the creditors' rights in India, Chapter 2 sets the context of our research by presenting the trends in the accumulation of bad assets in the banking sector and the recent reforms like the Indian Bankruptcy Code and Stressed Asset Resolutions to manage NPAs.

Chapter 3 proposes a novel measure of allocative efficiency as the index of credit allocative efficiency (ICAE) to evaluate the misallocation of credit towards firms with lower expected marginal returns compared to firms with higher expected marginal returns. The study makes a significant deviation from existing literature, which analyses the causes and trends of NPAs as an outcome after the allocation of bank credit. Instead, we carefully examine the efficiency of the allocation of bank credit at the point of disbursement. By focusing on the conditions before bank credit allocation, our research augments the existing knowledge on the lending decisions of the banking sector by investigating the maladies beyond NPAs. Our research is the first to provide a novel ex-ante measure of bank credit misallocation to the best of our knowledge. In subsequent chapters, we explore the macro- and micro-level determinants of misallocation and its impact on firm performance and behaviour. The findings contribute to the empirical literature of prodigal borrowing by the corporate sector and its consequences in emerging markets.

Chapter 4 investigates the pro-cyclicality in the banking sector's lending behaviour and misallocation of resources leading to unstable economic growth. Using the ICAE, a measure developed in Chapter 3, we explore the macroeconomic dynamics of the misallocation for a sample of Indian firms over the period 1990–2017 and test the nexus between pro-cyclicality and credit misallocation.

While this set of points draws macro-level inferences using our measure of bank credit misallocation, the data also allows us to conduct micro-level analyses to understand better the firm-specific characteristics that might influence credit misallocation. In Chapter 5, while exploring the firm-specific determinants of misallocation, we emphasize three main factors: (*a*) creditworthiness, (*b*) requirement of external funds, and (*c*) corporate governance structure. Based on our preliminary findings, we hypothesize that credit misallocation is attributed to firms with low creditworthiness, less requirement of external credit, and poor corporate governance mechanism.

Chapter 6 examines the downstream consequence of credit misallocation on firms' performance. Specifically, we explore whether credit misallocation impacts firms' performance and how persistent this impact is. Using multiple measures of firms' performance such as profitability, return on equity (ROE), return on capital employed (ROC), and return on total assets (ROTA), we empirically test our hypothesis by using a dynamic framework.

In contrast to earlier chapters that deal with credit booms and the efficacy of credit allocation, in Chapter 7 we consider a specific episode to understand how the Indian banking sector responds to a severe credit shock. We consider the GFC of 2008 as a natural opportunity to investigate whether Indian banks have responded optimally by using strategic lending policies in the aftermath of the global crisis. We test whether banks have chosen these attributes optimally in their allocation decision in the post-crisis period using three broad attributes: sector specificity, bank–firm relationship, and risk management.

Chapter 8 focuses on another critical objective of this research about the growing debate on whether the pro-cyclic credit bubble in the pre-crisis period and GFC has contributed to the rise in the 'evergreening of loans' and 'zombie lending' in the post-2010 period. Using a sample of listed firms for the period 1990–2017, we explore the causes, consequences, and persistence of zombie firms in the Indian economy. Further, we also explore the types of firms that have attracted more zombie lending than others in the post-crisis period.

Finally, Chapter 9 concludes the study with specific policy recommendations for Indian banks and the corporate sector.

Notes

1   See Ang (2008) for a comprehensive survey of recent developments in finance and growth literature.

2   However, the conflicting literature suggests that while bank monitoring improves the firm's corporate governance and ensures it takes efficient business actions, this better governance comes at the cost of an informational advantage that banks have over

other providers of capital. Banks can pursue rent-seeking activities by exploiting the private information it acquires from the firm. This informational monopoly over firms strengthens the bargaining position of the banks, which banks could use to cut off a firm's loan or even charge a high interest rate, direct the choice of projects, levy compensating balances, or refuse to relax covenants when the credit rating improves.

3   It is important to note that there had been few episodes of contraction in the economy during the late 1990s and the early 2000s due to various adverse external and domestic developments such as the Asian crisis, world recession, and poor monsoon.

4   Harshad Mehta Scam (1992), IPO Scam (1994), and Ketan Parekh Scam (the late 1990s).

5   Mayur Shetty, 'PM Modi's PSU Bank Spends Beat 45 Years' Investments', *Times of India*, 17 July 2019, https://timesofindia.indiatimes.com/business/india-business/modis-psu-bank-spends-beat-45-years-investments/articleshow/70252242.cms (accessed in January 2021).

6   The excerpts are quoted from the note prepared by Raghuram G. Rajan on 6 September 2018 – at the request of Murli Manohar Joshi, Member of Parliament and Chairman of the Parliament Estimates Committee – available at *Hindu Business Line*, https://www.thehindubusinessline.com/money-and-banking/article24924543.ece/binary/Raghuram%20Rajan%20Parliamentary%20note%20on%20NPAs (accessed in January 2021).

7   A Minsky moment refers to a collapse of asset values which marks the end of the growth phase of a cycle in credit markets.

2

The Indian Banking Sector
A Brief History

Evolution of Banking in India

The history of banking in India goes back to the 19th century. The first bank in India – the Bank of Bengal – was set up by the British in 1809. The primary interest of this bank was to cater to the needs of the colonial government. Following this, two other presidential banks – the Bank of Bombay and the Bank of Madras – were incorporated in 1840 and 1843. However, in modern parlance, the first commercial bank was the Imperial Bank of India, which evolved by merging the three presidential banks in 1935. The first Indian-owned bank, Allahabad Bank, which is still functional, was set up in 1865 in Allahabad, followed by the establishment of another large bank in 1985 – the Punjab National Bank. The subsequent years witnessed the setting up of many banks, such as Bank of India, Central Bank of India, Canara Bank, Indian Bank, Bank of Baroda, and Bank of Mysore. As the business activities centred in urban areas, these banks were all located in urban centres.

The British had already recognized the role of banks in the economy, and the need to regulate the money supply was the core theme of the Royal Commission on Indian Currency and Finance in 1926.[1] Before independence, the country had privately owned banks as joint-stock companies. Therefore, the areas of operation of the banks were localized. Consequently, the Reserve Bank of India Act, 1934, paved the way for establishing the Reserve Bank of India (RBI) as the central bank of India. The RBI commenced operations in April 1935 and exercised its control over other banks by setting the cash reserve ratio (CRR) and other statutory parameters for operations. Interestingly, many prominent banks collapsed in the pre-independence era (such as the Presidency Bank of

Bombay, Travancore National and Quilon Bank, and Bank of Upper India).[2] There were around 600 operational commercial banks at the time of independence in 1947. However, a marked shift in banking activities emerged shortly after Indian independence. The Government of India (GOI) started taking an active role in controlling the banking functions. The Banking Regulation Act, 1949, nationalized the RBI and made it the apex body to control, supervise, and regulate the banking activities of all the banks in the country.

Credit availability was a grave concern for India at the time of independence, particularly in the rural areas. In the pre-independence era, banks were mainly catering to traders and the business community's needs. There was a growing cry to spread the banking activities to other areas of the economy, such as agriculture. The nationalization of the Imperial Bank in 1955 (renamed as State Bank of India [SBI]) was one step in this direction. The newly created SBI's immediate objective was to create additional branches in all district headquarters, provide remittance and other facilities to co-operative and other banks, and mobilize rural savings. Further, the State Bank of India (Subsidiary Banks) Act, 1959, converted the erstwhile banks of princely states as SBI's associates.

Consequently, Bank of Patiala, Bank of Mysore, Bank of Bikaner, Bank of Jaipur, Bank of Indore, Bank of Hyderabad, Bank of Saurashtra, and Bank of Travancore became the subsidiaries of SBI. Later, two more banks, Bank of Bikaner and Bank of Jaipur, were amalgamated to incorporate State Banks of Bikaner and Jaipur. However, these measures were deemed insufficient as the industry and banks' close ties gave the former an advantage in obtaining credit (Reddy, 2002). The growing needs of the small-scale industries and the farmers remained unaddressed by the existing banks as the control of commercial banking in the country was concentrated in the hands of leaders of commerce and industry.[3] Consequently, the banks' capital base was eroded by a more than 75 per cent decline in the ratio of paid-up capital and reserves to deposits between 1951 and 1969 (Banking Commission, 1971). The failure of the banking sector set the stage for the banking sector reforms. Subsequent reforms over the next few decades mainly addressed the issues that were adopted by the country after independence; these included bank failures, the concentration of resources in the hands of wealthy businesses groups, neglect of agriculture in lending, and lack of financial inclusion.

We classify these reforms in three phases based on their focus. The first phase of reforms was between 1966–67 and 1990–91, focusing mainly on setting up social control and statutory pre-emptions in the banking sector. The second phase of reforms was initiated in 1991–92 and lasted up to 2007–08, transforming the banking sector as a part of financial sector liberalization. The focus in this phase was on strengthening the regulatory and supervisory norms by adopting international benchmarks of risk management, banking supervision, and performance measures. The third and most recent phase of reforms (2008–09 to 2019–20) focused on prudential norms following the global financial crisis (GFC). The next section briefly outlines the main features of these reforms and their impact on the banking sector in the country.

Phases of Banking Reforms in India

Reforms in the Early Phase (Phase 1: 1966–67 to 1990–91)

Realizing the need for planned growth and the widely held notion that banks' private ownership created a roadblock in distributing credit across all participants, the Indian government introduced the Banking Laws (Amendment) Act, 1968. The necessity of social control was recognized to develop the guidelines for effective bank management aligned with the country's priorities. The main objectives of social control were to expand the availability of bank credit across the country, reduce its misuse, ensure a large volume of credit to the priority sector, and make it an instrument of overall development and growth. Subsequently, in February 1968, the National Credit Council (NCC) was set up to support the RBI and the GOI in allocating credit based on the government's priorities and goals. The council estimated the demand for credit from different market participants and fixed priorities to grant loans based on the availability of funds. However, even after banks persuaded social control systems, credit for the organized sector was unavailable for a larger section of the population (Reserve Bank of India, 2008). Even though the number of branches increased significantly from 4,061 to 5,026 branches between 1952 and 1960 and further from 6,133 to 6,985 branches between 1960 and 1967, this expansion was mostly concentrated in urban areas.

Therefore, even after 20 years of independence, the two disturbing features regarding the nexus between the banks and industry and the neglect of the agricultural sector remained a concern to the authorities. Thus, as social control was not entirely successful in promoting financial inclusion for a large part of the population, the nationalization of banks became a necessity. As a result, the GOI passed the Banking Companies (Acquisition and Transfer of Undertakings) Act, 1969, which effectively nationalized 14 banks that had deposits of over INR 500 million.

These banks were directed to mobilize deposits to lend for all productive activities that generate growth, irrespective of the borrower's size and social status, particularly to the weaker sections of the society. Thus, the nationalization of banks reoriented bank lending to accelerate economic growth, specifically to the unserved priority sectors, which were ignored by the commercial banks. After recognizing the changes in lending behaviour and its benefits, six more banks were nationalized in 1980.[4] One of the significant achievements of the nationalization of banks was the spread of banking activities to every nook and corner of the country.[5]

Further, the NCC in July 1968 advised commercial banks to finance priority sectors, such as agriculture and small-scale industries. Subsequently, public sector banks (PSBs) were advised to allocate at least one-third of their outstanding credit to the priority sectors and maintain one-third of their total advances to the priority sectors by the end of March 1980. This was further extended to 40 per cent of aggregate advances. In addition, to uplift the weaker sections of society, the Differential Rate of Interest (DRI) Scheme was implemented to extend credit at a concessional rate to low-income groups in rural India.

However, commercial banks were not oriented to the needs and requirements of small and marginal farmers, and the co-operatives lacked resources to meet the expected demand. To address this, the Regional Rural Banks Ordinance, 1975, was enacted, which was later replaced by the Regional Rural Banks Act, 1976. Under the Act, Regional Rural Banks (RRBs) were established to boost the rural economy by providing credit to the small and marginal players.

Overall, the nationalization of banks in 1969 was instituted to ensure timely and adequate credit to all the productive activities of the economy. By the end of 1990, the country had 59,752 branches of commercial banks (including RRBs), of which 58.2 per cent of branches operated from rural areas. The rapid expansion of the branches since 1969 resulted in a significant decline in the average population per bank office from 65,000 in 1969 to 14,000 by the end of December 1990. This reflected substantial efforts made towards the spread of banking, particularly in unbanked rural areas. The banking sector expansion also increased the share of rural credit in total bank credit from 3.3 per cent in 1969 to 14.2 per cent in 1990.

This period also witnessed an increase in demands made on the banking system due to an increase in the fiscal deficit. The RBI tightened the monetary policy and also implemented financial discipline. This created an unbalance in the economy as traditional sectors faced credit constraints, whereas priority sector credit was mobilized at lower lending standards. The absence of competition combined with regulatory controls resulted in a decline in productivity and efficiency of the banking system and adversely affected its profitability. Further, deterioration in banks' capital position created significant non-performing assets (NPAs) in their books. In response to these developments, several measures were undertaken in the mid-1980s towards deregulation of the financial sector, facilitating consolidation and diversification.

To strengthen the banks' capital base, the government decided to infuse INR 2,000 crores for allocation among 20 nationalized banks during the Seventh Five Year Plan (April 1985–March 1990). This provided much-needed additional lendable resources in the hands of banks. Also, a Health Code System was introduced in 1985 to classify bank loans according to their performance. Under this mechanism, banks were required to classify their advances portfolio under the uniform grading system based on the quality or health of individual advances in eight categories. Each category was assigned a health code, of which codes numbered from 5 to 8 classified the NPAs: (5) debts recalled, (6) suit-filed accounts, (7) decreed debts, and (8) debts classified as bad and doubtful. Banks were advised not to charge and take to their income account interest on loans classified under the health codes 6, 7, and 8 from the quarter in which the individual accounts were classified under their categories.

Additionally, one of the significant pieces of legislation that aimed at addressing the sickness of the industries was the setting up of the Board for Industrial and Financial Reconstruction (BIFR) under the purview of the Sick Industrial Companies (Special Provisions) Act, 1985 (SICA). The objective of the BIFR was the revival and rehabilitation of potentially sick companies and the liquidation of non-viable industrial companies. Once the board of directors of a sick company reported its financial status to the BIFR, reasonable time was given to the company concerned to make its net worth positive. However, if the BIFR found that the company was not likely to increase its net worth to exceed its accumulated losses and was unlikely to become viable, proceedings for winding up the company could be taken up in the High Court. In the following years, several pieces of legislation came into place to address defaults, frauds, and malfeasance. One of the primary steps in this direction was Lok Adalats, under the Legal Services Authority Act, 1987, with judicial status to settle disputes between the bank and small borrowers. One of the primary ways of the Lok Adalats to settle disputes between parties was through mediation and conciliation, without going through the due procedure through courts, thereby saving time for all the parties involved. However, the inability to bring the parties together had been one of the major handicaps of this system.

Further, the mid-1980s also witnessed several operational reform measures in the banking sector. As the Banking Regulation Act, 1949, did not permit the banks to take up any non-banking activities, the Act was amended in 1984 to widen banks' role in other avenues of financial disintermediation. Subsequently, banks were allowed to undertake merchant banking activities through subsidiaries. Following this, many banks took up securities market-related activities, equipment leasing, hire purchase, mutual funds, housing finance, and venture capital. This diversification helped banks to enlarge the business portfolio and increase profitability through non-interest income.

To sum up, the reform measures introduced so far transformed the banking sector from a privately owned system to one dominated by the public sector. Box 2.1 presents a summary of major reforms undertaken between 1967 and 1991. However, as these efforts were only limited in their scope to liberalize the banking sector and improve its performance and soundness, major structural reforms were introduced in the next phase as a part of financial sector reforms.

Box 2.1   Major banking reforms in 1967–91

1967: Social control over banks was announced in December 1967 to secure a better alignment of the banking system to the needs of economic policy.

1968: National Credit Council (NCC) was set up in February 1968 to assist the Reserve Bank of India (RBI) and the Government of India (GOI) to allocate credit according to plan priorities.

1969: 14 banks with deposits of over INR 50 crores were nationalized.

1969: The Lead Bank Scheme was introduced to mobilize deposits on a massive scale throughout the country and for stepping up lending to the weaker sections.

1972: The concept of the priority sector was formalized. Specific targets were set out in November 1974 for public sector banks and in November 1978 for private sector banks.

1972: The Differential Rate of Interest (DRI) scheme was instituted to cater to the weaker sections of society and for their upliftment.

1973: A minimum lending rate was prescribed on all loans except for the priority sector.

1973: The District Credit Plans were initiated.

1975: Banks were required to place all borrowers with an aggregate credit limit from the banking system over INR 10 lakhs on the first method of lending, whereby 25 per cent of the working capital gap – that is, the difference between current assets and current liabilities, excluding bank finance – was required to be funded from long-term sources.

1976: The maximum rate for bank loans was prescribed in addition to the minimum lending rates.

1980: The contribution from borrowers towards working capital out of their long-term sources was placed in the second method of lending – that is, not less than 25 per cent of the current assets required for the estimated level of production – which would give a minimum current ratio of 1.33:1 (as against 25 per cent of working capital gap stipulated under the norms prescribed in 1975).

1980: Six banks with demand and time liabilities greater than INR 200 crores as on 14 March 1980 were nationalized on 15 April.

1988: Service Area Approach (SAA) was introduced, modifying the Lead Bank Scheme.

1989: The cash reserve ratio (CRR) was gradually raised from 5 per cent in June 1973 to 15 per cent by July 1989.

1990: The statutory liquidity ratio (SLR) was raised by 12.5 percentage points from 26 per cent in February 1970 to 38.5 per cent in September 1990.

Source: Adapted from Reserve Bank of India, *Report on Currency and Finance: 2006–08*, vol. 1, 4 September 2008, https://rbidocs.rbi.org.in/rdocs/Publications/PDFs/86722.pdf. Accessed in January 2021.

Reforms in the Post-liberalization Period (1991–92 to 2007–08)

By the end of the 1980s, the Indian economic crisis was recognized widely, and the first Narasimham Committee (Committee on the Financial Systems [CFS]) was appointed to realize the full potential of the structural reforms in the real economy. The CFS submitted its recommendations in November 1991, providing a basis of financial sector reforms relating to the banking sector, development financing, and capital markets. The committee noted the deteriorating health of the banking system and its adverse impact on depositor's and investor's confidence. Accordingly, banking sector reforms were initiated to improve efficiency and growth.

This phase of banking sector reform was structured on five principles, or 'Pancha Sutra': first, cautious implementation and sequencing of reform measures; second, introduction of the norms that were mainly reinforcing the existing structure; third, the introduction of complementary reforms across monetary, fiscal, external, and financial sectors; fourth, development of financial institutions; and, fifth, the development and integration of financial markets in the real economy (Reserve Bank of India, 2008). Thus, the post-liberalization banking sector reforms in phase 2 could be further divided into two sub-phases, from 1991–92 to 1997–98 (Phase 2a) and from 1997–98 to 2007–08 (Phase 2b).

Management of Financial Health and Soundness of the Banking System (Phase 2a: 1991–92 to 1997–98)

The early 1990s marked the weak banking sector period characterized by the weak capital base, lack of profitability, and fragile health condition of banks. In April

1992, internationally accepted prudential norms relating to income recognition, asset classification, provisioning, and capital adequacy were introduced in a phased manner for improving the banking sector's health. The reforms also addressed the problem of NPAs by providing a more precise definition of the NPAs based on objective criteria. In comparison to the existing system of health codes, banks needed to classify their advances into four broad groups: (*a*) standard assets, (*b*) sub-standard assets, (*c*) doubtful assets, and (*d*) loss assets. The new classification redrew the overall picture of the aggregate non-performing loans of all PSBs. According to the revised classification, the composition, which was 14.5 per cent of total outstanding advances as of March 1992 based on the old health code system, increased to 23.2 per cent in March 1993. Consequently, the banks' profitability declined substantially and prevented the bank from recycling funds, thereby constraining the growth of their balance sheets.

Therefore, restoring and maintaining the soundness of banks' financial health became a priority for the government. The government once again embarked on a recapitalization programme of nationalized banks from 1993 to 1994 to meet the burgeoning funding gap created by the newly introduced prudential measures. However, capital infusion by the government was inadequate to improve the balance sheet of the banks. To further fulfil provisioning norms and meet the additional capital needs, the PSBs were permitted to directly approach the capital market to mobilize equity funds from the public by amending the relevant Acts. However, while the government ensured that their ownership would remain at least 51 per cent of the nationalized bank's equity, many PSBs took up this opportunity, and by March 1998, nine PSBs raised capital aggregating INR 6,015 crores from the capital market, including the global depository receipt (GDR) issue of SBI aggregating INR 1,270 crores raised during 1996–97 (Reserve Bank of India, 2008).

Further, to contain fresh NPAs, the government enacted the Recovery of Debts Due to Banks and Financial Institutions Act, 1993, which led to the establishment of 29 Debt Recovery Tribunals (DRTs) and five Debt Recovery Appellate Tribunals (DRATs) to facilitate the expeditious adjudication and recovery of bad debts.

The impact of various measures of financial reforms was observed in terms of improvement in the quality of banks' balance sheets, as in a short span banks were able to bring down their NPAs significantly. Gross NPAs of PSBs declined from 23.2 per cent at the end of March 1993 to 16.2 per cent by the end of March 1998. At the same time, the overall profitability and financial soundness of the banking sector, in general, and PSBs, in particular, improved significantly. At the end of March 1998, all banks, except five banks (one PSB and four old private sector banks), could attain the stipulated 8 per cent capital adequacy requirement.

Two important factors contributed favourably to banks' profitability during the initial phase of reforms. First was the reduction in pre-emptions of resources of the banking sector in the form of CRR and statutory liquidity ratio (SLR), which recorded a high level of 63.5 per cent before the reforms were instituted. This removed the external constraints on banks improving their profitability and augmented banks' lendable resources for financing growth and employment in the private sector. Figure 2.1 presents the reduction in statutory pre-emptions. As shown in the figure, CRR was reduced in a phased manner and SLR was brought down progressively.

Second was the administered structure of interest rates before reforms did not allow market forces to play a role in pricing and, therefore, adversely affected credit allocation. The complex structure of interest rates was rationalized and regulated, which implied that banks were free to fix their deposit and lending rates. Banks were expected to use commercial judgement based on overall liquidity conditions and their risk perceptions. Box 2.2 shows a summary of several measures that were undertaken to deregulate interest rates. As a result, deposit interest rates softened significantly from 13 per cent per annum to 11.5–12 per cent, and lending rates witnessed innovations such as fixed, floating, and fixed interest rates, among others.

These steps had a significant positive impact on the profitability and reduction in NPAs of the banking sector during 1996–97. The number of loss-making scheduled commercial banks (SCBs) declined to eight (of which three were PSBs) in stark

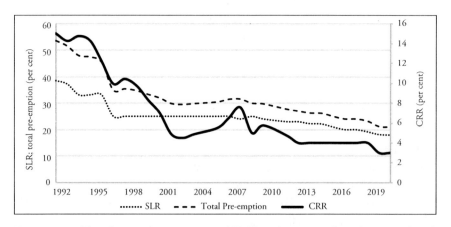

Figure 2.1 Trends in cash reserve ratio (CRR) and statutory liquidity ratio (SLR) in 1992–2019

Source: Reserve Bank of India, *Handbook of Statistics on Indian Economy*, various editions.

Box 2.2   Deregulation of interest rates

A. Deposit Interest Rates

October 1989: Interest rates were rationalized on domestic short-term deposits by merging two categories, 46 days to 90 days and 90 days to one year. Interest rates on both these were made payable at a uniform rate, effective on 11 October. A similar simplification for non-residential external (NRE) deposit rate was introduced, effective on 16 April 1990.

April 1992: The ceilings on deposit rates were simplified by replacing the existing maturity-wise ceiling prescriptions with a single ceiling rate of 13 per cent on all deposits above 46 days.

April 1993: A new Foreign Currency Non-Resident Deposits (Banks) (FCNR[B]) Scheme was introduced, under which the exchange risk was to be borne by the banks and interest rates prescribed by the Reserve Bank of India (RBI). The earlier scheme, Foreign Currency Non-Resident Accounts (FCNR[A]), was phased out by August 1994.

October 1995: To give flexibility to banks, deposits of maturity of over two years were exempted from the stipulation of ceilings.

April 1996: Interest rates on NRE term deposits of over two years were freed, effective on 4 April.

July 1996: Banks were given freedom to fix deposit rates for term deposits above one-year maturity. For better short-term management of funds, the minimum period of term deposit was brought down from 46 days to 30 days. For the maturity bucket of 30 days to 1 year, the banks could fix interest rates subject to a ceiling stipulated by the RBI.

April 1997: The ceiling interest rate on domestic term deposits of maturity of 30 days and up to 1 year was linked to bank rate. The interest rates on term deposits under NRE accounts of over one year were freed.

September 1997: Banks were given freedom to fix their own interest rates on NRE term deposits of six months and more.

October 1997: Deposit rates, other than those on savings deposits and FCNR(B), were fully deregulated.

April 1998: Banks were given freedom to offer a differential rate of interest for bulk deposits INR 15 lakhs and above and to set their own penal rates of interest on premature withdrawal of domestic term deposits and NRE deposits. The minimum period of maturity of term deposits reduced from 30 days to 15 days.

April 2001: The minimum maturity period of 15 days reduced to 7 days for wholesale deposits of INR 15 lakhs and above.

July 2003: Interest rate ceilings on NRE deposits were linked to London interbank offered rates (LIBOR, alternatively called swap rates).

November 2004: Minimum maturity period of 15 days reduced to 7 days for all deposits.

B. Lending Interest Rates

October 1988: The existing fixed-rate stipulations were converted into minimum (floors) rates, giving banks the option of raising the rates.

September 1990: Sector-specific and programme-specific prescriptions were discontinued, barring a few areas like agriculture, small industries, differential rate of interest (DRI) scheme, and export credit.

April 1992: The interest rates for advances of scheduled commercial banks (SCBs) (except DRI advances and export credit) were rationalized by bringing the six slabs of advances to four slabs according to the size of credit.

April 1993: Lending rates were further rationalized as the number of slabs were brought down from four categories to three categories by merging the first two slabs.

October 1994: Lending interest rates of scheduled commercial banks for credit limits of over INR 2 lakhs were deregulated, effective on 18 October.

October 1995: Banks were given freedom to decide the interest rate of advances against term deposits of INR 2 lakhs and above for both domestic and NRE deposits and to fix their own interest rates. The interest rate structure on post-shipment credit in foreign currency (PSCFC) was rationalized.

February 1997: Banks were allowed to prescribe separate prime lending rates (PLRs) and spreads separately for loan and cash credit components of loans.

April 1998: Banks were allowed to charge interest rate on loans against fixed deposits equal to or less than their PLR.

April 1999: Banks were provided freedom to operate tenor-linked PLR.

April 2003: With a view to ensuring transparency in banks' lending rates and also for reducing the complexity involved in pricing of loans, a scheme of benchmark PLRs (BPLRs) was introduced. Concurrently, the tenor-linked PLR system was discontinued.

Source: Adapted from Reserve Bank of India, *Report on Currency and Finance: 2006–08*, vol. 1, 4 September 2008, https://rbidocs.rbi.org.in/rdocs/Publications/PDFs/86722.pdf. Accessed in January 2021.

contrast to the fact that 14 banks (12 PSBs) had reported net losses in March 1993. During 1994–95, PSBs indicated a net profit of INR 1,116 crores in contrast to a net loss of INR 4,349 crores in 1993–94. This resulted in a significant increase in return on assets for SCBs to 0.8 per cent by 1997–98, from a negative 1.1 per cent in 1992–93. A similar trend was also observed for PSBs. Further, gross NPAs of PSBs as a percentage of gross advances, which was 23.2 per cent at the end of March 1993, declined to 17 per cent by the end of March 1998 (Figure 2.2).

Moreover, since one of the objectives of reforms was to bring in greater efficiency by creating a competitive environment, the RBI allowed the entry of

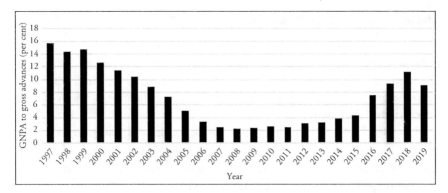

Figure 2.2 Trends in gross non-performing asset (GNPA) as a percentage of total advances – all banks

Source: Reserve Bank of India, *Handbook of Statistics on Indian Economy*, various editions.

new banks in the private sector in 1993 by amending the norms for the entry of new private sector banks. Further, as a step towards deregulation, it provided the banks greater freedom in the matter of opening of branches as well as the installation of automated teller machines (ATMs). To enhance competition, full operational freedom was provided to banks in their assessment of the working capital requirements of the corporate borrowers. Finally, banking consortium and syndicate arrangements were allowed for the corporate borrowers, and term-lending restrictions were lifted for commercial banks.

However, given the prudential norms, banks became wary of enlarging their loan portfolio during the initial stages of liberalization. Therefore, to ensure effective implementation of prudential regulation and to address the increased risks faced by banks in a liberalized environment, the Board of Financial Supervision (BFS) was established in 1994 to supervise and provide useful input in an integrated manner for banks and financial and non-banking financial companies. The BFS initiated several off-site monitoring and surveillance system (OSMOS) measures to strengthen banks' supervisory systems. Further, systems of evaluation based on the entire operations and performance of the banks were also initiated. Among these, CAMELS (Capital Adequacy, Asset Quality, Management, Earnings, Liquidity System and Controls) is applicable to domestic, commercial banks; and CALCS (Capital Adequacy, Asset Quality, Liquidity Compliance, and Systems) is applicable to foreign banks. Finally, the role of internal and external audits was also strengthened to reinforce the supervisory process of the RBI through the auditing requirements.

Management of NPAs (Phase 2b: 1997–98 to 2007–08)

Despite the significant step introduced early in the reforms phase towards the prudential norms relating to income regulation, asset classification, and provisioning, these norms fell short of international best practices. They hence necessitated measures to strengthen them further to be on par with the international best practices.

However, despite an increase in the lendable resources of banks, credit growth slowed down from 1996 to 1997 due to the factors on both the sides of demand and supply, and banks continued to invest in government securities, far more than the requirements. At the same time, the demand for funds by the corporate sector also slowed down due to enhanced competition in the product market.

Further, the East Asian currency crisis in 1997 had exposed the threats that a weak banking system could pose to the real economy. Therefore, the framework for further strengthening the banking sector was initiated by the Committee on Banking Sector Reforms (CBSR),[6] which suggested tightening the norms of income recognition, asset classification, and provisioning without inducing excessive risk aversion by banks.

In addition to the initiation of asset-liability management (ALM) practices, to mitigate the pro-cyclical behaviour, banks were asked to have a general provision on standard assets of a minimum of 0.25 per cent on 31 March 2000, which was subsequently increased to 1 per cent. The asset classification norms were also tightened for early reporting of bad quality of assets as the 'past due' concept was discontinued from March 2001. The revised norms required an asset to be treated as 'doubtful' if it remained in the sub-standard category for 18 months compared to 24 months, which was further reduced to 12 months by March 2005. In addition, income recognition norms were revised from March 2004 to classify an asset as NPA if it remained unpaid for 90 days, compared to six months as per earlier norms. The RBI further advised banks to adopt graded higher provisioning to the secured portion of NPAs in the 'doubtful' category for more than three years and NPAs which remained in this category for more than three years as of 31 March 2004. From 31 March 2005, provisioning was also increased from 60 per cent to 100 per cent over three years in a phased manner (Reserve Bank of India, 2008).

However, one of the serious consequences of applying aggressive prudential norms without an effective debt recovery system led to credit squeeze due to the exercise of excessive risk aversion by banks. While some measures were initiated to recover the past dues of the banks, they did not produce the desired results. For example, the efficacy of the DRTs and asset reconstruction companies (ARCs) remained painfully low due to legal and other structural factors. To provide the necessary legal underpinnings for ARCs, the GOI enacted the Securitization and Reconstruction of Financial Assets and Enforcement of Security Interest (SARFAESI) Act, 2002, which empowered the banks to foreclose properties (Box 2.3). Though the reform was passed in November 2002, it was in April 2004 when the Supreme Court declared SARFAESI to be constitutional, making it the landmark reform in the Indian banking sector.

Implementation of various measures to recover past due of banks facilitated banks to recover as much as INR 25,520 crores between 2003–04 and 2006–07. Further, while the asset quality had been improving after introducing prudential norms, it showed a distinct improvement in this phase as gross NPAs declined sharply (Figure 2.2).

Therefore, a reduction in NPAs and a reduction in CRR or SLR and deregulation of interest rates had a significant positive impact on the credit growth, which had

---

Box 2.3 Provisions under the Securitization and Reconstruction of Financial Assets and Enforcement of Security Interest (SARFAESI) Act, 2002

1. Secured creditors can recover their non-performing assets (NPAs) by taking possession of or selling the securities without court intervention or tribunal.

2. The secured creditors could start the recovery process by filing notice on an NPA loan, and if not paid by 60 days from the date of the notice, they were allowed to take possession of the secured assets, take over the management, appoint persons to manage the secure assets, or require the borrower to repay the secured creditor directly.

3. In cases of insufficient collateral, the creditors can file an application to the Debt Recovery Tribunal (DRT) for recovering the remaining dues.

4. This reform was only applied to the bank and financial institutions rather than non-banking financial companies (NBFCs), as clarified by the Supreme Court.

5. The Act also helped form specialized intermediaries, called asset reconstruction companies (ARCs), which managed the asset reallocation process.

6. Since the reform helped the creditors bypass the judicial process, the delinquent defaulters could not file the Board for Industrial and Financial Reconstruction (BIFR) and unnecessarily delay the recovery process.

Source: Authors' compilation.

decelerated significantly between 1996–97 and 2003–04 partly on account of risk aversion. As shown in Figure 2.3, the credit growth began to accelerate to over 30 per cent during 2004–05, particularly in the industrial sector. However, it is noteworthy that the banks' deposit growth rate could not cope with the pace of the rapid credit expansion, which led to the liquidation of the investment in SLR securities by banks, which had reached an all-time high level of 41.5 at the end of March 2003 and declined gradually to 28 per cent by the end of March 2007.

In April 2006, the RBI calibrated non-food bank credit growth to around 20 per cent during 2006–07 from growth of above 30 per cent. Further, the CRR was gradually raised to 6.5 per cent in 2007 from a low of 4.5 per cent in 2004, which moderated credit growth to 21.6 per cent in 2007–08. As we can observe from Figure 2.3, periods 2003–04 to 2009–10 are marked by higher industrial credit growth – highest in the last quarter of the century.

However, it is important to note that despite a sharp increase in credit between 2004–05 and 2006–07, banks were able to maintain their capital to risk-weighted asset ratio (CRAR) at 12.9 per cent in 2007, significantly higher than the statutory requirement due to improved profitability. As a result, the profitability of scheduled commercial banks improved from 0.8 per cent in 1997–98 to 1.11 per cent in 2008. The improved profitability was, among others, on account of a sharp decline in NPAs coupled with an increased credit volume.

Thus, it is important to note that the impact of reforms initiated in the early 1990s became evident in this phase as the Indian banking sector had become competitive, profitable, and strong.

Given the scope of banking that involves acceptance and deployment of a large amount of uncollateralized public funds to create credit in the economy, the

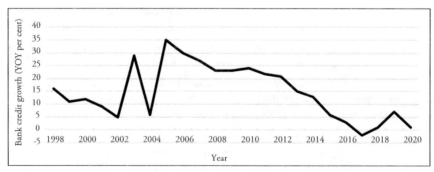

Figure 2.3 Bank credit growth in the industrial sector (YoY)

Source: Reserve Bank of India, *Handbook of Statistics on Indian Economy*, various editions.

corporate governance structure of banks becomes crucial. There were two primary concerns in the context of Indian banks. First is the concentrated ownership structure, where the controlling shareholders of private banks control the resources with their minor stake in the bank. Such divergence between control and ownership gives rise to agency problems which can lead to the expropriation of public funds in the hands of entrenched owners. Second is the quality of management of banks, which includes the structure of the board of directors. The Banking Regulation Act, 1949, had laid down the legal prescriptions relating to ownership and governance. However, the first effort towards formalizing the best practices in corporate governance of banks was made by the Advisory Group on Corporate Governance for the RBI Standing Committee on International Financial Standards and Codes, chaired by R. H. Patil. Subsequently, the RBI issued detailed guidelines on ownership and appointment of the board of directors on 3 February 2004.

Further, to strengthen the corporate governance structure of private sector banks, the RBI released a comprehensive policy framework of ownership and governance in February 2005. The framework prescribed norms to attain a well-diversified ownership structure by limiting the ultimate shareholding or control by a single group or entity up to 10 per cent of the paid-up capital. In addition, to ensure the quality of management, 'fit and proper' criteria were applicable to the directors and CEOs, and adherence to sound corporate governance principles was required. The framework also specified the transparency and fairness in the policy and essential processes and minimum net-worth requirement of INR 300 crores for system stability. Therefore, realizing the importance of corporate governance even in PSBs, necessary guidelines were issued to nationalized banks in November 2007, and new sections highlighting the applicability of 'fit and proper' criteria for elected directors on PSB boards were amended in the Banking Companies Act, 1970, and the State Bank of India Act, 1959.

Reforms after the Re-emergence of NPAs (Phase 3: 2007–08 Onwards)

However, the euphoria was short-lived since the economy underwent severe financial stress as an aftermath of the GFC in the late 2000s, leading to several detrimental challenges to the growth process. As a result, the credit growth that had accelerated to over 30 per cent in 2004–05 remained more or less at that level in the following two years. At the peak, infrastructure and construction constituted 27 per cent of the total industrial credit. However, the high growth period was followed by a sharp decline in the credit growth as it plummeted to 2.7 per cent in 2016 from an average annual growth of 24.62 per cent during 2003–10. The credit to industry further declined to an alarming 1.9 per cent in 2017 before recovering to 6 per cent in 2019 (Figure 2.3).

One of the major challenges that beleaguered the Indian banking sector was the re-emergence of NPAs. The bad loans in the bank's books started to witness an upward trend from 2011 and became alarming when the gross NPA ratio to advances, which was 2.4 per cent in 2010, increased to 7.5 per cent in March 2016 and 9.6 in March 2017. Further, the RBI's *Financial Stability Report* of September 2018 puts the gross NPA ratio of Indian banks at 11.5 per cent in March 2018. Figure 2.2 shows the disquieting growth trajectory of the gross NPA ratio of the scheduled commercial banks after 2010.

The NPA crisis that unfolded after 2000 had the following notable aspects. Figure 2.4 presents the trends of gross NPA ratio of the PSBs and private sector banks. The figure indicates that nearly 86 per cent of the total NPAs were contributed by the PSBs, which account for around 79 per cent of total banking assets. It is important to note that the NPA of PSBs that was subdued until 2014 showed a significant rise after the 2015–16 period as the RBI initiated the asset quality review (AQR) of banks in 2014. This initiative led to the recognition of many bank loans as NPAs, which banks so far considered as standard assets. However, while more than half of the bad loans of PSBs were waived off between 2013 and 2015, PSBs were able to write off a little under INR 1.9 lakh crores of bad loans between 2004 and 2014. As a result of the AQR, gross NPAs increased from 4.62 per cent in 2014–15 to 7.79 per cent in 2015–16 and reached as high as 10.41 per cent by December 2017. Gross NPAs of PSBs reached up to INR 7.70 lakh crores. Second, as depicted in Figure 2.5, the NPA problems affected the domestic banks significantly more in comparison to the foreign-owned banks during the same period, thus suggesting a lower efficacy of domestic banks (particularly the PSBs) in allocating credit. Third, it is also worth noting that loan quality was deteriorating for both priority and other sectors. In contrast to the conventional wisdom, Figure 2.6 shows that priority sector lending was not the main contributor to bad loans since 2011. While the priority sector always had a higher ratio of non-performing loans, the growth of NPAs was higher in the case of other sectors, particularly infrastructure and core industries (Chavan and Gambacorta, 2016).

Therefore, to mitigate the growing NPAs in the books of PSBs, the government had to infuse capital into public sector undertaking (PSU) banks to support credit expansion and help them tide over losses resulting from provisions for NPAs. Accordingly, the GOI had infused INR 3.8 lakh crores between the fiscal year 2011 and fiscal year 2020 and further sought parliamentary approval to infuse another INR 200 billion (USD 2.72 billion) in 2020–21 in the current fiscal year to help lenders mitigate the expected surge in bad loans due to the pandemic.

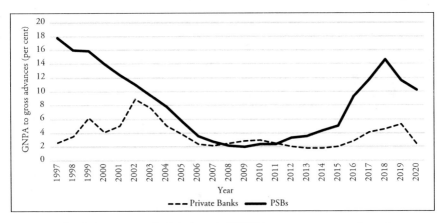

Figure 2.4 Gross non-performing asset (GNPA) as a percentage of total advances – public and private sector banks

Source: Department of Supervision, Reserve Bank of India.

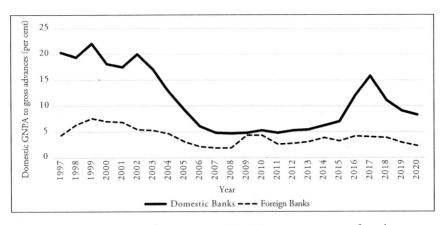

Figure 2.5 Gross non-performing asset (GNPA) as a percentage of total advances – domestic and foreign banks

Source: Department of Supervision, Reserve Bank of India.

However, as the government continued to strengthen the capital base of PSBs through equity capital infusion, the PSBs continued to report financial losses. According to the data published by the RBI, state-owned banks ended up writing off INR 3,16,500 crores of loans between April 2014 and April 2018 (even as they recovered INR 44,900 crores written off on a cumulative basis). To put this number in perspective, the amount of bad loans written off by PSBs during the four years is well over twice the projected budgetary expenditure on health, education,

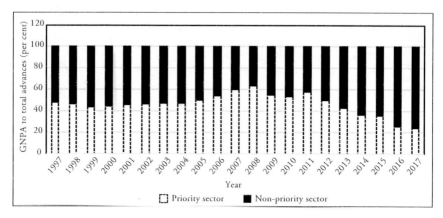

Figure 2.6 Gross non-performing asset (GNPA) as a percentage of total advances in public sector banks (PSBs) – sector-wise distribution

Source: Reserve Bank of India, *Handbook of Statistics on Indian Economy*, various editions.

and social protection for 2018–19 at INR 1.38 lakh crores. Further, from April 2014 to April 2018, the loans written off by the PSBs were over 166 per cent of the amount in the ten years till 2014.

The cumulative loss of PSBs crossed INR 87,357 crores in 2017–18 due to the scam-tainted Punjab National Bank (PNB) reporting a loss of nearly INR 12,283 crores, followed by Israel Discount Bank of New York (IDB) Bank.

Out of 21 state-owned banks, only two – Indian Bank and Vijaya Bank – posted profits during 2017–18 – INR 1,258.99 crores and INR 727.02 crores, respectively. In contrast, the aggregate loss of the rest of the PSBs stood at INR 54,854.3 crores in fiscal year 2019 as against INR 72,547.1 crores in the preceding year. It is important to note that the private lenders posted an aggregate profit of INR 47,583.82 crores during the same period. In 2019, PSBs' collective losses further escalated to over INR 66,000 crores due to aggressive provisioning, nearly double the nation's budgetary allocation for education. Figure 2.7 depicts the trends in capital infusion in PSBs along with the burgeoning losses.

It is important to note that the RBI had initiated several steps to manage the growing NPA crisis that had unfolded after 2010. Until 2008, the RBI targeted primarily to control private debt workout by laying out a mechanism for large distressed borrowers. The mechanism facilitated negotiations to bring debt burdens to manageable levels and relaxed the provisioning requirements for those banks that participated in the process. However, while these new insolvency mechanisms

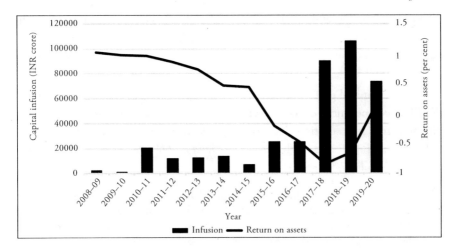

Figure 2.7   Capital infusion and profitability in public sector banks

Source: Reserve Bank of India, *Handbook of Statistics on Indian Economy*, various editions.

were targeted to replace the old and ineffective processes, they failed to deliver substantial gains due to inadequate legal provision, leading to a large amount of litigation. Therefore, to address the fragmented corporate insolvency and to set up a unified structure to expedite resolution of stressed assets, after 2014, the government has tried three debt resolution mechanisms: (*a*) the Strategic Debt Restructuring (SDR) Scheme of 2015, which allows creditors to take over firms unable to pay and sell them to new owners, (*b*) Sustainable Structuring of Stressed Assets (S4A) of 2016, which lets creditors take 50 per cent haircut to restore the financial viability of firms, and (*c*) Insolvency and Bankruptcy Code (IBC) of 2016, which addresses the NPA problem either by resolution or by the liquidation of indebted firms.

The most effective among these three measures, initiated by the IBC in 2016, was explicitly designed to improve India's lengthy and ineffective bankruptcy process. Notably, the RBI had introduced a 'Framework for Revitalizing Distressed Assets in the Economy' in January 2014 for early identification of weaknesses in loan accounts and initiation of remedial measures for each stage of stress. However, as banks allegedly continued evergreening of loans in fear of personal consequences of resolution proceedings and severely under-reported the NPAs, the RBI withdrew such forbearance from 1 April 2015 and initiated the AQR during 2015–16 to enforce correct classification of NPAs. This led to a sudden spike of gross NPAs from 4.62 per cent in 2014–15 to 7.8 per cent in 2015–16, reaching

10.4 per cent by December 2017 (INR 8.41 trillion). Thus, in conjunction with the AQR and the IBC, the RBI had referred 12 large delinquent corporate loan accounts constituting 25 per cent of total NPAs to the National Company Law Tribunal (NCLT).

While the initial performance of IBC is promising, it remains to be seen how the IBC becomes more effective over a period of time, in terms of both recovery rate and time to resolution. However, significant improvement in the recovery of bad loans is indicated by the *Report on Trend and Progress of Banking in India, 2019–20*, as follows:

> In absolute terms, of the total amount of Rs 1,72,565 crore recovered through various channels in 2019–20, IBC route accounted for Rs 1,05,773 crore. In 2018–19, of the total recovered amount of Rs 1,18,647 crore, the recovery via the IBC channel was Rs 66,440 crore. Further, in terms of duration, the IBC proceedings take 340 days on an average as compared to the duration of 4.3 years earlier.

Finally, complementing the structural reforms in 2017, the RBI reviewed the Prompt Corrective Action (PCA) framework of 2002 to evaluate monitoring and early intervention mechanisms. Regulatory trigger points relating to their CRAR, NPA, return on assets (ROA), and tier 1 leverage ratio were specified as a part of the revised PCA framework. Banks are deemed risky if the trigger points are hit and are instructed to initiate structured and discretionary actions. PCA framework complements the AQR that mainly targets the large non-performing borrowers by monitoring the financial health of commercial banks. As the NPA problem continues to persist since 2017, the RBI announced stringent guidelines for lenders in a circular called 'Resolution of Stressed Assets' on 12 February 2018, replacing the existing resolution mechanisms such as Corporate Debt Restructuring (CDR) and SDR. The salient features of the February 2018 circular were the following.

1. Guidelines were provided for the lenders that prompted identification of borrower defaults and laid time-bound rules for the referral of large defaulters to the IBC.

2. The banks were instructed to address the defaults within one day and mandated the lenders to pursue insolvency proceedings under IBC for any default for 180 days.

3. The circular was applicable for all borrowers with accounts over INR 20 billion and proposed to extend the same for INR 1 billion exposures.

Phase 1 (pre-liberalization period; 1966–67 to 1990–91)
- Social controls over banks
- Nationalization of banks
- Geographical spread of banking

Phase 2a (post-liberalization period; 1991–92 to 1997–98)
- Financial health and soundness
- Removal of external constraints
- Creation of competitive environment
- Strengthening of institutions
- Credit delivery to rural sector

Phase 2b (post-liberalization period; 1997–98 to 2007–08)
- Non-performing asset (NPA) management
- Intensification of competition
- Diversifiication and emergence of universal banks
- Corporate governance norms
- Credit delivery to small and mid-size enterprises (SMEs)
- Financial inclusion
- Customer service and financial literacy
- Banking technology

Phase 3 (post-global financial crisis period; 2008–09 onwards)
- Asset quality review
- Focus on financial stability
- Debt recovery and restructuring Systems
- Insolvency and Bankruptcy Code, 2016
- Prompt Corrective Action (PCA) framework
- Resolution Plan

Figure 2.8 Salient features of banking sector reforms in India
Source: Authors' compilation.

The circular directed lenders to recognize 'restructured assets' as non-performing.

Following the Supreme Court verdict against the February 2018 circular noting that the RBI does not hold an issuance power from the Banking Regulation, the circular was revised as 'Prudential Framework for Resolution of Stressed Assets' in June 2019. The circular emphasized initiating the Resolution Plan (RP) ahead of actual default and made it mandatory for all lenders to start RP in case of default. In addition, RPs involving the restructuring of bank accounts with INR 1 billion or more are required to undergo Independent Credit Evaluation (ICE) by RBI-approved credit-rating agencies.

To sum up, Figure 2.8 captures the evolution of the Indian banking sector and salient features of the reform process discussed in earlier sections.

Conclusion

As we have seen in this chapter, the impact of reforms initiated in the early 1990s became evident by 2010 since the Indian banking sector had witnessed a significant improvement in competitiveness, profitability, and financial health. However, the performance of the Indian banking sector went astray as an aftermath of the GFC, particularly after 2010. Despite several corrective measures taken by the RBI such as the SICA, the BIFR, DRTs, and the SARFAESI during the 2000s, the burgeoning NPAs had become one of the major challenges for the regulator and remain the top priority of the RBI to date.

Therefore, the chapter poses pertinent questions: why has the Indian banking sector, which displayed strong performance before 2008, become excessively overwhelmed with NPAs after 2010? Are these surging NPAs in the post-GFC world a mere reflection of the general business cycles, or do they reflect deeper systemic maladies? The following chapters in the study attempt to address some of these important questions.

Notes

1. It is also known as the Hilton Young Commission, 1926.

2. See the RBI's report on currency and finance. Reserve Bank of India, 'Evolution of Banking in India', 4 September 2008, https://rbi.org.in/scripts/publicationsview. aspx?id=10487 (accessed in January 2021). Also see Amol Agarwal, 'Banking Crises: An Indian History', *Mint*, 26 February 2018, https://www.livemint.com/Sundayapp/ fjheowjLjiFNsGcjzVZXsO/Banking-crises-An-Indian-history.html (accessed in January 2021).

3. Due to this feature, commercial banking principles were largely compromised. The persistence of crony capitalism in the Indian economy created oligarchies and slowed down growth, specifically in the early phase of banking. See *Business Standard*, 'How Crony Capitalism Impacts India: RBI Governor Rajan Explains', 14 August 2014, https://www.business-standard.com/article/economy-policy/how-crony-capitalism-impacts-india-rbi-governor-rajan-explains-114081400156_1.html (accessed in January 2021).

4. This is according to the Banking Companies (Acquisition and Transfer of Undertakings) Act, 1980.

5. Branch expansion rose to 20 per cent in the post-nationalization period and staggered at 12 per cent in the pre-nationalization period. The post-nationalization period witnessed an increase in gross credit allocation to the priority sectors, with all priority sectors receiving more than 35 per cent of gross bank credit. Overall, the nationalization of banks accelerated savings, investment, and growth of the Indian economy to a large extent (Ketkar and Ketkar, 1992).

6. See the CBSR's report. 'Committee on Banking Sector Reforms (Narasimhan Committee II: Action Taken on the Recommendations', https://rbidocs.rbi.org.in/rdocs/PublicationReport/Pdfs/24157.pdf (accessed in January 2021).

3

The Index of Credit Allocative Efficiency

In an efficient financial market, capital is expected to flow increasingly towards the profitable sectors and thereby generate more returns, ensuring overall growth of the economy (Rajan and Zingales, 1998, 2001). Liberalization of the economy is one step in the direction of increasing efficiency as it opens up the financial markets and boosts the participation of various market participants. A wave of liberalization of capital markets swept across various developing countries in the mid-1980s that replaced a flawed system characterized by government controls and provided the market forces an impetus in determining the interest rates and allocating credit efficiently (Bhaduri and Bhattacharya, 2018). As the markets steadily moved towards a free-market mechanism, the consequences of this process gained significant attention in the financial literature.

Two significant facets of financial liberalization and subsequent development have gained prominence in the empirical literature. One strand of literature focuses on the 'quantity effect', which examines the changes in the levels of savings and investment (McKinnon, 1974; Shaw, 1974 Beck, Levine, and Loayza 2000; Rajan and Zingales, 1998, 2001; Ueda, 2006). However, the empirical evidence favouring the quantity impact has been mixed (Devereux and Smith, 1994; Jayaratne and Strahan, 1996; Bandiera, 2000; Bhaduri and Kumar, 2014). In contrast, the second and the more recent literature examines the 'quality effect', which analyses whether the financial reforms led to improved allocation of savings and investment. It is often argued that if liberalization has to impact growth positively, it is more likely to be associated with the allocative efficiency of resources across firms and sectors (Bhaduri and Bhattacharya, 2018). While several studies have examined this aspect of reforms, the empirical findings remain contentious (Jaramillo, Schiantarelli, and Weiss, 1992; Wurgler, 2000; Galindo, Schiantarelli, and Weiss, 2007; Abaid, Oomes, and Ueda, 2008). Since the growth of industries through investment depends on the country's structure, country-specific studies can advance understanding of the efficiency of resources and their determinants (Carlin and Mayer, 2003). A few country-specific studies using the data of the 1980s and early 1990s suggest that financial liberalization has been associated with a substantial improvement in efficiency (Cho, 1988, Jaramillo, Schiantarelli, and Weiss, 1992; Harris, Schiantarelli, and Siregar, 1994; Galindo et al., 2002; Abaid, Oomes, and Ueda, 2008). More recently, single-country analyses suggest a strong case for the misallocation of resources in the liberalized regimes (Chari and Henry, 2002; Bhaduri and Kumar, 2014; Bhaduri and Bhattacharya, 2018).

In contrast to the extant literature, this research explores the less frequently researched dimension in bank credit allocation. As mentioned in the previous chapter, the banking sector contributes close to 50 per cent of the total flow of resources to the Indian corporate. Efficient mobilization and allocation of funds by banks help reduce the cost of capital to firms, increase capital formation, and improve productivity and growth (Levine, 2005). However, a country's institutional and regulatory environment can have different effects on banks' risk-taking, depending on their corporate governance structure (Laeven and Levine, 2009). Capital account liberalization in the country during the 1990s paved the way for banking sector reforms, increased competition, and the entry of foreign banks. Restructuring and corporatization of development financial institutions (DFIs) created a substantial capital base for newly privatized banks. At the same time, the entry of banks into stock and real-estate markets led to excessive risk-taking by banks which, coupled with a boom in India's stock market, increased financial fragility (Chandrasekhar and Pal, 2006). Despite the best efforts by the regulator and the government to promote alternate sources like private placements of debt and equity as well as foreign currency borrowings, banks remain the primary source of credit for Indian firms.[1] We argue that weak corporate governance mechanisms, poor institutional quality, and larger political interventions might lead to sub-optimal lending decisions, particularly in the context of emerging economies like India (Shah, 2015). Recent banking scams involving some of the largest nationalized banks, absconding promoters of defaulting firms, have exposed the fragility and quality of banks' governance in reducing the misappropriation of bank credit in the Indian economy. Against this backdrop, this chapter investigates the sources of misallocation of the bank credit extended to the corporate sector in the last two decades. Previous research has been constrained by the problem of how to measure efficiency in allocating capital. Most of the earlier studies define the efficiency of resource allocation in a narrow sense as purely technical efficiency, which is calculated using panel data estimates of a Cobb Douglas production function. More recent studies argue for measures based on the dispersion of returns and their elasticity with respect to investment across firms. One of the main contributions of our research is to propose a new measure of allocative efficiency based on the quality of allocative investment across firms.

Index of Credit Allocative Efficiency

The chapter proposes a measure of credit misallocation as an indicator of the prodigal borrowing behaviour of a firm. Credit misallocation, particularly 'borrowing exuberance' as a corporate behaviour and misallocation of resources by financial institutions, has been a contentious issue in the economic literature for a long time. Despite much anecdotal evidence suggesting borrowing exuberance in the popular press, precise quantification remains a vexing challenge for researchers.

In an efficient banking system, credit is expected to flow increasingly towards profitable firms, thereby generating more returns and ensuring the economy's overall growth. Therefore, to understand credit misallocation, particularly the borrowing exuberance, it is critical to start with the concept of efficient credit allocation. In a conventional neo-classical framework, we argue that firms in an efficient economy operate under competitive market interest rates. Consequently, the marginal returns to capital get equalized across all firms in the economy while optimizing their investment decisions.

To comprehend the idea, we present a simple neo-classical model (Abaid, Oomes, and Ueda, 2008). We write the typical profit function of a firm at time t as follows:

$$\pi(K_t, L_t) = f(K_t, L_t) - wL_t - \phi(I_t) - RK_t \qquad (3.1)$$

And standard capital formation equation:

$$K_t = (1 - \delta)K_{t-1} + I_t \qquad (3.2)$$

Here, K denotes capital, L denotes labour, w is the real market wage, I is an investment, and R is the gross interest rate. The function f is a constant-returns-to-scale (CRS) production function with partial derivatives $f'_1 > 0, f'_2 > 0, f'_{11} < 0, f'_{12} < 0$. The function $\varphi(I_t)$ measures the adjustment cost of investment and satisfies $\varphi' > 0$ and $\varphi'' > 0$.

Profit maximization gives us the unique steady-state optimal decision (K^*, I^*, L^*), which satisfies:

$$f_1(K^* L^*) - \phi'(I^*) = R \qquad (3.3)$$

$$f_2(K^* L^*) - w = 0 \qquad (3.4)$$

$$\delta K^* = I^* \qquad (3.5)$$

Note that as the production function is CRS, the labour market condition (3.2) determines the capital-to-labour ratio, given the real wage w. By substituting L^*

in 3.3 by the implicit function of K^* using 3.4 and substituting I^* from 3.5, the capital market condition (3.3) becomes a function of K^* only. This determines K^*, which is unique because the production function is concave while the adjustment cost function is convex.

Therefore, since in an efficient economy, each firm faces the same market interest rate, R, without any credit rationing, the model implies that the marginal returns to capital, given by 3.3, are equal across firms, and each firm uses capital to match its marginal returns to capital. This equalization of marginal returns across firms provides the foundation of the measure of misallocation proposed in this chapter.

As a corollary to this conjecture, we argue that an inefficient market, due to various sociopolitical reasons, including the government's direct interventions in the credit market, would generate wide variation in the marginal returns to capital across firms.

For example, consider the case where banks influence the allocation of credit. However, with no loss of generality, we consider that all firms face the same interest rates. Let us denote this amount by $\hat{I}$. In this case, firms maximize their profit function to the additional constraint $\hat{I} = I$. Defining λ as the Lagrange multiplier associated with this additional constraint, the credit market condition (3.3) can then be rewritten as

$$f_1(K^{**}, L^{**}) - \phi'(I^{**}) = R + \lambda \qquad (3.6)$$

Here ** indicates the new equilibrium.

Note, if firms are exuberant for the amount they can borrow and invest ($\hat{I} > I^*$), λ becomes negative. This implies that the marginal return to capital is lower than the market-based interest rate. The opposite is true for credit-constraint firms. Therefore, we argue that an inefficient economy is characterized by a persistent variation in marginal returns across firms that face the same production function, adjustment cost function, and real wage costs.

Hence, through efficient allocation of credit, we hypothesize that banks reduce these variations in the marginal returns to capital across firms. In other words, an efficient banking system directs less credit to firms with low marginal returns (that is, the overinvesting firms) and more credit to firms with high marginal returns (that is, the underinvesting firms), leading to an equal distribution of marginal returns to capital in the economy. We attempt to capture the extent of this transfer of credit from low-marginal-returns firms to the more productive firm with higher marginal returns to capital using a novel measure, the index of credit allocative efficiency (ICAE). In other words, we conceptualize misallocation as a flow of credit to firms with lower marginal returns to the capital from their counterpart firms with higher marginal returns to capital.

It is important to note that most of the existing studies deploy a total factor productivity (TFP) framework to ascertain the extent of misallocation.[2] This framework implicitly assumes that the funds are efficiently allocated when their alternative uses generate the same value-added for given amounts of factor inputs, or equivalently when the value of the marginal productivity of each factor is equalized across alternative uses (Di Mauro, Hassan, and Ottaviano 2018). Any deviation from equalization is interpreted as a signal of allocative inefficiency. Further, the misallocation of resources at the firm level is argued to lower aggregate efficiency (Hsieh and Klenow, 2009). The use of TFP in the context of misallocation of capital can be traced in several papers (for example, see Restuccia and Rogerson, 2008; Melitz, 2003; Gopinath et al., 2017). More recently, Schivardi, Sette, and Tabellini (2017) used the TFP framework specifically in the context of bank credit misallocation. However, it is to be noted that the TFP is a largely debated topic in the literature and makes it a non-reliable measure in deriving marginal productivity of capital (Banerjee and Duflo, 2014). Further, in order to find the TFP, a production function has to be defined, which often comes across several hurdles (Wurgler, 2000; Abaid, Oomes, and Ueda, 2008).

In this research, we build on an alternative notion of efficiency that suggests that misallocation arises if the funds do not flow from low-growth firms to high-growth firms (Wurgler, 2000; Di Mauro, Hassan, and Ottaviano, 2018). Notably, it is imperative to assess the marginal product of capital appropriately while calculating credit misallocation. However, quantifying the marginal product of capital is an arduous and contentious task as its accuracy critically depends on the reliable estimates of the underlying production function. To circumvent this, we use an approximation. Borrowing from the standard practices in the corporate finance literature, we use Tobin's Q as a proxy for expected marginal returns to capital. As efficient market prices help investors distinguish good investments from bad ones, measures such as Tobin's Q can provide a benchmark for the marginal returns to capital. Though not considered perfect, Tobin's Q is a frequently used measure of average returns to capital in finance literature.[3] Tobin's Q is the ratio of the market value of existing capital to its replacement cost. As the numerator represents investors' valuation of the firm, Tobin's Q is essentially the discounted sum of expected future profits per asset. In addition, the Q theory of investment argues that efficiency requires financing firms with a market value above the replacement value which signals that profits are expected to rise. This line of argument further hypothesizes that if the markets are reasonably efficient, any effort to channel the funds towards high-Q firms leads to an improvement in capital allocation. Therefore, by focusing on the flow of credit among firms based on Tobin's Q, our measure of misallocation, the ICAE circumvents the limitations of the TFP studies.[4] However, it is worth noting that the Q-based approach is only relevant with listed firms whose market value is directly observable.

Specifically, the ICAE is defined as a weighted average of quality of credit allocation to firms in the economy, where quality is measured by the amount of credit allocated to a firm commensurate with the marginal returns to its capital.

Mathematically, the ICAE is defined as

$$ICAE_t = \Sigma_{i=1}^{N} w_{it} CAE_{ijt} \text{ where } CAE_{ijt} = (q_{it} - \overline{q})(LTBB_{it} - \overline{LTBB}) \tag{3.7}$$

Here,

$$w_{it} = \frac{TA_{it}}{TA_t}$$

Here, q_{it} is the estimated Q for firm i at time t, $\overline{q}$ is the asset-weighted average of Q of each industry j at time t, TA_{it} is total assets of each firm i at time t, TA_t is the total assets of all the firms at time t, $LTBB_{it}$ is the long-term bank borrowing by firm i at time t, $\overline{LTBB}$ is the weighted average of long-term bank borrowing of each industry j at time t, and N is the total number of firms in year t.[5]

Specifically, the ICAE, for a firm i, is derived as a weighted sum of the two multiplicative factors: first, the firm's adjusted bank borrowing is defined as a deviation of the firm's bank borrowing from the asset-weighted average bank borrowing of the industry, while the second factor involves a similar deviation measure between the firm's Q and the asset-weighted average Q of the entire industry.[6] Therefore, assume that the average industry Q is a good proxy for the average expected Q for the economy; this attributes a market value to each bank credit allocation. Finally, the weighted transfer across all the firms in a year is added to arrive at $ICAE_t$. The $ICAE_t$, therefore, represents a measure of the overall value-added as a consequence of efficient credit allocation in the economy (Rajan, Servaes, and Zingales, 2000; Hovakimian, 2011).

It is worth noting that a positive (negative) value of the ICAE indicates that the banks are efficient (inefficient) in allocating credit, suggesting that, on average, more bank loans are flowing to high (low) Q companies from low (high) Q companies. Further, by construct, we can decompose $ICAE$ into two additive components: $ICAE^+$ and $ICAE^-$, where $ICAE^+$ incorporates all the positive CAE_{ijt}, while $ICAE^-$ captures all negative CAE_{ijt}.

$$ICAE_t^+ = \Sigma_{i=1}^{N} w_{it} CAE_{ijt} \text{ where } CAE_{ijt} = (q_{it} - \overline{q})(LTBB_{it} - \overline{LTBB}) > 0 \tag{3.8}$$

$$ICAE_t^- = \Sigma_{i=1}^{N} w_{it} CAE_{ijt} \text{ where } CAE_{it} = (q_{it} - \overline{q})(LTBB_{it} - \overline{LTBB}) \leq 0 \tag{3.9}$$

The intuitive rationale behind the concept of allocative efficiency can be explained using a scenario where two firms (with similar asset size) with different Q are provided with 300 units of bank credit. The credit is allotted among firms A and B in two alternative ways, as presented in Table 3.1.

In allocation scenario 1, firm A with a lower Q ratio receives more bank credit when compared to firm B, which has a higher Q ratio. On the contrary, in allocation scenario 2, firm B, which has a higher Q ratio, receives more bank credit when compared to firm A with a lower Q ratio. The preliminary observation suggests that allocation 2 seems more efficient, as the firm with a higher marginal product of capital is receiving more bank credit when compared to allocation 1. To fully understand the impact of these two types of allocation, we consider the following scenario in Table 3.2.

Let L^* and Q^* be the average bank credit and average Q ratio, respectively. Scenarios A_{11} and A_{22} are inefficient allocation scenarios, as in A_{11} a firm with $Q < Q^*$ receives more credit, and in A_{22} firms with $Q > Q^*$ receives lesser credit. We define the A_{11} scenario as 'borrowing exuberance' (BE) and A_{22} as 'borrowing constrained' (BC). However, the other two scenarios are efficient allocations. In scenario A_{21}, firms with a Q ratio higher than the industry average Q ratio receive

Table 3.1 Types of allocation

	Tobin's Q	Allocation 1	Allocation 2
Firm A	1	200	100
Firm B	2	100	200

Table 3.2 Impact of two types of allocation

	$L > L^*$	$L < L^*$
$Q < Q^*$	A_{11} (Borrowing Exuberance)	A_{12}
$Q > Q^*$	A_{21}	A_{22} (Borrowing Constrained)
Averages(*) $Q^* = 1.5,$ $L^* = 150$	ICAE = $(A_{11}+A_{22}) = -50$	ICAE = $(A_{21}+A_{12}) = 50$

Note: $A = (Q - Q^*)(L - L^*)$

a higher bank credit, while in A_{12}, firms with relatively lower Q receive credit lesser than the industrial average credit, representing efficient allocations.

As presented in equation 3.7, an allocative index (ICAE) is defined as $\Sigma \theta_f A_{ij}$, where θ_j is a set of weights. In our hypothetical example, the ICAE presents the allocative index for inefficient and efficient allocations. As presented in the last row of Table 3.2, the ICAE produces a value of −50 for inefficient allocations and a value of 50 for efficient allocations.

Finally, it is important to note that the ICAE highlights two potential sources of bank credit misallocation: (*a*) the firms with relatively low Q (having Q values less than the weighted average Q value of industry) attract more bank loans than an industry average, so the ICAE turns out to be negative and defined as BE, and (*b*) the firms with high Q values get less bank credit than average, so the ICAE also turns out to be negative and noted as BC. Therefore, to better understand the nature of misallocation, it is imperative to track both these possibilities – BC and BE – along with the overall trends in the ICAE. Equations 3.10 and 3.11 present the components of ICAE⁻ into BE and BC.

$$BE = \Sigma_{i=1}^{N} w_{it} CAE_{ijt} \text{ where } CAE_{ijt} = (q_{it} - \overline{q})(LTBB_{it} - \overline{LTBB}) \leq$$
$$0 \text{ with } (q_{it} - \overline{q}) \leq 0 \text{ and } (LTBB_{it} - \overline{LTBB}) > 0 \tag{3.10}$$

$$BC = \Sigma_{i=1}^{N} w_{it} CAE_{ijt} \text{ where } CAE_{ijt} = (q_{it} - \overline{q})(LTBB_{it} - \overline{LTBB}) \leq$$
$$0 \text{ with } (q_{it} - \overline{q}) \geq 0 \text{ and } (LTBB_{it} - \overline{LTBB}) < 0 \tag{3.11}$$

Estimation of Q Ratio

As mentioned earlier, an appropriate measure for the marginal product of capital is crucial to evaluate the allocation of bank credit. Using Q as a proxy for the marginal product of capital is often fraught with several limitations, particularly in emerging markets. One such limitation is that, since a large proportion of corporate debt in India is not actively traded in the debt market, the companies report asset value according to historical costs rather than replacement costs. To address this, we calculate the Q ratio as a proxy for Tobin's Q (Pandit and Siddharthan, 2003; Bhattacharyya and Saxena, 2009; Chadha and Oriani, 2010). The numerator is the firm's market value calculated as the sum of market capitalization and the book value of debt. The denominator uses the book value of total assets as a proxy for the replacement cost of assets. Mathematically, the Q ratio for firm i in the year t is measured as

$$q_{it} = \frac{Book\ value\ of\ debt_{it} + Market\ value\ of\ common\ stock_{it}}{Book\ value\ of\ assets_{it}} \tag{3.12}$$

Further, though the empirical literature suggests Tobin's Q as a reliable proxy to capture the expected marginal product of capital, it has limitations (Bhaduri and Bhattacharya, 2018), and it is often suggested that marginal Q, which is the ratio of the increment in market valuation to the cost of the associated investment, is a better estimate. The data constraints encourage us to use proxy average Q for marginal Q. However, this is based on the assumption that the marginal product of investment is proportional to the average product of capital, leading to measurement errors. In contrast to most studies that largely ignore such measurement errors, our research incorporates correction factors suggested by Abaid, Oomes, and Ueda (2008) to address these measurement errors.

Specifically, to reduce measurement errors in replacing marginal Q with an average Q, we adjust the estimates of Q for factors like industry, age, size, and leverage. The reasons behind this strategy are as follows: first, it would correct for the disparities between marginal Q and average Q, which can arise from industry-specific factors. Second, in many emerging economies, small firms are often not correctly valued. In contrast, large firms may be overvalued, suggesting that it is imperative to focus on the size of the firm while measuring Q. Third, empirical literature further suggests that a firm's age also plays an important role in defining Q as firms of different ages have machines and factories at different phases of their lifecycles, which gets reflected in the book value of assets. By controlling for age, we also account for the possibility that younger firms may not yet be correctly valued in the stock market. Finally, measurement errors may stem from underinvestment as a result of debt overhang.

Accounting for measurement errors, we run the following regression after controlling for industry, age, size, and debt overhang effects on average Q:

$$q_i = \Sigma_{j=1}^{J} \xi_j \cdot \text{Industry}_{ij} + \theta_1 \cdot \text{Age}_i + \theta_2 \cdot \text{Size}_i +$$

$$\theta_3 \cdot \frac{\text{Liability}_i}{\text{Asset}_i} + \theta_4 \cdot \left(\frac{\text{Liability}_i}{\text{Asset}_i}\right)^2 + e_i \tag{3.13}$$

Here, q_i is the logarithm of Q ratio for firm $I = 1, \ldots, i$; *Industry* is the dummy variable, which takes the value of 1 if firm i belongs to industry j, otherwise 0; *Age* is the age of firm i; and *Size* is measured as the natural log of total assets. To account for the non-linear relationship between the probability of default and leverage, both the linear and squared terms of leverage ratio are included. Further, the adjusted measure of Q is constructed using the residual of this regression model:

$$\hat{q} = \text{mean}(q_i) + e_i = \left(\frac{1}{I} \cdot \Sigma^I_{i=1} q_i \right) + e_i \qquad (3.14)$$

It is worth noting that although the measurement errors in Tobin's Q are unlikely to be fully eliminated through the aforementioned adjustment process, we argue that the change in the dispersion of adjusted Q would reflect a change in the dispersion of true marginal product of capital as long as the dispersion of any remaining measurement errors is uncorrelated with external shocks like financial liberalization.[7]

Data and Sample

The data is obtained from the Prowess IQ maintained by the Center for Monitoring Indian Economy (CMIE), a comprehensive database which provides all information on balance sheets and stock markets of Indian firms. The sample used in this research covers a period of 28 years, starting from 1990 to 2017. We arrive at our final sample by applying the following exclusions. First, we consider *only* the listed manufacturing firms whose total assets are INR one million or more. Second, we consider *only* firms with long-term bank borrowing of at least INR 1 lakh (that is, the difference between long-term bank debt at t and $t -1$, respectively). As a final step, after taking the distribution of the Q ratio, we limit the Q ratio at 1.5 to eliminate extreme values resulting in 1 per cent winsorizing of the data. This leaves us with an unbalanced panel of 7,871 firm-year observations.

Trends in the ICAE and Its Components

As a first step, we trace the credit allocation pattern of the Indian firms. The ICAE of Indian manufacturing firms over 28 years is presented in Figure 3.1. To avoid short-term fluctuations, we report the ICAE for four-years window. Observation of negative values in the ICAE in the figure suggests that there has been a case of misallocation in the economy for a long period, starting from 1994–97 to 2006–09.

Subsequently, the breakdown of the ICAEs into positive and negative ICAEs is presented in Figure 3.2. The figure plots three-year moving averages (MA3) of ICAE values during the study period.

As mentioned earlier, our primary interest is to investigate the negative ICAE that can be attributed to BE ($Q < Qbar$ and $B > Bbar$) or BC ($Q > Qbar$ and $B < Bbar$). To see the comparison between these two effects, we further plot the breakup of ICAE⁻ in Figure 3.3. The dominant region in the graph reveals that

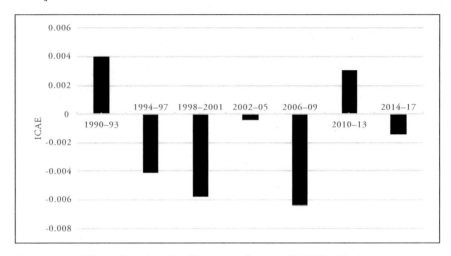

Figure 3.1 The index of credit allocative efficiency (ICAE) of Indian manufacturing firms in 1990–2017

Source: Authors' estimation.

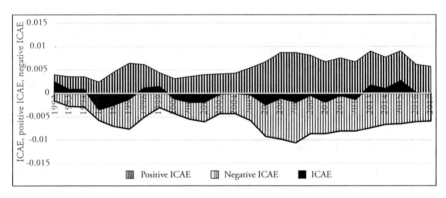

Figure 3.2 The breakup of the index of credit allocative efficiency (ICAE) – trends in negative and positive ICAE

Source: Authors' estimation.

Note: The graph shows a three-year moving average for the ICAE, and negative and positive values of the ICAE.

firms with a lower Q ratio received more bank credit. In other words, we observe that BE is dominating compared to the BC phenomenon as a source of credit misallocation.

We also observe three distinct cycles of excess borrowings during our sample period (1992–2017): 1992–98, 2000–03, and 2004–10, as shown in

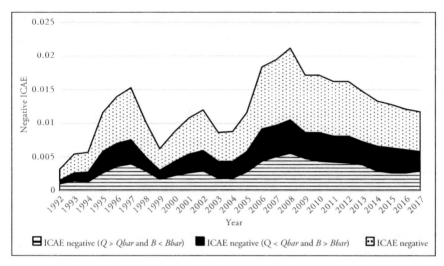

Figure 3.3　The breakup of the index of credit allocative efficiency (ICAE)

Source: Authors' estimation.

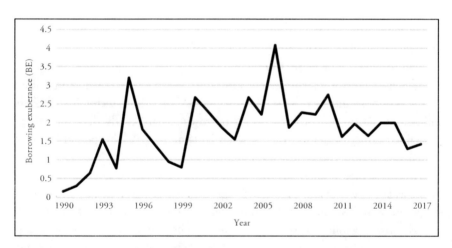

Figure 3.4　Trends in borrowing exuberance (BE) in 1990–2017, normalized

Source: Authors' estimation.

Figure 3.4. Further, the trend depicts that the excess borrowing peaked and witnessed significant growth during 2004–07, right before the global financial crisis (GFC) of 2008.

To further corroborate our observations, we also carried out a structural break analysis (Phillips and Perron, 1998), which also confirms two structural breaks

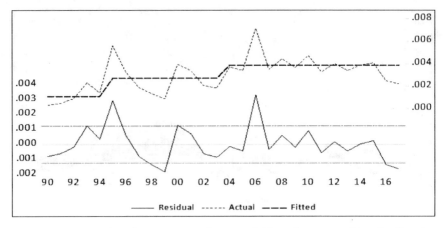

Figure 3.5 Trends in borrowing exuberance (BE) with structural breaks (fitted versus residual)

Source: Authors' estimation.

Note: Actual and fitted values are plotted on the secondary axis.

in our data – the first one is initiated in 1994 and the second one in 2004. The residuals of the fitted structural model are shown in Figure 3.5.

The first period between 1994 and 1997 was the post-liberalization regime when banking sector reforms were institutionalized to ease the credit constraints in the economy and increase the loan supply to the private sector. The second episode of the rise in corporate sector borrowing, particularly the exuberance, as defined earlier in the study, is between 2004 and 2010. This period includes India's dream run, during which the economy enjoyed a boom in growth with a 9 per cent average annual growth rate between 2003–04 and 2007–08 – one of the world's highest in this period. This growth was primarily led by the private corporate sector, which contributed to domestic output significantly.[8] However, excess borrowing following the GFC of 2008 can be attributed to the evergreening of loans where banks continue to lend firms with poor credit quality to avoid declaring debt as NPAs.

To gain further insight into the intensity of the cycles of BE as mentioned earlier, we estimate the attribution across various periods. The results are presented in Figure 3.6.[9] We observe that the two episodes, 1994–97 and 2004–10, spanning nine years, contribute more than 50 per cent of overall BE. While further decomposing these two episodes, we note that the 2004 credit boom attributes 37 per cent of overall BE. Out of this, 17 per cent is attributed during 2004–06, and 20 per cent is attributed during the remaining period of 2007–10.

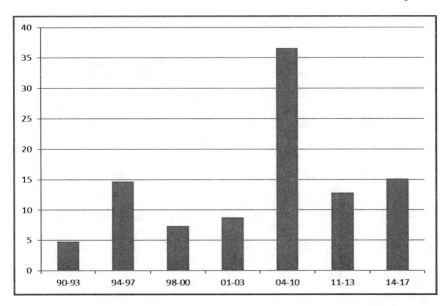

Figure 3.6   Attribution of borrowing exuberance (BE) across time in 1990–2017

Source: Authors' calculation.

Note: Time windows are not symmetrical and are adjusted for the credit boom cycles (1994–97 and 2004–10).

Next, in order to get a better insight into the determinants of misallocation, we present the trends in negative ICAE across various firm-specific characteristics. These firm characteristics are drawn from the empirical literature in corporate finance, such as size, age, business group affiliation, interest cover ratio, leverage, and external capital requirement. In the following section, we present the distribution of the negative ICAE and its components – BC and BE – across quartiles of firm characteristics, with Q1 representing the lowest quartile and Q4 representing the highest quartile. To begin with, the negative ICAE and the cases of BC and BE across firm age quartiles are presented in Figures 3.7a–3.7b. It is observed that misallocation, including BE, is higher among firms belonging to the oldest category (Q4).

The next firm-specific attribute considered is the firm size. The breakup of the negative ICAE and the cases of BC and BE are presented in Figures 3.8a–3.8b. The figure reveals that misallocation as well as the BE is significantly higher among big firms (firms belonging to Q4).

In the following section, we present the distribution of bank credit misallocation across various industrial sectors of the economy. The breakup of the negative ICAE

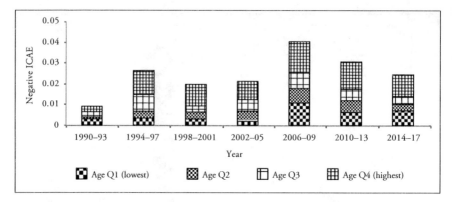

Figure 3.7a The negative index of credit allocative efficiency (ICAE) and age quartiles

Source: Authors' compilation.

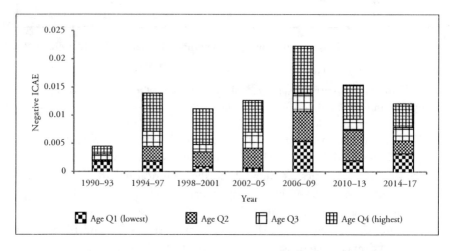

Figure 3.7b The negative index of credit allocative efficiency (ICAE) – borrowing constrained (BC) ($Q > Qbar$ and $B < Bbar$) and age quartiles

Source: Authors' compilation.

and the cases of BC and BE are presented in Figures 3.9a–3.9c. We observe that the misallocation is higher among the metals, chemicals, and construction industries. This is also true for the BE across these industrial sectors.

Next, the misallocation in bank credit is plotted against leverage, where the leverage is measured by one-year lag value of the debt-to-asset ratio. The distribution of the negative ICAE and its classification in terms of BC and BE are

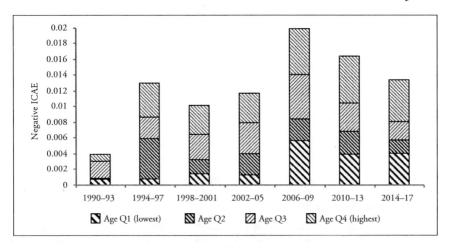

Figure 3.7c   The negative index of credit allocative efficiency (ICAE) – borrowing exuberance (BE) ($Q < Qbar$ and $B > Bbar$) and age quartiles

Source: Authors' compilation.

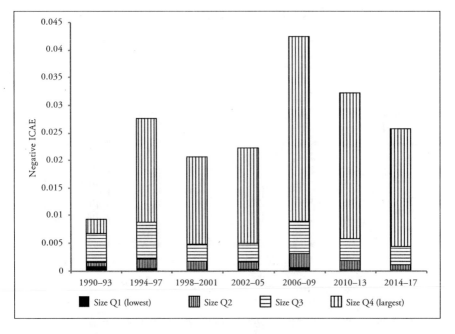

Figure 3.8a   The negative index of credit allocative efficiency (ICAE) and size quartiles

Source: Authors' compilation.

presented in Figures 3.10a–3.10c. The figures depict that misallocation is higher among highly levered firms, and the same trend is corroborated for the BE.

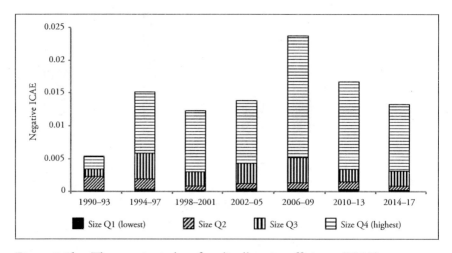

Figure 3.8b The negative index of credit allocative efficiency (ICAE) – borrowing constrained (BC) (*Q* > *Qbar* and *B* < *Bbar*) and size quartiles

Source: Authors' compilation.

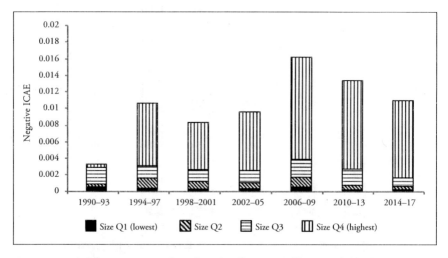

Figure 3.8c The negative index of credit allocative efficiency (ICAE) – borrowing exuberance (BE) (*Q* < *Qbar* and *B* > *Bbar*) and size quartiles

Source: Authors' compilation.

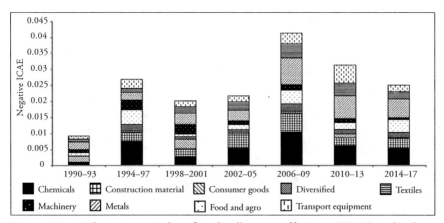

Figure 3.9a The negative index of credit allocative efficiency (ICAE) and industry

Source: Authors' compilation.

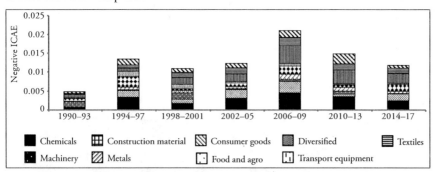

Figure 3.9b The negative index of credit allocative efficiency (ICAE) – borrowing constrained (BC) ($Q > Qbar$ and $B < Bbar$) and industry

Source: Authors' compilation.

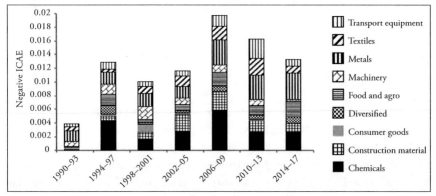

Figure 3.9c The negative index of credit allocative efficiency (ICAE) – borrowing exuberance (BE) ($Q < Qbar$ and $B > Bbar$) and industry

Source: Authors' compilation.

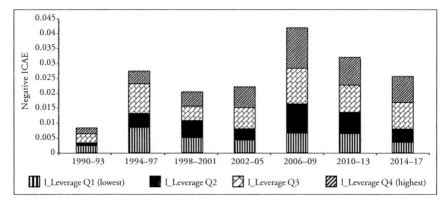

Figure 3.10a The negative index of credit allocative efficiency (ICAE) and previous year leverage

Source: Authors' compilation.

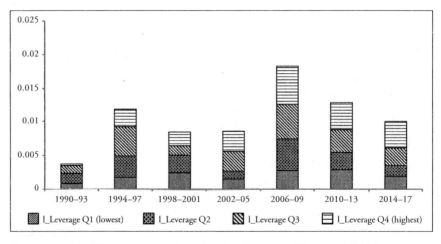

Figure 3.10b The negative index of credit allocative efficiency (ICAE) – borrowing constrained (BC) ($Q > Qbar$ and $B < Bbar$) and previous year leverage

Source: Authors' compilation.

Now, we examine the bank credit misallocation across the previous year's interest coverage ratio (ICR). Following conventional wisdom, we focus on the distribution of the negative and the positive ICAE across two categories of firms – firms with previous year's ICR of less than 2 and firms with previous year's ICR greater than 2. The firms with the ICR less than 2 are usually considered as having poor financial health. In Figures 3.11a–3.11c, we observe that bank credit misallocation is higher among firms with a higher ICR, and this is also prominent with respect to BE.

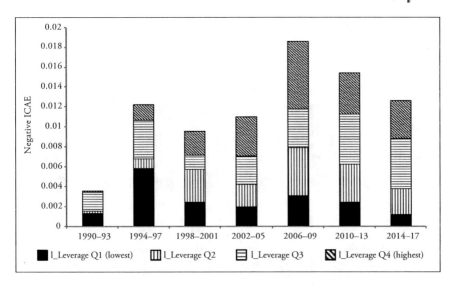

Figure 3.10c The negative index of credit allocative efficiency (ICAE) – borrowing exuberance (BE) ($Q < Qbar$ and $B > Bbar$) and previous year leverage

Source: Authors' compilation.

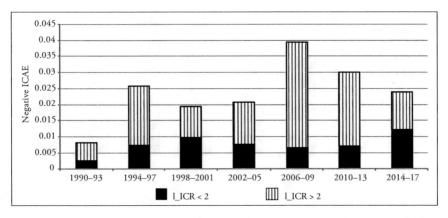

Figure 3.11a The negative index of credit allocative efficiency (ICAE) and the previous year's interest coverage ratio (ICR)

Source: Authors' compilation.

Next, we explore the nature of bank credit misallocation based on the financial deficit faced by the firms in the previous year. The deficit is defined, following Shyam-Sunder and Myers (1999), as the sum of dividends, net investment, and change in the net working capital, net of cash flow after interest and taxes expressed as a proportion of total assets. The deficit is used as a proxy for a

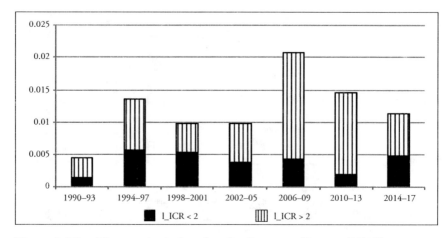

Figure 3.11b The negative index of credit allocative efficiency (ICAE) – borrowing constrained (BC) ($Q > Qbar$ and $B < Bbar$) and previous year's interest coverage ratio (ICR)

Source: Authors' compilation.

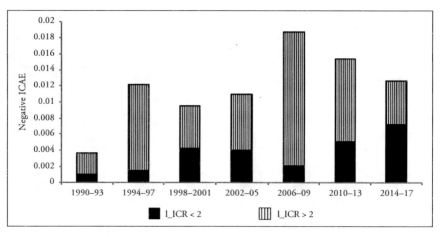

Figure 3.11c The negative index of credit allocative efficiency (ICAE) – borrowing exuberance (BE) ($Q < Qbar$ and $B > Bbar$) and previous year's interest coverage ratio (ICR).

Source: Authors' compilation.

firm's requirement for external capital. Therefore, a negative deficit indicates a financial surplus. In the context of allocative efficiency, such firms with low or negative deficit should borrow less and hence not be exposed to misallocation.

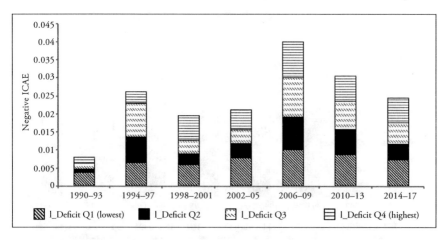

Figure 3.12a The negative index of credit allocative efficiency (ICAE) and previous year's deficit

Source: Authors' compilation.

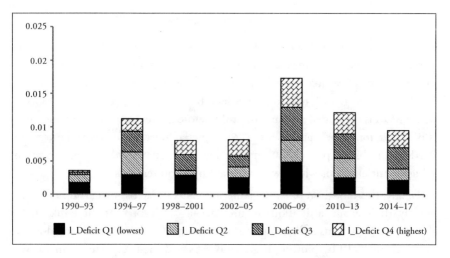

Figure 3.12b The negative index of credit allocative efficiency (ICAE) – borrowing constrained (BC) (*Q* > *Qbar* and *B* < *Bbar*) and previous year's deficit

Source: Authors' compilation.

Figures 3.12a–3.12c present the distribution of the negative ICAE and its breakup across BC and BE. We observe that the misallocation is higher among firms with lower levels of the deficit.

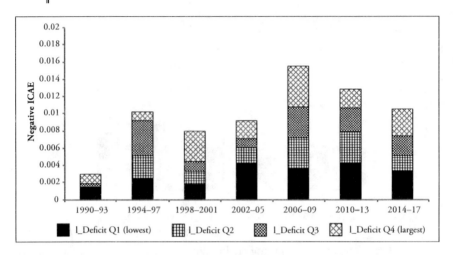

Figure 3.12c The negative index of credit allocative efficiency (ICAE) – borrowing exuberance (BE) ($Q < Qbar$ and $B > Bbar$) and previous year's deficit

Source: Authors' compilation.

The firm's external capital requirement is less if the firm generates sufficient capital through internal sources. To understand the distribution of bank credit misallocation across firms' capital requirements, we present the bank credit misallocation across quartiles of the external financing, where external financing is defined as the growth of return on assets (ROA) – that is, [ROA– (1 – ROA)], where ROA is calculated as a ratio of profit before depreciation, interest and taxes (PBDIT) to total assets. Figures 3.13a–3.13c present the distribution of the negative ICAE and its breakup across BC and BE. The figures reveal that the misallocation is higher among firms with lower external fund requirements.

Finally, the allocation of bank credit also can vary across ownership of firms, namely their group affiliation. Figures 3.14a–3.14c present the bank credit allocation across firms affiliated to business groups (Group = 1) and stand-alone firms (Group = 0) by plotting negative ICAEs and their respective sources. We observe that misallocation is higher among business-group-affiliated firms.

Conclusion

Existing studies on the allocation of bank credit to stock market firms have found little or no evidence of misallocation. This is partly due to the methodological issues in estimating allocative efficiency. This chapter proposes a simple model to measure the misallocation of bank borrowing in Indian listed firms. The primary

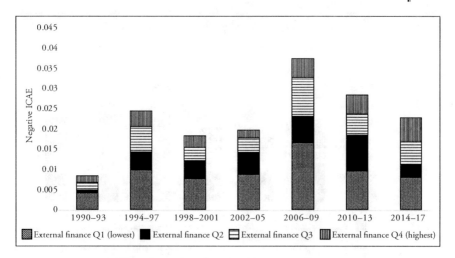

Figure 3.13a The negative index of credit allocative efficiency (ICAE) and external financing

Source: Authors' compilation.

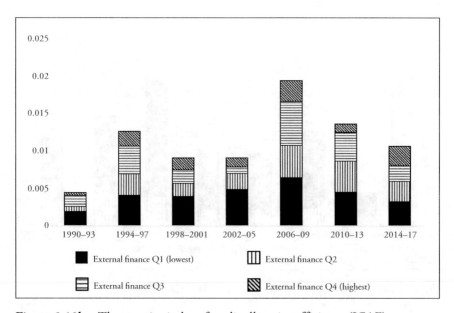

Figure 3.13b The negative index of credit allocative efficiency (ICAE) – borrowing constrained (BC) ($Q > Qbar$ and $B < Bbar$) and external financing

Source: Authors' compilation.

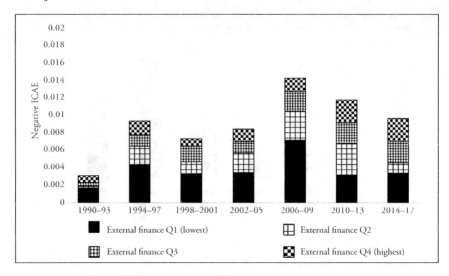

Figure 3.13c The negative index of credit allocative efficiency (ICAE) – borrowing exuberance (BE) (*Q* < *Qbar* and *B* > *Bbar*) and external financing

Source: Authors' compilation.

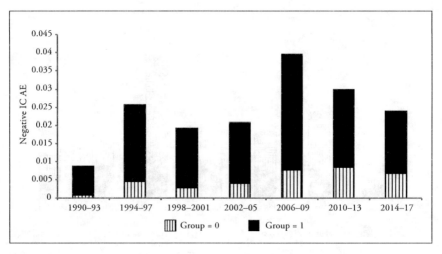

Figure 3.14a The negative index of credit allocative efficiency (ICAE) and business-group affiliation

Source: Authors' compilation.

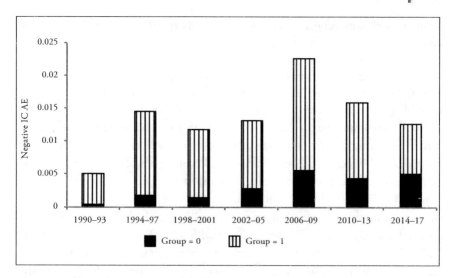

Figure 3.14b The negative index of credit allocative efficiency (ICAE) – borrowing constrained (BC) (*Q* > *Qbar* and *B* < *Bbar*) and business-group affiliation

Source: Authors' compilation.

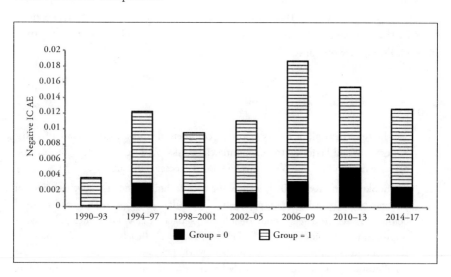

Figure 3.14c The negative index of credit allocative efficiency (ICAE) – borrowing exuberance (BE) (*Q* < *Qbar* and *B* > *Bbar*) and business-group affiliation

Source: Authors' compilation.

finding of this exercise reveals that the overall trend in the credit allocation efficiency along with the BE in India has witnessed several cycles, the most prominent being the one of 2004–07. Incidentally, this period is also marked by substantial growth in credit. Therefore, the chapter reveals sure tell-tale signs of the pro-cyclical nature of the credit misallocation in India. The issue of pro-cyclicality in misallocation is further explored in the next chapter.

While decomposing the ICAE across various firm characteristics, we observe a few interesting trends: on average, bank credit misallocation is higher among the older and larger firms. Specifically, misallocation is widespread in industries like metals, construction, and chemicals. Further, misallocation is more prevalent among the firms which already had a higher leverage ratio. On the contrary, the misallocation also happened among firms with a higher ICR. Notably, firms that did not require funds – that is, firms with lower levels of deficit and lower external capital requirement – also demonstrated higher levels of misallocation on an average. Finally, the misallocation was widespread among the business-group-affiliated firms compared to standalone firms. Overall, the preliminary findings from this section suggest that banks might have allocated credit to the firms that were not ideal candidates for receiving it. However, it is important to note that while these findings are extremely valuable and provide the necessary background to develop the formal empirical models in the later chapters, these findings need to be further investigated for statistical validity. We aim to achieve these objectives in the following two chapters.

Notes

1   See the Reserve Bank of India's report on commercial banks. Reserve Bank of India, 'Operations and Performance of Commercial Banks', 21 December 2017, https://rbi. org.in/scripts/PublicationsView.aspx?Id=18061 (accessed in January 2021).

2   Chen, Skully, and Kym (2005) analyse the cost, technical, and allocative efficiency of Chinese banks by using a non-parametric DEA (data envelopment analysis) method before and after the deregulation. Their findings suggest that while the deregulation has improved the overall efficiency of allocation, technical efficiency of banks scores over the cost and allocative efficiency. Another growing stream of literature looks into the misallocation of resources, particularly in terms of investment funds and availability of internal sources of funds. For example, Richardson (2006) examines the extent of firm-level over-investment of free cash flow. The findings on the association between over-investment and free cash flow are consistent with works suggesting poor future performance following firm-level investment activity (Titman, Wei, and Xie 2004; Fairfield, Whisenant, and Yohn 2003). Further seminal work by Wurgler (2000), in the

wake of Hubbard (1998), suggests using the elasticity of investment growth (measured as growth in financing) to value-added growth (as a proxy for growth in investment opportunities). Wurgler (2000) used a large sample of countries with industries to show a positive correlation between Tobin's Q and value-added growth. Hence, higher elasticity of investment growth to value-added can be reliably interpreted as an indicator of better allocative efficiency as funds are more quickly reallocated to sectors offering higher opportunities.

3   See, for example, Lindenberg and Ross (1981) and Kaplan and Zingales (1997).

4   Note that, in spirit, our measure closely mirrors the measure of misallocation of capital by Abaid, Oomes, and Ueda (2008), Bhaduri and Kumar (2014), and Bhaduri and Bhattacharya (2018).

5   To control for scale effects, we define bank borrowing as a ratio of bank borrowing to total borrowings.

6   Rajan, Servaes, and Zingales (2000) refer to this as transfers while testing the efficiency of internal capital markets in diversified firms. Later, this was modified by Hovakimian (2011) to study the extent to which conglomerates face friction in the capital market in their internal capital allocation across various divisions. We have adopted it to capture the efficiency of bank capital allocation for the Indian economy.

7   For simplicity, we assume that the stock market valuation of firms is efficient in that Tobin's Q correctly reflects discounted future expected profits. However, as Morck, Yeung, and Yu (2000) suggest, the efficiency of stock market valuation itself may improve with external shocks like financial liberalization. In this case, an observed decline of dispersion in Tobin's Q could be attributed solely to the improvement in stock market valuation. Our approach of considering deviation in firm's q ratio from the industry average allows us to distinguish the allocation from the valuation.

8   The minor episode between 2000 and 2002 is marked by privatization of banks, entry of foreign banks, and privatization of DFIs. This period was also the beginning of corporate sector reforms by institutionalizing norms for corporate governance and regulating the market for corporate control.

9   Attribute measures the percentage contribution of BE in a particular time window proportional to the total BE over the total study period.

4

Macroeconomic Analyses of Bank Credit Misallocation in the Indian Corporate Sector
Investigation of Pro-cyclicality

Pro-cyclicality in the lending behaviour and misallocation of resources by financial institutions has been a contentious issue in economic literature for a long time. Pro-cyclicality in the banking sector can be defined as the reinforcing interaction within the financial sector and between the functioning of the banking sector and the real economy, leading to unsustainable economic growth during the upturns and deeper recessions in the downturns (BIS, 2010; Clement, 2010). It is often argued that the upswing of business cycles, characterized by rapid increases in credit and asset prices and higher cash flows, improves borrowers' creditworthiness, thereby forcing banks to dilute the underwriting standards in a competitive environment (Lowe, 2002). Notably, during an economic boom, the optimistic perception underestimates risk, and the higher cash flows ensure that assets turning to non-performing assets (NPAs) are muted. Consequently, the credit flow accelerates during economic upswings. However, this scenario reverses during a recession as sales and income drop and asset prices become stagnant, resulting in loan delinquencies. Subsequently, bank credit slows down during economic recessions (Samantaraya, 2016), and therefore, the banking sector can exacerbate cyclical fluctuations, hindering the efficient allocation of resources in the economy and adversely affecting credit growth and financial stability (Athanasoglou, Daniilidis, and Delis, 2014).

A vast body of literature has addressed the pro-cyclicality of bank credit and its downstream consequences (Berger and Udell, 2004; Caporale, Colli, and Lopez, 2014; Xie, 2016; Chavan and Gambacorta, 2019). However, it is important to note that the existing studies on the pro-cyclicality of bank lending and its adverse impact on the economy often analyse an outcome ex-post to the banks' funding decisions such as loan growth and NPA. Such ex-post outcome is influenced by various external factors that are over and above the wrong decisions made by the banks at the time of sanction of loans. Notably, most empirical studies on India examine the NPA crisis in the background of events such as the credit boom in the mid-2000s, the subsequent downturn in the economy, currency depreciation, and the tightening of norms by the regulators. More recently, the NPA-based approach has gained wide popularity among economists and academicians (Misra and Dhal, 2010; Samantaraya, 2016; Bawa et al., 2019).[1] However, any correlation between pro-cyclicality and credit issuance decision and its outcome at an ex-post level is fraught with several biases. In particular, any analysis of the ex-post outcome of misallocation at a later period could be contaminated with several factors like changes in the law and regulations, unfavourable macroeconomic environment, and other external shocks, information that is not available at the time of the lending decision taken by the banks.

In contrast to these studies, our research looks at the circumstances at the time of credit disbursement, where we critically examine the lending decisions made by the banks with the available information. Specifically, we evaluate misallocation at the point of loan disbursal, where the bank is supposed to use all available information about the firm's prospects prudently. By examining the loan decision at the point of origin, we can potentially observe any laxity on the part of the bank in allocating credit to a low-quality firm, thereby eliminating the impact of any ex-post factors in the economy. Thus, this approach can pin down the origin of bad loans to poor decision-making by banks without getting contaminated by the impact of factors that may occur at later periods of the firm's life cycle and affect its ability to service the loan.

Precisely, to capture the sub-optimality in banks' lending decisions, we use a measure of credit allocation efficiency called the index of credit allocative efficiency (ICAE), which was developed in the previous chapter. As discussed earlier, the ICAE is proposed as a measure of misallocation of resources due to inappropriate allocation of bank credit to firms with lower marginal returns to capital. Therefore, the ICAE is inherently designed to compare bank credit allocation in a firm to that of the average bank credit in the industry based on the returns to capital (Q ratio). It is worth noting that a positive (negative) value for the ICAE indicates that the banks are efficient (inefficient) in allocating credit, suggesting that, on average, more bank loans are flowing to high (low) Q companies from low (high) Q companies. Therefore, the use of the ICAE provides a framework that could pinpoint the exact source of misallocation of bank credit. In this chapter, we apply the ICAE framework to explore the pro-cyclicality in bank lending behaviour.

Pro-cyclicality in Bank Lending around the World

It has been well established in theoretical literature that banks often overstretch both the quantum and the quality of their credit over the expansionary phase, leading to misallocation and non-performing credit. This is because banks as rational agents are driven by two short-term concerns: earnings and reputation, and, therefore, they tend to 'herd' their peers in terms of lending several times after diluting the lending standards (Rajan, 1994). Furthermore, banks' lending decisions could be a sub-optimum solution because high reputation firms tend to borrow at arm's length to minimize the monitoring costs and bargaining power by banks (Diamond, 1991; Rajan, 1992).

Moving away from rational behaviour, several cognitive biases like disaster myopia or short-sightedness in underestimating the likelihood of high-loss, low-probability events afflict banks (Guttentag and Herring, 1986). Even though banks can mitigate these biases by acquiring information about market conditions and borrowers, their short-sightedness often stops them from performing such actions. For example, cognitive dissonance suggests that banks tend to interpret it in a biased way despite having the necessary information at their disposal, reinforcing their existing beliefs about market conditions (Borio et al., 2001). This often results in underestimating the prevailing risks, leading to a more pro-cyclical risk-taking response by banks.

Further, pro-cyclicality in loan growth and risk-taking gets amplified due to the fading institutional memory of credit busts that occurred previously, and this phenomenon is observed more during the expansionary phase of business cycles (Berger and Udell, 2004). Also, the existence of principal–agent problems between shareholders and managers, with the latter more interested in short-term gains, can result in a more pro-cyclical risk-taking response by banks during credit upturns (Saunders et al., 1990).

Besides, collateral is another source of pro-cyclicality of bank lending. During credit growth, banks tend to expand their credit limit as the value of underlying collateral increases due to the upswing in the asset price cycle (Borio et al., 2001; Jimenez, Salas, and Saurina, 2006; Adrian and Shin, 2010). The continuous increase in asset prices and credit growth further increases the collateral valuation and amplifies the asset price cycle (Kiyotaki and Moore, 1997). Consequently, driven by an increase in collateral valuation, banks provide credit to those firms that may not have otherwise been financed. However, this cycle breaks down whenever there is a downturn in asset prices and loan losses start accumulating. This is further accentuated by the fact that banks tend to look for newer borrowers during an upturn in the credit cycle as all the existing good borrowers already possess a mortgage. In the process, banks may finance sub-prime borrowers who were not deemed credit-worthy and hence did not have access to the credit market earlier (Adrian and Shin, 2010).

There is an existing body of empirical literature that provides evidence for the theoretical arguments about pro-cyclical lending behaviour by banks in general and factors that impact the quality of bank loans and subsequent banking crisis. For example, Keeton (1999) found a positive impact of credit growth on loan delinquencies among US banks. In a related study, Salas and Saurina (2002) and Jimenez, Salas, and Saurina (2006) show that there exists a positive relationship between credit growth and growth in loan losses, indicating that apart from a rise in bank loan losses with higher credit growth, the loans extended during periods of booms were riskier than those extended during periods of busts. Subsequently, studies documenting a positive impact of bank credit on bad loans across other economies (Festic et al., 2011; Messai and Jouini, 2013; Caporale, Colli, and Lopez, 2014) as well as emerging economies (De Bock and Demyanets, 2012; Skarica, 2013) provide evidence on the pro-cyclicality in bank credit.

Apart from the direct relationship between the business cycle and the quality of bank loans, a set of literature looks into the variations in loan delinquencies and factors determining such variations. In a pioneering study, Keeton and Morris (1987) report the variations in bad bank loans attributed to local economic conditions and the weaker performance of sectors like agriculture and energy. Gavin and Hausman (1996) show the impact of macroeconomic factors such as interest rates, expected inflation, disposable income, credit growth, monetary policy, and exchange rate on the quality of bank loans during the Latin American banking crisis in the 1990s. The emergence of a banking crisis due to a boom in lending is studied in cross-country and time-series studies. Using a large sample of developed and developing countries between 1980 and 1994, Demirgüç-Kunt and Detragiache (1998) suggest that banking crises tend to erupt when the macroeconomic environment is weak, characterized by low gross domestic product (GDP) growth, excessively high real interest rates, and high inflation. In a related study, using a contemporaneous framework, Hardy and Pazarbaşioğlu (1999) highlight that credit flow to the private sector shows both boom and bust patterns following a banking crisis. Gourinchas, Valdes, and Landerretche (2001) examine many episodes characterized as lending booms and find that the probability of having a banking crisis significantly increases after such episodes. Using credit provisions as a measure of credit quality, Bikker and Metzemakers (2005) investigate the relationship between credit losses and several macroeconomic variables, finding that the reversal of the economic cycle eventually worsens bank asset quality. Similar studies include Arpa et al. (2001) and Hoggarth, Logan, and Zicchino (2005) for UK banks during the period 1988–2004.

The literature on pro-cyclical bank lending also includes macro-stress testing studies pioneered by Gambera (2000), which finds that factors like unemployment, income from the agricultural sector, GDP, and the number of bankruptcy cases are good predictors for the quality of loans among US commercial banks. Measuring credit quality as a ratio of bad loans to loan portfolios, Baboucek and Jancar (2005) validate the effects of macroeconomic stress on the quality of the Czech banking sector. On the contrary, Filosa (2007) finds the Italian banking sector to be weakly pro-cyclical even under tight monetary conditions that affected the soundness of banks. Further, Bofondi and Ropele (2011) analyse the macroeconomic determinants of credit quality measured by the ratio of new bad loans to the outstanding loans in the previous period. The findings show that changes in macroeconomic conditions generally affect loan quality with a lag.

In the context of the subprime crisis of 2008, Messai and Jouini (2013) examine the determinants of bad loans for a sample of 85 banks in three countries that faced a financial crisis – that is, Italy, Greece, and Spain. By incorporating macroeconomic variables like rate of growth of GDP, unemployment rate, and real interest rate and bank-specific variables like return on assets, the change in loans, and the loan-loss-reserves-to-total-loans ratio in explaining the bad loan problems, their findings show that the bad loans are negatively associated with the growth rate of GDP and the profitability of banks and positively associated with the unemployment rate, the proportion of loan-loss reserves, and the real interest rate.

More recently, Caporale, Colli, and Lopez (2014) analysed non-performing loans during contractionary periods. Their results confirm the argument that bad loans, which are relatively muted during economic upswings, grow exponentially during the economic crisis. Moreover, the findings show that the excess credit channelized during economic booms can give rise to NPAs when the economy eventually contracts. There is also an argument that pro-cyclicality of the banking sector and high economic activities are signs of an overheating economy, and any reversal of this scenario could accelerate the growth of the NPAs (Festic, Kavkler, and Repina, 2011; Cucinelli, 2015).

Finally, a set of studies also highlight that the legal, political, sociological, economic, and banking institutions and entry of foreign banks into the economy affect the share of NPAs and credit allocation in banks (Breuer, 2006; Kozak 2016). For example, with respect to the entry of foreign banks, Degryse, Kim, and Ongena (2009) find that greenfield foreign banks allot more credit to transparent firms with a reliable balance sheet, healthy credit history, and collateral assets. In contrast to the belief that foreign bank entry should improve credit access for all firms, information asymmetries can exacerbate misallocation. Consistent with the adverse effects of information asymmetries, Gormley (2010) finds that foreign banks financed only a small set of very profitable firms upon their entry into India during the 1990s. The entry of foreign banks further reduced the likelihood of firms receiving bank loans by 8 percentage points and adversely affected the performance of small firms with a greater need for external finance.

Apart from focusing on the banking structure, a few studies report pro-cyclicality in bank credit allocation. The pro-cyclicality of bank credit has been ascribed to the market imperfections and deviations from the efficient market hypothesis. A vast body of literature argues that factors like implementation of the Basel-type regulations, accounting standards norms, and NPA provisioning requirements have intensified pro-cyclical bank lending (Ghosh and Nachane, 2003; Nachane, Ghosh, and Ray 2006; Samantaraya, 2009; Samantaraya, 2016. Further, the problems of moral hazard and adverse selection are also fundamental to explaining the pro-cyclicality of bank credit. Using a case study of India, a recent study by Chavan and Gambacotra (2019) shows that poor quality of loans increases by 4.3 per cent in the long run due to a 1 per cent increase in loan growth. Thus, bad loans can pose a serious threat to the Indian economy when it implodes.

Overall the empirical literature presents three main scenarios where pro-cyclicality affects the efficient functioning of banks. First, during an economic upturn, the risk appetite of banks increases, and consequently, they lend funds to investments that have marginally positive or even a negative net present value. However, during the economic meltdowns, they do precisely the opposite. Therefore, the banking system, rather than compensating for swings in economic activity over the cycle, makes them even more intense. Second, the pro-cyclicality in the credit allocation distorts the efficient allocation of bank credit in the economy. Notably, during an economic boom, banks lower the lending standards and the due-diligence procedures due to increased competition from other sources of funds like capital markets and underestimation of risk. Consequently, the loans are disbursed to low-quality firms, whereas during downturns, even investments with positive net present value do not receive bank financing (Jimenez, Salas, and Saurina, 2006). Third, pro-cyclicality hinders stakeholders' ability to control banks' management, leading to an intensifying banking crisis (Berger and Udell, 2004).

Finally, it is evident from the extant literature that the correlation between pro-cyclicality and loan quality has been examined by using ex-post outcomes of misallocation such as NPA. However, as argued earlier, this approach could be fraught with several biases as NPAs could be contaminated with several other ex-post factors and external shocks that are not observed at the time of the lending decision. Therefore, we fill this gap in the literature by analysing misallocation at the time of making lending decisions to investigate pro-cyclicality in bank credit misallocation further.

Data, Sample, and Variables

The data used in this research is obtained from various sources for a period between 1990 and 2017. To derive our dependent variable, which is a measure of bank credit misallocation (*ICAE*), we obtain firm-specific variables from Centre for Monitoring Indian Economy (CMIE) Prowess for a sample of non-financial firms. This measure is derived in Chapter 3. In addition to *ICAE*, we also focus on borrowing exuberance (*BE*), a source of bank credit misallocation captured through negative *ICAE*. In particular, *BE* captures the dimension of credit misallocation when *ceteris paribus* credit flows from high *Q* firms to low *Q* firms. Finally, our primary variable of interest is bank credit growth (*Credit Growth*), calculated as the growth in the gross advances made by banks, which is taken from various volumes from the Reserve Bank of India (RBI) statistical tables related to Indian banks, a flagship publication of the RBI.

To check for the robustness of our model, we also use a modified variable of interest as excess credit growth, which is derived from the credit growth using the Hodrick–Prescott (HP) Filter. The HP Filter technique de-trends the data, and the residuals represent the excess credit growth, which is over and above the long-term trend in the bank credit supply (Hodrick and Prescott, 1981).

A set of control variables is included to account for the macroeconomic and structural components that could affect banks' lending decisions. These include the following: (*a*) the lending interest rate, which represents the change in the average bank lending rate for the given financial year obtained from the International Financial Statistics published by the International Monetary Fund; (*b*) growth in the stock markets, which depicts the annual growth rate of Sensex, the flagship index of the Bombay Stock Exchange (BSE) (the necessity to control for the stock market arises from the fact that the stock market is an alternate source of funds for the firms and can substitute for bank lending as the capital markets of country grow); (*c*) industrial growth in the economy, measured as the growth of the index of industrial production (IIP). The IIP is a composite indicator that measures the short-term changes in the production volume of various industrial products such as minerals mining, electricity, and manufacturing. The IIP data is taken from the Central Statistics Office (CSO) of the Ministry of Statistics and Programme Implementation, Government of India (GOI). In addition, following Bouvatier, López-Villavicencio, and Mignon (2012), we also account for the structure of the banking sector to control for the changes due to the introduction of new private banks and foreign banks in the post-liberalization period. This variable holds importance in the Indian economy as there has been a steady rise in the share of foreign banks in the banking system's total assets. Therefore, similar to Chavan and Gambacorta (2019), we define banking structure as a ratio of a log of assets held by the foreign banks to overall assets held by the banking industry.

Further, we add the Herfindahl–Hirschman index (HHI) of banking sector assets to measure market concentration because asset concentration reflects the degree of consolidation in the banking sector. The extent of asset concentration can potentially affect the prudence shown by banks in taking loan decisions, which serves as a proxy for competition in the banking sector. The HHI of the banking assets is calculated by the sum of the square of the market share of public, private, and foreign banks. The asset size of all types of banks in India is taken from the RBI statistical tables related to Indian banks.

This chapter aims to test the empirical association between pro-cyclicality and misallocation of credit in the Indian banking sector. The macroeconomic dynamics of the misallocation is explored in a time-series framework covering 28 years. A two-pronged strategy is adopted to analyse the determinants of bank credit misallocation over the years. The first model analyses the overall bank credit allocation in the economy as a function of credit growth and a set of control variables. The following strategy delves deeper into the sources of misallocation and explores the pro-cyclicality of the specific phenomenon of BE in bank credit allocation among firms.

Specification of Pro-cyclicality in Bank Credit Misallocation and Credit Growth

First, to empirically establish the link between misallocation and pro-cyclicality of credit, this research uses an auto-regressive moving average (ARMA) framework, which models our primary variable of interest for the degree of misallocation, $ICAE_t$, as a function of the credit growth and a set of control variables. The first empirical assessment follows the model presented in equation 4.1.

$$ICAE_t = \theta_0 + \theta_1 \; Credit \; Growth_t + \Sigma_j^k \delta_j X_t + \varepsilon_t \qquad (4.1)$$

Here, $ICAE_t$ is the index of credit allocative efficiency for time t. As discussed in the previous chapter, negative values of $ICAE$ indicate misallocation. The variable *Credit Growth* captures the credit growth at time t. X_t is a vector of control variables like lending interest rate, BSE Sensex growth, lagged IIP growth, banking structure, and HHI of banking assets at time t.

In order to determine the order of AR and MA functions, we use the autocorrelation function (ACF) and partial autocorrelation function (PACF), which are standard procedures in time-series analysis, to select appropriately adjusted AR and MA terms based on the time-series nature of the data.

As argued earlier, under the pro-cyclicality hypothesis, we expect a negative association between $ICAE$ and credit growth or excess credit growth as we hypothesize that the banks relax their underwriting standards during credit booms and allocate credit inefficiently. Further, a positive association between the lending rate and allocative efficiency is expected as the increased cost of borrowing will result in high-quality firms demanding less bank capital (reflecting the borrowing constraint [BC] among firms). We also expect a positive association between Sensex growth and the ICAE as the better access to equity markets during an economic upturn might reduce the demand for bank loans, and this could dampen the effect on the extent of misallocation. In addition, allocative efficiency increases during an economic boom as funds are likely to be utilized in total capacity to generate output. Therefore, the IIP is expected to have a positive association with the ICAE. Further, a decline in banking concentration (HHI) is predicted to share a positive association with the $ICAE$ as competitive pressures in the banking industry from private and foreign banks could enhance the monitoring by banks in allocating credit to more productive firms to ensure recovery of their funds. Finally, banking structure is expected to be positively associated with allocative efficiency in bank credit as an increase in the assets held by foreign banks can result in banking sector innovations and adaptation of global best practices.

Specification of Pro-cyclicality in Borrowing Exuberance and Credit Growth

The second empirical model used in this research goes one step ahead by examining the source of misallocation in bank credit. As argued in the previous chapter, the misallocation of credit can take place under two scenarios: first, when firms with high Q ratios receive lower levels of bank credit and, second, when firms with lower Q ratios receive higher levels of bank credit. As described in the previous chapter, while the first source of misallocation is attributed to *borrowing constraint* (*BC*), the second one is captured in terms of *borrowing exuberance* (*BE*) in firms. BE becomes a crucial concern when low-quality firms receive more credit than their industry peers. A higher level of *BE* presents a case for the laxity from the bank's side while allocating credit despite having information on the quality of the firms represented by the *Q* ratio.

We run the baseline model outlined in equation 4.1 with *BE* as a dependent variable. This model is outlined in equation 4.2:

$$BE_t = \beta_0 + \beta_1 \; Credit \; Growth_t + \Sigma_j^k \delta_j X_t + \varepsilon_t \tag{4.2}$$

Here, BE_t measures the degree of misallocation because of low *Q* ratio firms getting loans disproportionate to their peers in the same industry at time *t*. *Credit Growth* corresponds to the credit growth at time *t*. X_t is a vector of control variables that includes the lending interest rate, Sensex growth, lagged IIP growth, banking structure, and the HHI of banking assets.

Similar to the baseline model strategy, appropriately adjusted AR and MA terms are selected based on the time-series nature of the data. It is also important to note that while BE is negative in all scenarios by construction, we multiply it by a factor minus one for better interpretation of results.

Accordingly, we expect a positive association between BE and credit growth or excess credit growth as during such times the banks dilute their lending standards, leading to a higher misallocation. Further, we predict a negative association between the lending interest rate and misallocation as risky borrowers will crowd out with the increased cost of capital. We also expect a negative association between Sensex growth and BE as misallocating firms may seek the stock market as an alternate source of external capital to minimize the bank monitoring costs. The IIP is predicted to be positively associated with BE because the latter is expected to accentuate during economic upswings. Also, the banking concentration (HHI) is predicted to share a positive association with BE as lack of competition in the banking sector can lead to laxity in selecting borrowers. The higher presence of foreign banks is expected to be negatively associated with BE as access to banking innovations and global best practices should help banks carefully select loan applications. The empirical analysis and the results of these two models are presented in the next section.

Tests of Stationarity

As a first step in the time-series analysis, we test for the stationarity of the variables used in our models using unit root tests. We present results of three unit root tests: Augmented Dickey and Fuller (1979), KPSS (Kwiatkowsky–Phillips–Schmidt–

Shin, 1992), and Phillips and Perron (1988) tests. The test statistics reported in Table 4.1 confirm that the variables used in this research are all stationary.

Trends and Patterns of the ICAE and Macroeconomic Variables

Before we present the results of our empirical models, we focus on the cycles of credit growth to understand the pro-cyclicality of BE. Figure 4.1 illustrates the trends in misallocation in general and BE in particular, along with the trends in credit growth over the study period. The figure shows telltale signs of pro-cyclic behaviour of bank credit misallocation and BE to the credit growth as evident, particularly during 1994–97 and 2003–09, which were also the prominent episodes of credit growth in the economy. The high credit growth episode occurred during the early 1990s after liberalization when the quantum of funds from banks was channelled to the corporate sector to increase the output. The second episode of the credit boom was during India's dream run, which witnessed high GDP growth coupled with the boost in the bank credit to the commercial sector.

Next, a graphical representation of the association between other independent variables and the ICAE is presented in Figures 4.2–4.6. The association between the ICAE and the credit growth gives some early hints about the misallocation of credit during a boom phase. Notably, in the years 2004–06, when the bank credit market in India witnessed its largest credit boom in history, the ICAE values are in

Table 4.1 Unit root analysis

Variable	Augmented Dickey and Fuller	Phillips–Perron	Kwiatkowsky–Phillips–Schmidt–Shin
Credit growth	−2.7922	−2.8000	0.1442
Excess credit growth	−4.6289	−4.6289	0.0593
Lending interest rate	−3.0447	−2.2695	0.1387
Growth Sensex	−6.1088	−6.0953	0.2643
Growth index of industrial production	−2.8082	−2.7806	0.2566
Herfindahl–Hirschman index assets	−18.4169	−17.4135	0.1649
Banking structure (log)	−3.3809	−3.3828	0.1829

Source: Authors' calculations.

Note: *t*-statistics are reported in the second and third column in the table, while Lagrange multiplier (LM) statistics are reported in the last column.

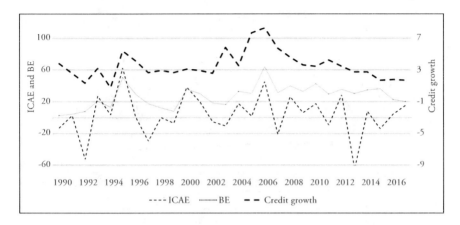

Figure 4.1 Trends in the index of credit allocative efficiency (ICAE), borrowing exuberance (BE), and credit growth in 1990–2017, normalized

Source: The ICAE and BE are estimated by the authors. Credit growth is sourced from Reserve Bank of India, *Handbook of Statistics on Indian Economy*, various editions.

Note: For better comparison, we present normalized time series.

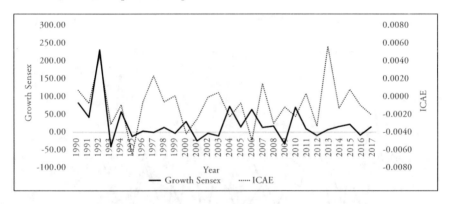

Figure 4.2 Trends in the index of credit allocative efficiency (ICAE) and Bombay Stock Exchange (BSE) Sensex growth in 1990–2017

Source: The ICAE is estimated by the authors. The Sensex growth is sourced from Reserve Bank of India, *Handbook of Statistics on Indian Economy*, various editions.

the negative zone, suggesting that the scale of misallocation was prominent during this period. This supports the literature that argues that banks relax their lending standards during the credit boom times. Further, the association between the growth in the Sensex and the ICAE numbers reveals that bank credit misallocation was lower when the markets registered a higher growth rate. With the higher growth

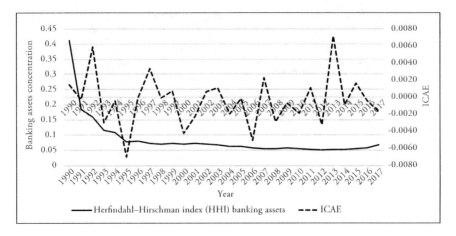

Figure 4.3 Trends in the index of credit allocative efficiency (ICAE) and banking sector concentration in 1990–2017

Source: The ICAE is estimated by the authors. The HHI is computed using banking assets sourced from Reserve Bank of India, *Handbook of Statistics on Indian Economy*, various editions.

Note: The ICAE is plotted on the secondary vertical axis.

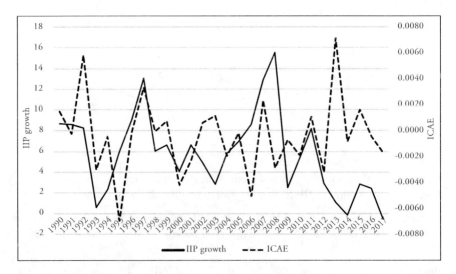

Figure 4.4 Trends in the index of credit allocative efficiency (ICAE) and growth in index of industrial production (IIP) in 1990–2017

Source: The ICAE is estimated by the authors. The IIP growth is sourced from the Central Statistics Office (CSO) database.

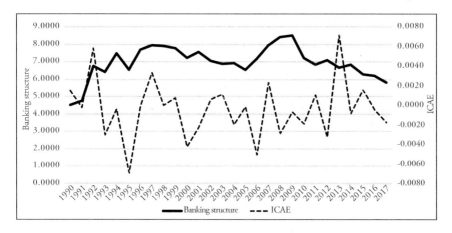

Figure 4.5 Trends in the index of credit allocative efficiency (ICAE) and banking structure in 1990–2017

Source: The ICAE is estimated by the authors. The banking structure is computed from the data sourced from Reserve Bank of India, *Handbook of Statistics on Indian Economy*, various editions.

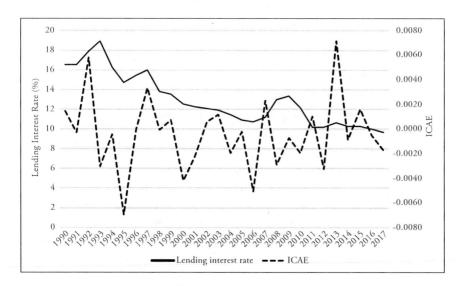

Figure 4.6 Trends in the index of credit allocative efficiency (ICAE) and lending interest rate in 1990–2017

Source: The ICAE is estimated by the authors. The lending interest rate is sourced from the International Finance Corporation (IFC) database.

of equity markets, the demand for a bank loan might have reduced due to better access to funds. This could dampen the effect on the extent of misallocation in the market. The association between the growth of the IIP and the ICAE also portrays a similar picture where the high growth phase in the industry typically witnessed higher levels of misallocation. Therefore, the preliminary observation based on the trend analysis suggests telltale signs of pro-cyclicality in bank credit allocation, which needs further investigation to prove the relationship statistically.

Relationship between Bank Credit Misallocation and Macroeconomic Factors

Using the ICAE as a measure of allocation efficiency, the study carries out a time-series model in an ARMA framework. The findings of the first empirical model in this research, that is, equation 4.1, are presented in columns 2–4 in Table 4.2.

The results confirm the statistical significance and consistency of our central hypothesis that bank credit misallocation is associated and pro-cyclical to the credit growth cycles. Model 1, the baseline model, shows a negative association between the ICAE and credit growth, suggesting the pro-cyclicality in credit allocation. This significant negative association substantiates our argument that the efficiency in allocating bank credit deteriorates during the credit boom. The findings also imply that the lending standards of the banks deteriorate during a credit upswing. Our evidence corroborates with the findings of works by Caporale, Colli, and Lopez (2014) and presents evidence for the impact of the credit cycle in the lending decisions by the banks.

Next, the control variables presented in this research also highlight the factors determining allocation efficiency. As predicted, we report a positive association between the change in the lending interest rate and the ICAE. This shows a second-order effect of interest rate on the ICAE, suggesting that a positive change in the interest rate improves allocation efficiency. This further implies that both the banks and firms become more cautious about the project's credibility due to the increase in the opportunity costs. Furthermore, although insignificant, the allocative efficiency shares a positive association with the growth in the equity market as reported by the coefficient of growth in the Sensex. In addition, the findings also suggest that industrial growth seems to have no significant association with allocative efficiency.

To check the robustness of these findings, we use an alternative measure of credit growth – excess credit growth. Model 2 in Table 4.2 presents the findings of the ICAE as a function of excess credit growth. We continue to find evidence favouring our hypothesis as the empirical results show a significant and negative association between the two. As presented in Models 2 and 3, the excess credit supply seems to play a major role in influencing allocation efficiency. The banking sector concentration and banking structure do not have a significant relationship with the ICAE. These findings are in line with Chavan and Gambacorta (2019) and Gormley (2010).[2]

Table 4.2 Pro-cyclicality in the index of credit allocative efficiency (ICAE) and bank credit growth

Variables	Model 1	Model 2	Model 3
Credit growth	−0.0001**		
	(−1.9136)		
Excess credit growth		−0.0002**	−0.0002*
		(−2.1816)	(−1.7993)
ΔLending interest rate	0.0009**	0.0013**	0.0012**
	(2.3590)	(2.5857)	(2.3543)
Sensex growth	0.0001	0.0001	0.0001
	(0.9363)	(0.7654)	(0.7756)
Index of industrial production growth (IIP) (lag 1)	−0.0001	−0.0003**	−0.0002
	(−0.9549)	(−2.2310)	(−0.9599)
Herfindahl–Hirschman index (HHI) banking assets			−0.0056
			(−0.2905)
Banking structure			−0.0050
			(−0.2007)
C	0.0019	0.0015	0.0058
	(1.6036)	(1.7209)	(0.2788)
MA (1)	Yes		
MA (3)	Yes	Yes	Yes
R square	0.5827	0.6386	0.6415
Adj R square	0.4289	0.5302	0.4822

Note: Values in the parentheses are *t*-statistics. ***, **, and * indicate statistical significance at 1, 5, and 10 per cent levels.

We examine the autocorrelations and partial autocorrelations of the equation residuals up to 12 lags, as shown in Tables 4.3–4.5. We do not find any significant values of Q-statistics at the 1 per cent level, once again suggesting a good fit. Therefore, all the residuals are free from any correlation suggesting a satisfactory fit of our empirical model to the sample.

Testing for the Pro-cyclicality in the Source of Misallocation (BE)

Once we establish the association between allocative efficiency and pro-cyclicality, we decompose the overall ICAE to analyse the exact source of misallocation of credit and examine the phenomenon of BE further. As discussed in the previous chapter, the negative value of ICAE can be broken down into two components. The BE scenario arises when the low Q firms receive more bank credit than high Q firms. This section of the study investigates the relationship between BE and credit cycles. As mentioned earlier, we multiply BE by a factor of –1 for a better interpretation of results.

Similar to the ICAE, we present a graphical presentation of the association between the BE phenomenon and macroeconomic variables in Figures 4.7–4.11. We observe that the relationship between BE and credit growth is more pronounced. In fact, BE moves in tandem with the changes in credit growth.

Table 4.3 Autocorrelation function (ACF) and partial autocorrelation function (PACF) of residuals (Model 1, Table 4.2)

Sample: 1990–2017
Included observations: 27
Q-statistics probabilities adjusted for 2 ARMA terms

Autocorrelation	Partial correlation		AC	PAC	Q-Stat	Prob*
		1	-0.168	-0.168	0.8548	
		2	0.085	0.058	1.0791	
		3	-0.113	-0.093	1.4987	0.221
		4	-0.122	-0.165	2.0039	0.367
		5	-0.004	-0.040	2.0046	0.571
		6	0.170	0.181	3.0760	0.545
		7	-0.206	-0.197	4.7374	0.449
		8	0.208	0.113	6.5141	0.368
		9	-0.035	0.087	6.5672	0.475
		10	-0.051	-0.08	6.6849	0.571
		11	0.110	0.083	7.2736	0.609
		12	-0.205	-0.163	9.4682	0.488

Source: Author's compilation from times-series estimation in EViews.

Table 4.4   Autocorrelation function (ACF) and partial autocorrelation function (PACF) of residuals (Model 2, Table 4.2)

Sample: 1990–2017
Included observations: 27
Q-statistics probabilities adjusted for 1 ARMA term

Autocorrelation	Partial correlation		AC	PAC	Q-Stat	Prob*
		1	-0.341	-0.341	3.4957	
		2	0.184	0.077	4.5542	0.033
		3	-0.073	0.012	4.7304	0.094
		4	-0.091	-0.142	5.0119	0.171
		5	-0.134	-0.231	5.6549	0.226
		6	0.147	0.084	6.4613	0.264
		7	-0.223	-0.140	8.4122	0.209
		8	0.337	0.203	13.092	0.070
		9	-0.102	0.071	13.548	0.094
		10	-0.043	-0.156	13.634	0.136
		11	0.13	0.106	14.463	0.153
		12	-0.261	-0.200	18.015	0.081

Source: Author's compilation from times-series estimation in EViews.

Table 4.5   Autocorrelation function (ACF) and partial autocorrelation function (PACF) of residuals (Model 3, Table 4.2)

Sample: 1990–2017
Included observations: 27
Q-statistics probabilities adjusted for 1 ARMA term

Autocorrelation	Partial correlation		AC	PAC	Q-Stat	Prob*
		1	-0.409	-0.409	5.0260	
		2	0.131	-0.043	5.5641	0.018
		3	-0.115	-0.092	5.9949	0.050
		4	0.067	-0.011	6.1491	0.105
		5	-0.194	-0.201	7.4826	0.112
		6	0.013	-0.185	7.4892	0.187
		7	-0.047	-0.14	7.5750	0.271
		8	0.184	0.113	8.9740	0.255
		9	-0.114	-0.006	9.5412	0.299
		10	-0.046	-0.197	9.6378	0.381
		11	0.156	0.061	10.836	0.370
		12	-0.326	-0.346	16.387	0.127

Source: Author's compilation from times-series estimation in EViews.

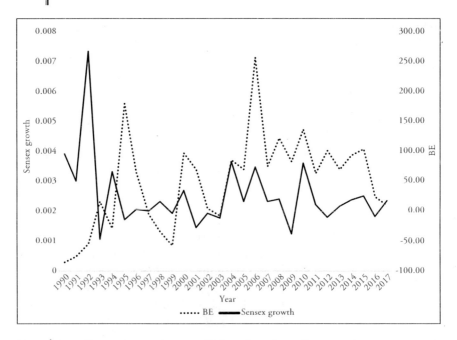

Figure 4.7 Borrowing exuberance (BE) and stock market growth

Source: BE is estimated by the authors. Sensex growth is sourced from Reserve Bank of India, *Handbook of Statistics on Indian Economy*, various editions.

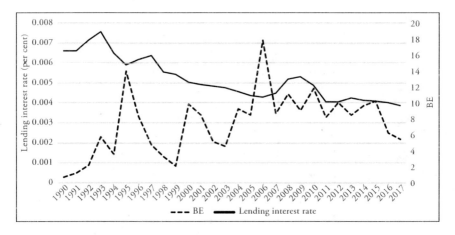

Figure 4.8 Borrowing exuberance (BE) and lending interest rate

Source: BE is estimated by the authors. The lending interest rate is sourced from International Monetary Fund, *International Financial Statistics*, various editions.

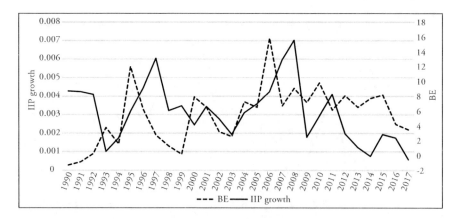

Figure 4.9 Borrowing exuberance (BE) and the index of industrial production (IIP) growth

Source: BE is estimated by the authors. IIP growth is sourced from the Central Statistics Office (CSO) database.

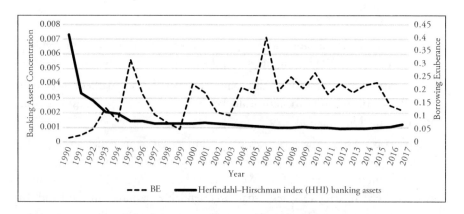

Figure 4.10 Borrowing exuberance (BE) and banking assets concentration

Source: BE is estimated by the authors. The HHI is computed using banking assets sourced from Reserve Bank of India, *Handbook of Statistics on Indian Economy*, various editions.

Furthermore, we observe that BE is higher when there is a bank credit boom in the market. This is similar to the trends in the overall ICAE, which also shows that misallocation increases during credit booms. This contemporaneous association

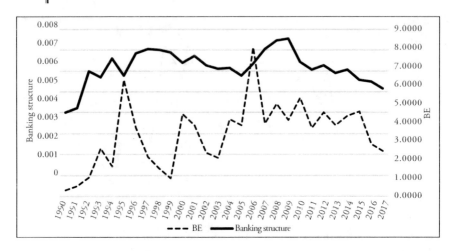

Figure 4.11   Borrowing exuberance (BE) and banking structure

Source: BE is estimated by the authors. The banking structure is computed from the data sourced from Reserve Bank of India, *Handbook of Statistics on Indian Economy*, various editions.

further strengthens our argument that the banks seem to continue providing additional loans despite having signals on the poor quality of the firm.

In addition, the trends in BE also follow the overall stock market movements and IIP growth. In order to statistically verify the relationship, we estimate the model outlined in equation 4.2.

Table 4.6 presents the estimates of the model given in equation 4.2. The findings reported in Model 1 present evidence for the credit boom being one of the significant determinants of BE. We report a positive and significant association between the two, which suggests that large lendable resources in the hands of banks encourage banks to increase lending to non-credit-worthy firms. Laxity in the underwriting and lending standards by the banks during the boom phase overlooks the quality of the borrowing firms. This eventually leads to firms with a lower Q ratio receiving a large volume of credit.

Further, we use the alternate specification for credit growth, that is, excess credit growth, to establish the robustness of our findings. The results of the models using excess credit growth, which is reported in Models 2 and 3, further corroborate the findings reported in Model 1. We observe that the excess credit growth shares a significant positive association with BE in all scenarios with alternate specifications. The lending interest rate, as hypothesized, shares a negative relationship with BE.

While Model 2 incorporates the growth of Sensex and the growth of the IIP, Model 3 includes the HHI of banking assets and banking structure as additional variables. Importantly, only Sensex growth shows a significant positive association with the BE phenomenon in Model 3. Notably, the IIP growth and banking structure remain insignificant throughout. However, consistent with our hypotheses, all variables carry the correct signs.

Table 4.6 Pro-cyclicality of borrowing exuberance (BE) and credit growth

Variables	Model 1	Model 2	Model 3
Credit growth	0.0001**		
	(2.5467)		
Excess credit growth		0.0001**	0.0001**
		(2.4122)	(2.3430)
ΔLending interest rate	–0.0002**	–0.0003***	0.0001
	(–2.3796)	(–3.1788)	(0.2324)
Sensex growth	0.0001	0.0001	0.0001*
	(0.2551)	(0.7974)	(1.9581)
Index of industrial production (IIP) growth (lag 1)	–0.0001	0.0001	0.0001
	(–0.3852)	(0.7724)	(0.3508)
Banking structure			–0.0019
			(–0.1667)
Herfindahl–Hirschman index (HHI) banking assets			–0.0366
			(–1.2575)
C	0.0042***	0.0064***	0.0063
	(3.0356)	(6.7388)	(0.7649)
MA (1)	Yes		
MA (3)	Yes	Yes	Yes
R-squared	0.5176	0.4890	0.6269
Adjusted R-squared	0.3399	0.3358	0.4610

Note: Values in the parentheses are *t*-statistics. ***, **, and * indicate statistical significance at 1, 5, and 10 per cent levels.

The autocorrelations and partial autocorrelations of the equation residuals up to 12 lags are reported in Tables 4.7–4.9. The Q-statistics are not significant for any of our models, further suggesting the good fit of the model.

Table 4.7 Correlogram of residuals (Model 1, Table 4.6)

Sample: 1990–2017
Included observations: 27
Q-statistics probabilities adjusted for 2 ARMA terms

Autocorrelation	Partial correlation		AC	PAC	Q-Stat	Prob*
		1	0.028	0.028	0.0234	
		2	0.258	0.257	2.1071	
		3	-0.058	-0.076	2.2175	0.136
		4	0.094	0.034	2.5185	0.284
		5	0.027	0.061	2.5454	0.467
		6	0.222	0.196	4.3763	0.357
		7	-0.040	-0.075	4.4394	0.488
		8	-0.085	-0.203	4.7349	0.578
		9	-0.001	0.070	4.7350	0.692
		10	-0.238	-0.224	7.3530	0.499
		11	0.137	0.136	8.2673	0.507
		12	-0.040	0.039	8.3518	0.595

Source: Author's compilation from times-series estimation in EViews.

Table 4.8 Correlogram of residuals (Model 2, Table 4.6)

Sample: 1990–2017
Included observations: 27
Q-statistics probabilities adjusted for 1 ARMA term

Autocorrelation	Partial correlation		AC	PAC	Q-Stat	Prob*
		1	0.166	0.166	0.8523	
		2	0.299	0.280	3.6322	0.057
		3	-0.019	-0.113	3.6442	0.162
		4	0.200	0.151	5.0008	0.172
		5	0.149	0.157	5.7863	0.216
		6	0.331	0.225	9.8836	0.079
		7	-0.034	-0.190	9.9295	0.128
		8	0.013	-0.127	9.9361	0.192
		9	-0.051	0.042	10.048	0.262
		10	-0.180	-0.321	11.541	0.240
		11	-0.064	-0.085	11.742	0.303
		12	-0.051	0.071	11.880	0.373

Source: Author's compilation from times-series estimation in EViews.

Table 4.9   Correlogram of residuals (Model 3, Table 4.6)

Sample: 1990–2017
Included observations: 27
Q-statistics probabilities adjusted for 1 ARMA term

Autocorrelation	Partial correlation		AC	PAC	Q-Stat	Prob*
		1	-0.058	-0.058	0.1010	
		2	-0.007	-0.011	0.1026	0.749
		3	-0.106	-0.107	0.4665	0.792
		4	-0.039	-0.052	0.5183	0.915
		5	-0.017	-0.025	0.5280	0.971
		6	0.204	0.192	2.0822	0.838
		7	-0.176	-0.170	3.2886	0.772
		8	-0.183	-0.217	4.6621	0.701
		9	0.013	0.033	4.6696	0.792
		10	-0.253	-0.298	7.6184	0.573
		11	0.042	-0.049	7.7053	0.658
		12	-0.190	-0.318	9.5875	0.568

Source: Author's compilation from times-series estimation in EViews.

Conclusion

The chapter critically examines the possibility that the banking sector, particularly in the context of an emerging market, can exacerbate cyclical fluctuations, hindering the efficient allocation of resources in the economy and adversely affecting credit growth and financial stability (Athanasoglou, Daniilidis, and Delis, 2014). In contrast to the existing studies that analyse the impact on the economy as an ex-post outcome which is often influenced by various external factors, this chapter looks at the ex-ante circumstances where we critically examine the lending decisions made by the banks with the already available information. Mainly, using a measure of misallocation at the point of loan disbursal where the banks are supposed to use all available information about the prospects of the firms prudently, this chapter validates the pro-cyclicality in bank lending behaviour.

The findings reported in this research provide evidence for the significant positive relationship between credit growth and misallocation of bank credit in general and BE in particular in the context of Indian markets. The pro-cyclicality in the ICAE suggests that the efficiency of bank credit allocation drops when the bank loan market is in a high growth phase. The BE phenomenon where banks lend more funds to low-quality firms further aggravates the situation. This might suggest a laxity and poor judgement from banks in allocating credit, despite having signals on the low quality of the firm. Finally, it is important to note that while the macro analysis provides valuable insights into the pro-cyclicality of lending behaviour, we note that most of the selected explanatory variables remain statistically insignificant, suggesting that the corporate borrowing behaviours in India are largely governed by the firm-specific attributes (Bhaduri, 2000; Guha-Khasnobis and Bhaduri, 2000). Therefore, in the next chapter, we attempt to explore these hypotheses further, using the firm-level panel data.

Notes

1   See *Business Line*, 'Rajan Traces NPA Mess to Banks' Excesses in 2006-08', 11 September 2018, https://www.thehindubusinessline.com/money-and-banking/rajan-traces-npa-mess-to-banks-excesses-in-2006-08/article24928727.ece (accessed in January 2021); T. T. Ram Mohan and C. Rangarajan, 'Resolving India's Banking Crisis', *The Hindu*, 11 May 2019, https://www.thehindu.com/opinion/lead/resolving-indias-banking-crisis/article27097047.ece (accessed in January 2021).

2   The negative sign of banking structure on allocative efficiency suggests that the information asymmetry resulting from foreign banks' selection of borrowers can exacerbate the misallocation. Similar results were suggested by Gormley (2010) with respect to banks' profitability after the entry of foreign banks in the country.

5

Determinants of Bank Credit Misallocation
Firm-level Analysis

One of the key contentions of economic studies, as discussed earlier, is the efficient allocation of resources among the various market participants in the economy. Among them, efficient allocation of capital remains the most discussed and debated topic among policy-makers and academicians across the world. The availability of external funding, especially bank credit and ease of access to bank credit, contributes to the financial deepening of an economy, facilitating the aggregate output and overall economic activity (King and Levine, 1993). Therefore, efficient credit allocation becomes critical where companies continue to rely on bank lending for financing (Booth et al., 2001; Giannetti, 2003). This is further aggravated in the economies where we observe weakly developed capital markets and weak shareholder and creditor protection.

Interestingly, when the narrative shifts to emerging markets like India, where banks are the largest suppliers of credit, several questions are posed on efficient allocation of bank credit among many firms operating in different settings of industry, the scale of operation, and performance. Although the growing body of literature has examined the misallocation of bank credit, particularly with respect to the emerging markets, the overall conclusion remains ambiguous so far. For example, in a cross-country study, Taboada (2011) reports that higher bank credit is allocated to less productive industries and those firms with less dependence on external finance. In contrast, Chen, Skully, and Kym (2005) and Firth et al. (2009) find the evidence of allocation of bank credit to better governed and more profitable firms in various country-specific studies. Among the several reasons for misallocation discussed in the literature, ownership structure of banks, agency problems, weak legal system, political influence, poor corporate governance both at the firm and at the bank level, fraud and corruption, and biased lending by banks have been referred to as prominent factors of emerging economies (La Porta, Lopez-de-Silanes, and Shleifer, 2002; Sapienza, 2004; Ding and Ge, 2005; Illueca, Norden, and Udell, 2014). At the same time, each emerging market has its own unique institutional and operating environment, which, on the one hand, restricts us from applying a universal model across all such economies and, on the other hand, calls for country-specific studies.

This chapter attempts to fill the gap in the literature where there is limited microeconomic evidence on bank credit misallocation and its determinants. By investigating the firm-level determinants of bank credit misallocation using a case study of one of the largest emerging markets, India, we add to the empirical literature on bank financing. A large body of literature on misallocation of credit often considers misallocation as an *ex-post* outcome such as quantum of bad loans – for example, NPAs. However, the findings of these studies could be contaminated with several factors like changes in the law and regulations, unfavourable macroeconomic environment, and other external shocks whose information is not available at the time of the lending decision. In contrast to these studies, we analyse the *ex-ante* circumstances in which banks issued the credit based on the firm-specific information available at the point of disbursal. Thus, we check the extent to which banks misallocate credit during loan disbursal despite having all available information about a firm's prospects. Therefore, this research attempts to delve into the dynamic nature of bank credit misallocation at the point of origination through a microeconomic perspective by using firm-level information.

The primary objective of this research is to identify the firm-specific attributes that correlate with the misallocation of bank credit. Specifically, we focus on three main factors of misallocation of bank credit. The first factor involves the creditworthiness of the firm receiving bank loans. It is often argued that when the economy is on an upswing, the banks tend to ease their lending norms and the due-diligence process. This laxity from banks often leads to non-credit-worthy firms receiving bank credit, which would not have happened if there was no excess credit supply. Therefore, the possibility of non-credit-worthy firms obtaining loans has detrimental consequences downstream.

The second factor comprises the requirement of external funds. During credit booms, firms tend to obtain loans over and above their actual requirement, given the excess supply of credit in the market.[1] The actual requirement and the productivity of the investment are often underestimated in such cases. The sudden availability of excess capital combined with reckless spending and mismanagement could probably turn this into a poor quality loan, mainly when the economic conditions reverse.

The third factor highlights the importance of the corporate governance structure of firms and banks. While government control of banks exists due to financial and credit market failures in general, such control is pervasive globally, including those in developed markets (Stiglitz and Weiss, 1981; Greenwald and Stiglitz, 1986; La Porta, Lopez-de-Silanes, and Shleifer, 2002). The agency view goes hand in hand with the social view that state-owned enterprises are created to maximize social welfare and generate corruption and misallocation (Banerjee, 1997; Hart, Shleifer, and Vishny, 1997). Such misallocation of credit is identified in the literature owing to related lending, politically influenced lending by government-controlled banks, and inadequate bank monitoring (Sapienza, 2004; Dinç, 2005; La Porta, Lopez-De-Silanes, and Shleifer, 2006). More often, a long-term bank–firm relationship leads to evergreening of the loans to companies already in financial trouble (Albertazzi and Marchetti, 2010). Further, poor corporate governance at the firm level aggravates the improper utilization of funds which is more apparent in emerging markets where the corporate governance mechanisms are weaker. In sum, we hypothesize that the bank credit misallocation initiated at the firm level is associated with low creditworthiness, a lesser requirement for external credit, and poor corporate governance mechanisms. We carry out the investigation based on the literature on misallocation of bank credit which provides two distinct perspectives. The first strand of literature focuses on credit allocation from the banks' perspective by analysing the nature of their lending decisions. In contrast, the other strand of literature examines credit misallocation using firm-specific information.

Overall, the bank-specific studies advance our understanding of the sources of misallocation from the supply side, while firm-specific studies focus more on the demand side. Our research specifically fits into the second strand of literature by providing the microeconomic evidence of misallocation of bank credit.

Determinants of Credit Misallocation: Bank-specific Factors

Bank-based studies have primarily looked at the efficiency of banking systems across countries. For example, Chen, Skully, and Kym (2005) report that financial deregulation improved the efficiency of large state-owned and smaller banks compared to medium-sized banks. The studies examining the effect of financial liberalization and efficiency of banking systems were further extended to emerging markets from Southeast Asia (Williams and Nguyen, 2005; Thoraneenitiyan and Avkiran, 2009; Sufian, 2010; Chan et al., 2015).

Taboada (2011) investigates how the change in ownership of banks affects credit allocation of the top 10 banks from 63 countries. The study reveals that an increase in domestic block-holder ownership increases the lending to less productive industries and firms that do not need external capital. This is particularly relevant for emerging economies, where the banks controlled by domestic block-holders tend to influence a significant portion of their lending activities to the firms, which might be inefficient.

The adverse impact of government involvement in credit markets is noted in both cross-country and standalone studies. At the macro level, countries with higher government ownership of financing institutions show lower growth (Barth, Kasznik, and McNichols, 2001; La Porta, Lopez-de-Silanes, and Shleifer, 2002; Dinç, 2005). In addition, microeconomic evidence drawn from single-country studies finds support for political influence in bank lending (Sapienza, 2004, for Italy; Khwaja and Mian, 2005, for Pakistan; Cole, 2009, for India; Carvalho, 2014, for Brazil; Cull et al., 2015, for China). In contrast, Srinivasan and Thampy (2017) find that corporate-sector lending by government-owned banks in India increases the sensitivity of investment to firm valuation. While these are direct evidence of bank lending behaviour, literature has also highlighted indirect evidence of misallocation by focusing on factors like bank–firm relationships. For example, suggesting evergreening, Peek and Rosengren (2005) report that relationship lending often leads to banks extending credit to weaker firms. Further, Laeven (2001) concludes that there exists a widespread practice of banks' lending huge volumes of loans to insider parties that are connected to banks through ownership structure. Finally, Borensztein and Lee (2005) find that there is relatively higher access to bank credit by conglomerates without proper project evaluation and monitoring.

Determinants of Credit Misallocation: Firm-specific Factors

In contrast to bank-based studies on misallocation, a small but growing body of literature provides microeconomic evidence of misallocation using firm-level data. For example, using a cross-country study, Wurgler (2000) argues that the efficiency of capital allocation is associated with three prominent factors – developed capital markets with efficient prices reflecting all the relevant information, less invasive government control, and strong stakeholder rights.[2]

Using the data from East European countries, Giannetti and Onegena (2009) show that foreign banks' entry improves capital allocation by mitigating the related lending problems for small and young firms. In contrast, the entry of foreign banks in an emerging market can exacerbate information asymmetries and a systematic drop in credit availability (Gormley, 2010).

Focusing on China's economic stimulus plan during 2009–10, Cong et al. (2019) found evidence for widespread misallocation as firms with a lower product of capital received higher volumes of bank loans, specifically from the state-owned enterprises. Another stream of literature that analyses the firm-specific determinants of misallocation explores the role of corporate governance practices of firms and banks. Among them, bank–firm relationships are another widely discussed factor in the misallocation of credit. More often, firms tend to maintain a close relationship with banks in emerging markets and predominantly rely on a single bank (Rajan and Zingales, 1998; Gup, 1998). In such an institutional setup, a bank's ability to lend effectively to the right set of firms leads to severe credit constraints that prevent the firms from opting for projects with a high marginal return to capital (Stein, 2002; Banerjee and Duflo, 2005). By looking into the allocation of loans by the government-controlled banks to private firms in China, Firth et al. (2009) find that state-owned banks provided loans to financially healthier firms with better governance practices. However, with respect to the credit to larger firms, the study observed that the political connection plays a significant role. In contrast to these findings, Yeh et al. (2013) and Chen et al. (2014) show that a firm's political connections are positively correlated with the allotment of preferential bank loans.

Dependent Variable

The dependent variable in our empirical analyses is the index of credit allocative efficiency (ICAE), as developed in Chapter 3, and the constituents of the negative ICAE, namely borrowing exuberance (BE).

Variables of Interest I: Corporate Finance

Firm Size (*size_ta*)

It is often argued that larger firms enjoy better visibility and reputation in the credit market, enabling them to obtain loans even when the performance is below par (Easterwood and Kadapakkam, 1991). For example, using a sample of US firms, Hooks (2003) examines the determinants of the concentration of bank debt and finds that it varies by the size of the firm. Alonso et al. (2005) observe a positive association between the firm size and the proportion of bank debt among the Spanish firms and corroborate the view of Diamond (1991) that reputation plays a significant role. A small firm is often screened out of the financial markets since it is more difficult for outsiders to observe any public information about a small firm, and also, there is a lack of outside reputation. In contrast, a large established firm with a good reputation taps cheap credit in external credit markets.

Further, banks often tend to relax the lending norms for big firms because the reputation (or collateral) effect scores over the quality aspect (Ekpu, 2011). In another study, Smith (1987) suggests that a small firm with a very high ex-ante default risk will be denied credit, a firm in the middle-risk category will obtain only trade credit, while a firm with relatively low risk will be most likely to obtain a bank loan (substitution between trade credit and bank loan; monitoring). Therefore, it is critical to control for the firm's size while assessing the misallocation of credit. Keeping in line with the literature, we define the variable *size_ta* as a natural log of total assets to proxy firm size.

Firm Age (*age*)

We hypothesize that the older firms share a better reputation and perhaps a longer credit history, encouraging banks to lend loans. The impact of age of the firm is presented in the screening view of bank debt by Smith (1987), which argues that the proxy for ex-ante default risk depends on firm age. Particularly in the context of emerging economies which are characterized by acute information asymmetries, it is observed that size and age, if used in bank loan screening, often result in a lower bank credit (Ghosh, 2007). Firm age is measured as the difference between the listing year and the year of observation.

Collateral (*Tangibility*)

The collateral offered by the firm often forms the basis of the amount it can obtain as loans. This is because tangible assets provide the observability of a firm's activities to outsiders (Hoshi, Kashyap, and Scharfstein, 1990) and helps to limit the moral hazard problem (Boot, Thakor, and Udell, 1991; Leeth and Scott, 1989). However, the probability of misallocation of credit increases if the banks ignore the underlying value of the collateral. The literature also emphasizes the role of collateral as an explanation for the pro-cyclical nature of credit and risk-taking by banks (Kiyotaki and Moore, 1997; Adrian and Shin, 2010; and Borio, Furfine, and Lowe, 2001). An increase in the credit flow leads to a rise in the collateral value, thus amplifying the asset price cycle (Kiyotaki and Moore, 1997). Under such circumstances of hyper-credit growth, banks increase their credit limit as the value of the underlying collateral assets increases.

Consequently, the increase in collateral value enables banks to finance those borrowers that may not have been otherwise financed. Additionally, Adrian and

Shin (2010) argue that banks look for newer borrowers whenever there is a credit boom as all the existing good borrowers already possess a mortgage. However, when the asset price cycle breaks down during a downturn, these loans pile up as bad loans. Therefore, in line with the literature, we proxy firm collateral by defining *tangibility* as the ratio of net fixed assets to total assets.

Financial Constraints (*KZindex*)

A financially constrained firm is often challenged to access bank credit as it displays higher financial risk.[3] This is aggravated particularly when the economy is facing a crisis and, therefore, the bank credit supply is limited (Bernanke and Gertler, 1995). However, during good times this trend reverses, and financially constrained firms are likely to get funds over and above their requirement. Financial constraint is measured using the *KZ index* (Kaplan and Zingles, 1997),[4] which provides a relative measure of external financing. Firms with a higher value KZ index are more likely to experience difficulties in financing their ongoing operation when their overall financial condition deteriorates. We argue that the misallocation of bank credit can be closely related to the extent of financial constraints faced by the firm. For example, a firm having a low KZ index (suggesting financially non-constrained firms) associated with a low (or negative) ICAE suggests an acute case of misallocation of capital as the firm continues to undertake bank borrowing despite having a relatively low return on capital. In contrast, a firm with a high KZ index associated with a high ICAE suggests a better allocation of resources. A similar argument holds for BE. Therefore, a firm's financial constraints have implications for individual firms and aggregate economic activity.

Financial Distress (*ZScore_em*)

We also account for the fact that a firm may be accessing bank borrowing despite facing financial distress, leading to the possible misallocation of resources. The distress becomes severe when the firms are close to bankruptcy as the liquidity constraints grow manifold. Therefore, any additional loans to such firms should be evaluated with the utmost caution (Bongini, Ferri, and Hahm, 2000). Nevertheless, it is often seen, when misallocation is rampant, firms that are close to bankruptcy receive more credit while firms with a better risk profile are deprived of their desired credit. This is also corroborated by Taboada (2011), documenting that firms closer to bankruptcy are more likely to use bank debt. We use Altman Z-score for emerging markets as a proxy of financial distress,[5] where a lower Z-score indicates a higher probability of bankruptcy.

Leverage (*leverage_ta*)

It is argued that when financial leverage is higher, firms face constraints in raising additional funds, specifically debt in the form of bank loans. Higher leverage increases the probability of bankruptcy, and it goes hand in hand with the poor performance of the firms (Bongini, Ferri, and Hahm, 2000). Consequently, an excess loan extended to high leverage firms will lead to higher default risk. Further, the leverage ratio has a critical impact on the ability of firms to service debt obligations as it limits the ability of firms with low income to make interest payments. Following the existing literature, we define firm *leverage* as the ratio of long-term debt to total assets.

Interest Coverage Ratio (*ICR_dummy*)

In the context of bank borrowings, the interest coverage ratio (ICR) also plays an important role. A lower ICR suggests that the firm has a debt burden and its ability to service its debt is questionable. In contrast, a high ICR decreases the probability of a firm going bankrupt. Therefore, a firm with a lower ICR does not appear to be an ideal candidate for receiving the loans. We hypothesize that firms with lower ICR are more likely to misallocate if they continue to borrow. Following the literature, we measure the ICR as the ratio of earnings (profit before depreciation, interest, taxes, and amortization [PBDITA]) to interest expenses. Similar to McGowan et al. (2018), we use a cut-off for ICR value greater than or equal to 2 to identify less creditworthy firms. Following this convention, we define a dummy variable *ICR-dummy* which takes a value equal to 1 if the ICR is greater than or equal to 2 and 0 otherwise.

Internal Financing (*growth_internal_funds*)

Another important factor that deserves attention in corporate finance literature is the ability of the firm to generate internal capital. A firm's external financing need depends on the magnitude of its internal cash flows relative to its investment opportunities (Demirgüç-Kunt and Maksimovic, 1998). Therefore, a firm's external capital requirement would be less if the firm generates a sufficient amount through internal sources. Typically, such firms are not expected to approach the banks for funding. We hypothesize that a firm generating sufficient internal funds is more likely to misallocate if it continues to borrow. As followed in the literature, we define *growth_internal_ funds* as the growth of return on assets (ROA), where the ROA is calculated as a ratio of PBDITA to total assets (for example, see Ding and Ge, 2005).

External Funds Requirement (*deficit_ta*)

Measurement of the requirement of external funds is equally critical among factors that influence corporate financing. A firm with a lower requirement of external funds is not an ideal candidate for bank borrowing. To check if the firms that borrow are the ones that need external capital, we incorporate a financial deficit variable into our research following Shyam-Sunder and Myers (1999).[6] A low (negative) deficit indicates a financial surplus. In the context of allocative efficiency, if such firms continue to borrow, they are likely to misallocate.

Variables of Interest II: Corporate Governance

The institutional and regulatory environment of a country can have differential impacts on banks' risk-taking ability, depending on banks' ownership and corporate governance structure (Laeven and Levine, 2009).[7] The next set of variables of interest includes variables that capture corporate governance mechanisms from banks' perspectives. The existing literature identifies the role of banks in the corporate governance structure of firms through banks' ownership and banking relationships at the firm level.

Government–Bank Relationship (*n_psb*)

Government control of banks, particularly in emerging markets, is often argued as one of the major contributing factors of credit misallocation due to agency problems, corruption, fraudulent activities, and political influence (La Porta, Lopez-de-Silanes, and Shleifer, 2002; Sapienza, 2004; Illueca, Lars, and Udell, 2012). This is particularly important in emerging markets where government ownership of banks is negatively associated with financial development and growth (La Porta, Lopez-de-Silanes, and Shleifer, 2002). Specifically, in the Indian context, Cole and Turk (2007) find that government-controlled banks are often associated with inefficiency and poor performance. Also, Chavan and Gambacorta (2019) report that the pro-cyclicality of public sector banks (PSBs) is relatively high compared to their private counterparts. Furthermore, in a recent study, Kumar (2020) finds that politically motivated lending by government-controlled banks led to excessive indebtedness in India's agricultural sector. In this backdrop, a firm's relationship with a government-owned bank could affect the access and utilization of funds. While Cole and Turk (2007) find that firms having a relationship with state-owned banks are more likely to maintain a single bank relationship, Srinivasan and Thampy (2017) find that firms that maintain exclusive relationships with state-owned banks have significantly lower investment cash flow sensitivity. To account for the relationship with government-owned banks in our research, we define the *n_psb* as the total number of public sector bankers reported at the firm level. In addition to this, we use an interaction term between credit growth and *n_psb* to test the argument whether the pro-cyclicality in the misallocation of resources is exacerbated for firms having a public sector banking relationship.

State Bank and Its Associates (*d_sbi*)

Further to isolate the effect of one of the dominant players in the public sector banking space that is, State Bank of India (SBI), we define a dummy variable that equals 1 if the firm is holding at least one relationship with SBI or its associates.

Multiple Bank–Firm Relationships (*n_bank*)

The literature argues there are two major purposes for the existence of multiple banking relationships: (*a*) unavailability of credit from one bank and (*b*) insurance against deterioration of firm's credit-worthiness. In the context of emerging markets like India, the existence of multiple banking relationships can address misallocation to some extent as the competition among banks is relatively restricted, and the cost of monitoring to a single bank tends to be high due to poor disclosure practices (Berger et al., 2008). However, empirical evidence suggests that firms in emerging markets usually rely on a single bank (Nam, 1996; Rajan and Zingales, 1998; Gup, 1998). This could potentially encourage crony capitalism and connected lending, which could further accentuate the misallocation of resources (Dewatripont, 1995). To account for the multiple-banking relationship, we incorporate a variable that captures the total number of banking relationships at a firm level.

Bank Directors (*d_bank_nominee*)

The presence of a nominee director is a corporate governance mechanism with several advantages (Ferreira and Matos, 2012). Banker participation in a company board would increase the scope of the long-term banking relationship and strengthen existing banking relationships (Sisli-Ciamarra, 2012). The amount of proprietary information that the bank acquires about the company would increase, monitoring would become more effective, and the cost of acquiring firm-specific information to the bank would decrease (Qian and Yeung, 2015). Therefore, we hypothesize that the presence of a bank nominee director on the borrowing firm's board reduces the misallocation of bank credit. This variable is defined as a dummy variable that takes a value of 1 if the firm has a bank nominee director as a member of the board and 0 otherwise.

In the following section, we highlight the corporate governance structure of firms that could potentially impact the extent of bank credit allocation. While corporate governance mechanisms at the firm level are frequently studied with respect to firm performance (for example, Sarkar and Sarkar [2000]; Ghosh [2007]; Nachane, Ghosh, and Ray [2006]), and capital structure decisions in general (Harris and Raviv, 1991), evidence for the utilization of bank credit is largely unavailable.

Outsider Ownership (*sh_mutual_funds* and *sh_banks_fi*)

Outside ownership reduces the agency problem between insiders and outsiders. The monitoring of a firm's activities implied by the use of bank-borrowed funds is a control mechanism chosen discretionally by a firm's managers (Denis and Mihov, 2003). However, the presence of banks or financial institutions in the ownership structure of firms also has a strong impact on firms' borrowing decisions due to the monitoring activity by banks as owners. Similarly, the shareholder activism by mutual funds, which generally hold block ownership, can impact the strategic activities of firms. We account for both these factors by including the percentage of ownership of banks and financial institutions (*sh_banks_fi*) and mutual funds (*sh_mutual_funds*). A higher share of this ownership is expected to reduce misallocation.

Insider Ownership (*sh_promoters*)

Another essential dimension of corporate governance structure is the promoters' shareholding in the firm. Promoters are the individuals or corporations that are in control of the management of the firm. There are two advantages of higher promoter ownership of the firm. As suggested by Jensen (1986), a higher proportion of management ownership facilitates alignment of interest with that of shareholders, while higher promoter shareholding is often perceived as the promoter's trust in the prospect of the firm. Therefore, such firms are expected to use the borrowed funds prudently. Empirical evidence provides further strength to this argument. A firm with a higher ownership concentration finances its deficit of internal funds with bank debt (Dewatripont and Tirole, 1994; John and Kedia, 2000). However, firms with promoter control are also found to mismanage the resources through tunnelling activities (Bertrand, Mehta, and Mullainathan, 2002). As argued by Qian and Yeung (2015), when inefficient state-owned banks dominate the financing system, firms' access to the bank loan is positively associated with controlling shareholders' tunnelling activities. Therefore, the effect of promoter ownership on bank credit misallocation is ambiguous.

Board Governance (*board_size* and *board_independence*)

The next strand of corporate governance variables accounts for the firm's board of directors. The board of directors is appointed to monitor management to ensure alignment with shareholders' interests (Germain, Galy, and Lee, 2014). Among various measures of board governance, board size and the presence of independent directors have been most commonly used. The presence of independent directors and more board members are healthy signs of an independent board that has potentially more monitoring power (Raheja, 2005). Independent directors can better challenge CEOs than are grey or inside directors, and they have incentives to develop a reputation as skilled decision control experts in the corporate directorship market (Fama, 1980). In addition, institutional investors and regulators often advocate the independent representation of directors to strengthen the board's oversight (Guo and Masulis, 2015). However, it is equally important to note that independent directors often face limited access to firm-specific information and high costs in assessing the reliability of the information, and these limitations can, in turn, reduce their monitoring incentives and effectiveness (Raheja, 2005; Adams and Ferreira, 2007; Masulis and Mobbs, 2011). Therefore, building on monitoring and limited resources hypotheses, independent directors can both reduce and increase the misallocation problem.

Control Variables

We found in the previous chapter that there exists a pro-cyclicality in bank credit misallocation. Therefore, we add credit growth to control for the effects of business cycles on firm-level misallocation. We also control for the growth of firm and business group affiliation. These variables are defined as follows.

Credit Growth (*Creditgrowth*)

In continuation with the previous chapter, which analyses the macro impact of credit growth, we further test the validity of the hypothesis at a micro level using credit growth as one of the independent variables in our specification. The empirical evidence of the impact of credit growth on misallocation has been unambiguous. Franco, Hope, and Lu (2017) report that among European countries, higher availability of credit reduces capital misallocation. In contrast, it is also observed that during the growing phase of the credit cycle, practices such as lower bank lending standards, increased competition, and the underestimation of risk result in loans that are granted to investments with marginally positive or even a negative net present value (Breuer, 2006; Festic, Kavkler, and Repina, 2011; Athanasoglou, Daniilidis, and Delis, 2013; Caporale, Colli, and Lopez, 2014), while during downturns, investments with positive net present value fail to receive bank financing (Jimenez, Salas, and Saurina, 2006). We measure credit growth as the annual growth rate of advances provided by the scheduled commercial banks. While we use the contemporaneous credit growth as the primary variable, we also incorporate a one-year lagged term for credit growth into our model to control for any autocorrelation effects.

Firm Growth (*growth_ta*)

One of the fundamental premises of efficiency in allocating resources argues that when the markets are efficient, capital should flow from a low growth industry or firm to a high growth industry or firm (Wurgler, 2000; Di Mauro, Hassan, and Ottaviano, 2018). This suggests that in the event of misallocation or BE, low-growth firms would receive more credit, and the worthy high-growth firms would be in shortage of funds. This could consequently cripple the growth of the economy. Therefore, if the allocation is efficient, bank credit is expected to flow to high-growth firms. Hence, we control for firm growth by adding the growth rate of total assets (*growth_ta*) in our empirical specification.

Business Group Affiliation (*d_group*)

In India, business groups form an important part of the private sector as close to 45 per cent of the firms in our sample are affiliated with business groups. It is also argued that business-group firms have better access and are likely to be less capital constrained when compared to standalone firms (Lensink, van der Molen, and Gangopadhyay, 2003). This is driven by the fact that financial relationships exist between affiliated firms, and these financial interlinkages may serve to mitigate moral hazard problems within the group (Berglöf and Perotti, 1994). Further, in an imperfect market characterized by asymmetric information, group membership may signal the firms' quality (Ghatak and Kali, 2001) or relative stability in cash flows (Gangopadhyay and Lensink, 2001), reducing the harmful effects of adverse selection. Especially in an emerging country like India, reputation effects may be of great importance since the absence of strong creditor rights and a reliable legal system may make contract enforcement via a court very costly (Lensink, van der Molen, and Gangopadhyay, 2003). However, this might also indicate that group-affiliated firms are receiving bank credit disproportionately, ignoring the firm's quality in question. Following the literature, we add a dummy variable that takes 1 if a firm is affiliated to a business group and 0 otherwise.

Table 5.1 represents the description and sources of all variables used in this research. All the variables are constructed using firm-level data obtained from Centre for Monitoring Indian Economy (CMIE) Prowess. Credit growth is calculated using total advances obtained from the Reserve Bank of India's *Handbook of Statistics on Indian Economy*.

Table 5.1 Description and source of the variables

Variable	Description of the variable
ICAE	Credit allocative efficiency (see Chapter 3 for computation)
Misallocation	Negative values of CAE * (–1)
BE	Borrowing exuberance (ICAE of firms with Q < Qbar; B > Bbar) * (–1))
size_ta	Total asset of a firm (natural log of total assets)
age	Age of the firm since its incorporation
ICR_dummy	Dummy variable = 1 if previous year's ICR (ratio of PBDITA to interest expenses) < 2; 0 otherwise
deficit_ta	Deficit = (dividend + net investment + change in net working capital – cash flow after interest and taxes); expressed as proportion of total assets
growth_internal_funds	Growth of internal funds
zscore_em	Altaman Z-score for emerging markets
tangibility	Expenditure on plant and machinery or total assets
leverage _ta	debt or total assets
KZindex	KZ= (–1.002 * ((total income – prior period and extraordinary income)/l_total assets)) + (0.283 * tobin's q) + (3.139 * leverage1) – (39.368 * (dividend/l_total assets)) – (1.315 * ((cash and bank balance + book value of market able securities)/l_total assets))
d_group	Dummy = 1 if firm belongs to a business group; 0 otherwise
growth_ta	Growth in total assets
n_psb	Number of PSBs as bankers
d_sbi	Dummy = 1 if SBI or associates are reported as bankers; 0 otherwise
n_bank	Total number of banking relations
board_size	Board Size measured as total number of directors
board_independence	Proportion of independent directors

(Contd)

(Contd)

Variable	Description of the variable
d_bank_nominee	Dummy=1 if the board has a bank nominee director; 0 otherwise
sh_mutual_funds	Mutual funds shareholding (per cent)
sh_banks_fi	FI and bank shareholdings (per cent)
sh_promoters	Promoter shareholding (per cent)

Empirical Specification: Determinants of Bank Credit Misallocation

This research investigates the determinants of misallocation and BE of bank credit among Indian firms. As described earlier, the primary variable of interest is *misallocation*, which is essentially the negative ICAE with two main constituents: firms with relatively lower Q ratio receiving a higher proportion of bank credit *(BE)* and firms with relatively higher Q receiving a lower proportion of bank credit *(BC)*. Therefore, by construct, in both cases, the ICAE will be a negative quantum.

Since the dependent variable, the negative ICAE, has a natural censoring at 0, we adopt a Tobit regression model as it is the most commonly used methodology for handling truncated data. Further, to account for the firm-specific unobserved heterogeneity and time-variant effects, we use a random-effects Tobit model. For ease of interpretation, we further multiply the dependent variable by a factor of -1. Also, to account for the potential endogeneity, all the independent variables are lagged by one year. Our baseline model for negative ICAE is defined as

$$Misallocation_{it} = \alpha_i + \Sigma\beta_p Creditgrowth_{t-p} + \Sigma_j^k \beta_j X_{it} + \varepsilon_{it}\, p = 0,1 \qquad (5.1)$$

Here, $Misallocation_{it}$ is the negative ICAE of firm i at time t. X_{it} is a vector of the previous year's firm characteristics such as the size, age, ICR, financing deficit, growth of assets, and Z score. In addition, tangibility, business group affiliation, and the growth of internal funds are added as contemporaneous variables in vector X_{it}. The baseline model of misallocation is augmented to incorporate these variables into various specifications as described in Box 5.1.

Next, to gain further insight into the nature of misallocation, we focus on BE, where firms with relatively lower Q receive a higher proportion of bank credit. While both the elements of misallocation are important, misallocation caused through borrowing exuberance could be potentially more detrimental for the economy. The baseline model for borrowing exuberance is as specified below:

$$BE_{it} = \alpha_i + \sum \beta_p Creditgrowth_{t-p} + \sum_j^k \beta_j X_{it} + \varepsilon_{it} \, p = 0,1 \qquad (5.7)$$

Here, X_{it} is a vector of variables that includes the size, age, ICR, financial deficit, growth, Z, growth of internal funds, and business-group affiliation of the firms. Similar to the misallocation regression specifications, we augment our baseline model for borrowing exuberance for the robustness checks as reported in Box 5.2.

As argued earlier, corporate governance mechanisms at the firm level can be associated with credit misallocation by firms due to underlying agency theory postulating the entrenched behaviour by insiders and lack of monitoring by outside investors. Unfortunately, the corporate governance information in India is available from 2001 after the introduction of Clause 49, which mandated the disclosure

---

Box 5.1 Model specifications of bank credit misallocation and firm-specific characteristics

$Misallocation_{it} = \alpha_i + \beta_0 Creditgrowth_t + \beta_1 Creditgrowth_{t-1} +$
$\beta_2 Size\_ta_{it-1} + \beta_3 Age_{it-1} + \beta_4 ICR\_dummy_{it-1} + \beta_5 Deficit\_ta_{it-1} +$
$\beta_6 Growth\_ta_{it-1} + \beta_7 Zscore\_em_{it-1} + \beta_8 d\_group_{it} + \varepsilon_{it}$ $\qquad (5.2)$

$Misallocation_{it} = \alpha_i + \beta_0 Creditgrowth_t + \beta_1 Creditgrowth_{t-1} +$
$\beta_2 Size\_ta_{it-1} + \beta_3 Age_{it-1} + \beta_4 ICR\_dummy_{it-1} + \beta_5 Deficit\_ta_{it-1} +$
$\beta_6 Growth\_ta_{it-1} + \beta_7 Zscore\_em_{it-1} + \beta_8 d\_group_{it} +$
$\beta_9 Tangibility_{it} + \varepsilon_{it}$ $\qquad (5.3)$

$Misallocation_{it} = \alpha_i + \beta_0 Creditgrowth_t + \beta_1 Creditgrowth_{t-1} +$
$\beta_2 Size\_ta_{it-1} + \beta_3 Age_{it-1} + \beta_4 ICR\_dummy_{it-1} + \beta_5 Deficit\_ta_{it-1} +$
$\beta_6 Growth\_ta_{it-1} + \beta_7 d\_group_{it} + \beta_8 KZindex_{it-1} + \varepsilon_{it}$ $\qquad (5.4)$

$Misallocation_{it} = \alpha_i + \beta_0 Credit\ Growth_t + \beta_1 Credit\ Growth_{t-1} +$
$\beta_2 Size\_ta_{it-1} + \beta_3 Age_{it-1} + \beta_4 ICR\_dummy_{it-1} + \beta_5 Deficit\_ta_{it-1} +$
$\beta_6 Growth\_ta_{it-1} + +\beta_7 d\_group_{it} + \beta_8 KZindex_{it-1} +$
$\beta_9 Leverage\_ta_{it-1} + \varepsilon_{it}$ $\qquad (5.5)$

$Misallocation_{it} = \alpha_i + \beta_0 Credit\ Growth_t + \beta_1 Credit\ Growth_{t-1} +$
$\beta_2 Size\_ta_{it-1} + \beta_3 Age_{it-1} + \beta_4 ICR\_dummy_{it-1} +$
$\beta_5 Growth\_ta_{it-1} + \beta_6 d\_group_{it} + \beta_7 KZindex_{it-1} +$
$\beta_8 Leverage\_ta_{it-1} + \beta_9 Growth\_internal\_funds_{it} + \varepsilon_{it}$ $\qquad (5.6)$

Box 5.2 Model specifications of borrowing exuberance (BE) and firm-specific characteristics

$$BE_{it} = \alpha_i + \beta_0 Creditgrowth_t + \beta_1 Creditgrowth_{t-1} +$$
$$\beta_2 Size\_ta_{it-1} + \beta_3 Age_{it-1} + \beta_4 ICR\_dummy_{it-1} +$$
$$\beta_5 Deficit\_ta_{it-1} + \beta_6 Growth\_ta_{it-1} +$$
$$\beta_7 Zscore\_em_{it-1} + \beta_8 d\_group_{it} + \varepsilon_{it} \tag{5.8}$$

$$BE_{it} = \alpha_i + \beta_0 Creditgrowth_t + \beta_1 Creditgrowth_{t-1} +$$
$$\beta_2 Size\_ta_{it-1} + \beta_3 Age_{it-1} + \beta_4 ICR\_dummy_{it-1} +$$
$$\beta_5 Deficit\_ta_{it-1} + \beta_6 Growth\_ta_{it-1} + \beta_7 Zscore\_em_{it-1} +$$
$$\beta_8 d\_group_{it} + \beta_9 \operatorname{Tan} gibility_{it} + \varepsilon_{it} \tag{5.9}$$

$$BE_{it} = \alpha_i + \beta_0 Creditgrowth_t + \beta_1 Creditgrowth_{t-1} +$$
$$\beta_2 Size\_ta_{it-1} + \beta_3 Age_{it-1} + \beta_4 ICR\_dummy_{it-1} +$$
$$\beta_5 Deficit\_ta_{it-1} + \beta_6 Growth\_ta_{it-1} + + \beta_7 d\_group_{it} +$$
$$\beta_8 KZindex_{it-1} + \varepsilon_{it} \tag{5.10}$$

$$BE_{it} = \alpha_i + \beta_0 Creditgrowth_t + \beta_1 Creditgrowth_{t-1} +$$
$$\beta_2 Size\_ta_{it-1} + \beta_3 Age_{it-1} + \beta_4 ICR\_dummy_{it-1} +$$
$$\beta_5 Deficit\_ta_{it-1} + \beta_6 Growth\_ta_{it-1} + + \beta_7 d\_group_{it} +$$
$$\beta_8 KZindex_{it-1} + \beta_9 Leverage\_ta_{it-1} + \varepsilon_{it} \tag{5.11}$$

$$BE_{it} = \alpha_i + \beta_0 Creditgrowth_t + \beta_1 Creditgrowth_{t-1} +$$
$$\beta_2 Size_{it-1} + \beta_3 Age_{it-1} + \beta_4 ICR\_dummy_{it-1} +$$
$$\beta_5 Deficit\_ta_{it-1} + \beta_6 group_{it} + \beta_7 KZindex_{it-1} +$$
$$\beta_8 Leverage_{it-1} + \beta_9 Growth\_internal\_funds_{it} + \varepsilon_{it} \tag{5.12}$$

of corporate governance structure for listed firms. Therefore, we undertake a sub-sample analysis between 2001 and 2017. For this purpose, we augment the baseline model for borrowing exuberance as follows:

$$BE_{it} = \alpha_i + \sum \beta_p Creditgrowth_{t-p} + \sum_j^k \beta_j CG_{it} + \sum_j^k \beta_j X_{it} + \varepsilon_{it}\, p = 0,1 \tag{5.13}$$

Various corporate governance (CG) variables are added in the baseline model as presented in Box 5.3.

Empirical Findings and Discussion

To obtain an initial insight, we present the summary statistics of all the variables in Table 5.2. Panel A of Table 5.2 gives the basic descriptive statistics of the

---

Box 5.3 Model specifications of BE and corporate governance structure

$$BE_{it} = \alpha_i + \beta_0 Creditgrowth_t + \beta_1 Creditgrowth_{t-1} + \beta_2 Size\_ta_{it-1} + \beta_3 Age_{it-1} + \beta_4 ICR\_dummy_{it-1} + \beta_5 Deficit\_ta_{it-1} + \beta_6 Growth\_ta_{it-1} + \beta_7 Zscore\_em_{it-1} + \beta_8 d\_group_{it} + \beta_9 n\_PSB + \varepsilon_{it} \tag{5.4}$$

$$BE_{it} = \alpha_i + \beta_0 Creditgrowth_t + \beta_1 Creditgrowth_{t-1} + \beta_2 Size\_ta_{it-1} + \beta_3 Age_{it-1} + \beta_4 ICR\_dummy_{it-1} + \beta_5 Deficit\_ta_{it-1} + \beta_6 Growth\_ta_{it-1} + \beta_7 Zscore\_em_{it-1} + \beta_8 d\_group_{it} + \beta_9 Creditgrowth \# n\_PSB_{it} + \varepsilon_{it} \tag{5.5}$$

$$BE_{it} = \alpha_i + \beta_0 Creditgrowth_t + \beta_1 Creditgrowth_{t-1} + \beta_2 Size\_ta_{it-1} + \beta_3 Age_{it-1} + \beta_4 ICR\_dummy_{it-1} + \beta_5 Deficit\_ta_{it-1} + \beta_6 Growth\_ta_{it-1} + \beta_7 Zscore\_em_{it-1} + \beta_8 d\_group_{it} + \beta_9 d\_SBI_{it} + \varepsilon_{it} \tag{5.6}$$

$$BE_{it} = \alpha_i + \beta_0 Creditgrowth_t + \beta_1 Creditgrowth_{t-1} + \beta_2 Size\_ta_{it-1} + \beta_3 Age_{it-1} + \beta_4 ICR\_dummy_{it-1} + \beta_5 Deficit\_ta_{it-1} + \beta_6 Growth\_ta_{it-1} + \beta_7 Zscore\_em_{it-1} + \beta_8 d\_group_{it} + \beta_9 n\_bank_{it} + \varepsilon_{it} \tag{5.7}$$

$$BE_{it} = \alpha_i + \beta_0 Creditgrowth_t + \beta_1 Creditgrowth_{t-1} + \beta_2 Size\_ta_{it-1} + \beta_3 Age_{it-1} + \beta_4 ICR\_dummy_{it-1} + \beta_5 Deficit\_ta_{it-1} + \beta_6 Growth\_ta_{it-1} + \beta_7 Zscore\_em_{it-1} + \beta_8 d\_group_{it} + \beta_9 sh\_banks\_fi_{it} + \beta_{10} sh\_mutual\_funds_{it} + \beta_{11} sh\_Promoters_{it} + \beta_{12} d\_bank\_no\min ee_{it} + \varepsilon_{it} \tag{5.8}$$

$$BE_{it} = \alpha_i + \beta_0 Creditgrowth_t + \beta_1 Creditgrowth_{t-1} + \beta_2 Size\_ta_{it-1} + \beta_3 Age_{it-1} + \beta_4 ICR\_dummy_{it-1} + \beta_5 Deficit\_ta_{it-1} + \beta_6 Growth\_ta_{it-1} + \beta_7 Zscore\_em_{it-1} + \beta_8 d\_group_{it} + \beta_9 sh\_banks\_fi_{it} + \beta_{10} sh\_mutual\_funds_{it} + \beta_{11} sh\_Promoters_{it} + \beta_{12} d\_bank\_no\min ee_{it} + \beta_{13} Board\_size_{it} + \beta_{14} board\_independence_{it} + \varepsilon_{it} \tag{5.9}$$

negative ICAE firms, and Panel B shows the summary statistics of firms with BE. We observe that the characteristics of firms with BE are very similar to that of misallocating firms because these firms are a subset of misallocating firms. Based on descriptive statistics, we observe that BE firms are larger, older, and affiliated

Table 5.2 Summary statistics of variables

	All values of ICAE			Negative ICAE			BE		
	Mean	Median	SD	Mean	Median	SD	Mean	Median	SD
Full sample (1990–2017)									
size_ta	7.56	7.48	1.75	7.56	7.46	1.76	7.66	7.55	1.77
age	30.08	25.00	20.03	29.48	24.00	20.08	30.72	24.00	20.45
ICR_dummy	0.51	1.00	0.50	0.53	1.00	0.50	0.52	1.00	0.50
deficit_ta	0.04	0.02	0.13	0.04	0.02	0.13	0.06	0.04	0.14
growth_ internal_funds	0.15	0.13	0.65	0.16	0.13	0.94	0.17	0.13	1.37
zscore_em	4.75	4.87	1.58	4.77	4.88	1.59	4.81	4.83	1.43
tangibility	0.26	0.24	0.15	0.26	0.25	0.15	0.27	0.26	0.15
leverage_ta	0.42	0.41	0.20	0.43	0.41	0.20	0.40	0.40	0.19
KZindex	0.40	0.38	3.54	0.36	0.39	1.78	0.24	0.31	1.71
d_group	0.47	0.00	0.50	0.47	0.00	0.50	0.49	0.00	0.50
growth_ta	0.18	0.12	0.30	0.19	0.13	0.31	0.22	0.16	0.34
Sample size	**7871**	**7871**	**7871**	**3692**	**3692**	**3692**	**1727**	**1727**	**1727**
Sub-sample (2001–17)									
n_psb	1.60	1.00	2.24	1.57	1.00	2.22	1.74	1.00	2.55
d_sbi	0.53	1.00	0.50	0.52	1.00	0.50	0.56	1.00	0.50
n_bank	3.34	2	3.39	3.34	2	3.38	3.49	2	3.80
board_size	7.57	8.00	3.46	7.56	8.00	3.52	7.57	8.00	3.46
board_ independence	44.24	50.00	23.69	43.91	50.00	23.90	44.61	50.00	23.50
d_nominee	0.34	0.00	0.47	0.35	0.00	0.48	0.35	0.00	0.48
sh_mutual funds	1.53	0.02	3.50	1.65	0.02	3.61	1.31	0.02	3.12
sh_banks_fi	0.61	0.00	2.71	0.61	0.00	2.72	0.75	0.00	3.07
sh_promoters	51.76	52.19	15.60	51.67	52.09	15.72	51.71	52.04	14.87
Sample size	**6284**	**6284**	**6284**	**2933**	**2933**	**2933**	**1388**	**1388**	**1388**

Source: Authors' calculations using a sample of 7,871 firm-year observations.

to a business group with lower interest coverage and a lower deficit. In addition, these firms have lower growth, higher tangible assets, and a lower debt ratio. Finally, BE firms have relatively lower financial constraints and lower Z-score when compared to the overall misallocation sample.

To further understand how these firm-specific characteristics are associated with misallocation, we estimated the multivariate Tobit model as explained earlier.

Determinants of Misallocation

We begin our empirical analysis by looking into the determinants of misallocation of bank credit. The results of the Tobit regression are presented in Table 5.3. It is also important to note that all the coefficients are raised by a factor of 10^5 for better interpretation of results. Model 1 is our baseline model, and subsequent models are estimated as alternative specifications described in Box 5.1. Results from Model 1 show that the contemporaneous credit growth in the economy has a significant and positive association with overall bank credit misallocation. These findings corroborate with the previous chapter, where the pro-cyclicality of credit was found to be one of the important determinants of misallocation. In order to control for persistency in the influence of credit growth, we add lagged credit growth as appropriate. As a result, the credit growth of the previous year has a negative impact on misallocation.

As noted earlier, we try to understand the nature of misallocation from three distinct firm-specific attributes – namely, creditworthiness, the requirement of external funds, and corporate governance structure, respectively. Looking from the standpoint of creditworthiness, the significant positive coefficient on the ICR in Model 1 and the significant negative coefficient of leverage in Models 4 and 5 suggest that misallocating firms are reasonably creditworthy. This clearly shows that banks grant loans to the right set of firms and have an effective and prudent risk-management process in place.

However, when we focus on the external funds' requirement as captured by deficit (Models 1–4) and alternatively as internal growth of funds (Model 5), our results indicate that misallocating firms have either no apparent requirement for an external source of funds (that is, the insignificant coefficient on the deficit) or have sufficient internal source of funds (that is, significantly positive coefficient on *growth_internal_funds*). Also, the positive and insignificant coefficient on Z score (Models 1–2) indicates that misallocating firms are not in danger of imminent default. Similarly, the positive and insignificant coefficient on tangibility (Model 2) shows that misallocating firms do not show any deficit in terms of the availability of the collateral. To further substantiate our findings, we also augment our model with a measure of financial constraints, namely the KZ index (Models 3–5). The significant negative coefficient on the KZ index clearly shows that misallocating firms do not face any severe financial constraints. Finally, among firm-specific control variables, our results show that, in general, misallocating firms are larger and younger. This could be because big firms enjoy greater visibility in the market, scale and magnitude of operation of these firms, and reputation scores over the quality aspects of the firms. On the other hand, misallocating firms being younger are in contrast to the view that the older firms share a better reputation and longer credit history, which could encourage the banks to lend loans.

Finally, we do not observe any apparent trend in misallocating firms being affiliated to business groups (that is, the insignificant coefficient on *d_group*). However, we undertake a detailed analysis of corporate governance on misallocation later in this section. In sum, our initial findings suggest that misallocation is driven by excessive credit growth, and misallocating firms are larger, younger, and creditworthy but do not show any obvious requirement of external funds.

Table 5.3 Determinants of misallocation

	Model 1	Model 2	Model 3	Model 4	Model 5
Credit growth	0.1196***	0.0919***	0.121***	0.1250***	0.1240***
	(4.799)	(3.655)	(4.869)	(5.033)	(4.977)
L. Credit growth	−0.0862***	−0.0248	−0.0869***	−0.06340**	−0.0622**
	(−3.356)	(−0.952)	(−3.385)	(−2.501)	(−2.454)
L.size_ta	1.8300***	1.85***	1.8400***	1.9200***	1.9200***
	(12.78)	(13.00)	(12.91)	(13.33)	(13.34)
L.Age	−0.0593**	−0.0061	−0.0612**	−0.0651***	−0.0659***
	(−2.428)	(−0.245)	(−2.509)	(−2.637)	(−2.676)
L.ICR_dummy	2.2200***	1.8600***	2.1900***		
	(5.411)	(4.509)	(5.578)		
L.Deficit_ta	−1.0100	−1.5000	−1.0500	−0.9660	
	(−0.732)	(−1.071)	(−0.759)	(−0.683)	
L.Growth_ta	−0.0272	−0.0604	−0.1070	−0.1280	−0.1320
	(−0.507)	(−0.486)	(−0.624)	(−0.621)	(−0.579)
L.Zscore_em	0.1340	0.1190			
	(1.019)	(0.905)			

(Contd)

(*Contd*)

	Model 1	Model 2	Model 3	Model 4	Model 5
D_group	0.7510	0.4070	0.7110	0.7580	0.7640
	(1.577)	(0.835)	(1.496)	(1.583)	(1.596)
Tangibility		1.610			
		(1.159)			
L.KZindex			−0.1360*	−0.1920**	−0.1880**
			(−1.799)	(−2.346)	(−2.204)
L.Leverage_ta				−2.5400**	−2.6900**
				(−2.004)	(−2.157)
Growth_internal_ funds					0.7750***
					(3.337)
Constant	−20.19***	−21.49***	−19.48***	−18.95***	−19.48***
	(−15.06)	(−15.11)	(−17.66)	(−16.90)	(−16.96)
Observations	7,276	6,264	7,287	7,287	7,281
Number of comp	1,401	1,334	1,403	1,403	1,402

Note: This table presents the results of Tobit regression on misallocation and firm-specific factors. The dependent variable is misallocation estimated using the negative index of credit allocative efficiency (ICAE). Independent variables include lagged and contemporaneous firm characteristics as described in the text. *t*-statistics are reported in parentheses. ***, **, and * represent statistical significance at 1, 5, and 10 per-cent levels. L. indicates one period lag. All the coefficients are raised by a factor of 10^5 for better interpretation of results.

Determinants of BE

Next, we focus on the nature of misallocation. Specifically, we examine BE – a relatively severe form of misallocation – wherein firms with a relatively lower Q ratio receive a higher proportion of bank credit. The findings of the Tobit regression are presented in Table 5.4. While the results presented in Table 5.4 closely mirror our earlier findings on misallocating firms, the degree of association is more pronounced for the BE as a source of misallocation.

The findings of the base model (Model 1) continue to corroborate the findings of misallocation as well as the findings of Chapter 3. The significant positive coefficient on credit growth shows that firm-level BE is driven by excessive credit supply. As discussed in the earlier chapter, the excess credit supply and the associated optimism in the markets may encourage banks to relax the lending standards and due-diligence process. Consequently, the firms that ideally would not have been eligible for a bank loan in normal circumstances because of relatively lower *Q* end up receiving more bank credit than their industry peers. Similar to the earlier analysis, we now turn our focus to the firm-specific determinants of BE. Consistent with the results on overall misallocation, the significant positive and negative coefficient on firm size and age (Models 1–5) show that the BE phenomenon is more prevalent across larger and younger firms.

The significant positive coefficient on *icr_dummy* (Models 1–3) indicates that BE firms on average are creditworthy. Models 1–4 show that the negative coefficient on deficit has turned significant with respect to the BE firms. This further strengthens our hypothesis that the BE firms did not have any apparent need for external financing. The significant negative coefficient on KZ index (Model 3) further suggests that BE firms are not financially constrained. The coefficient turns out to be insignificant in Models 4 and 5 where we introduce leverage and *growth_internal_funds*, which turn out to be significantly positive and negative, respectively. The negative coefficient on leverage and the positive coefficient on *growth_internal_funds* substantiate our hypotheses that BE firms are low leverage (that is, creditworthy) and have sufficient internal funds.

Consistent with misallocating firms, collateral (*tangibility*) and financial stability (*z-score*) measures are insignificant. Interestingly, the coefficient on the group is positive and significant (Models 1–5). This essentially substantiates our argument that corporate governance plays a key role in the allocation of bank credit. Our findings suggest that the nature of misallocation is more severe among business-group-affiliated firms.

In the next section, we further examine the role of corporate governance in a sub-sample analysis by introducing a series of variables related to corporate governance at the firm as well as banks.

BE and Corporate Governance

This section reports the findings of sub-sample analysis for the period between 2001 and 2018. As stated earlier, the choice of sample period is governed by the availability of detailed corporate governance information from 2001 onwards. Table 5.5 presents the results of our augmented model with a set of corporate governance variables, which includes corporate governance mechanisms related to the lending banks (bank–firm relationship, SBI and associates, nominee director) and internal control mechanisms adopted by firms (insider ownership, board size, board independence, institutional ownership), respectively.

Table 5.4 Determinants of borrowing exuberance (BE)

	Model 1	Model 2	Model 3	Model 4	Model 5
Credit growth	0.0885***	0.0573**	0.0905***	0.093***	0.0914***
	(2.61)	(1.76)	(2.42)	(2.76)	(2.706)
L.Credit growth	–0.0541	0.0037	–0.053	–0.042	–0.040
	(–1.54)	(0.11)	(–1.52)	(–1.21)	(–1.154)
L.Size_ta	1.1400***	1.2100***	1.200***	1.400***	1.3900***
	(5.57)	(6.34)	(5.95)	(6.83)	(6.773)
L.Age	–0.0832**	–0.0692**	–0.085**	–0.1080***	–0.1070***
	(–2.43)	(–2.10)	(–2.47)	(–3.12)	(–3.108)
L.ICR_dummy	1.4900**	0.7920	1.090**		
	(2.64)	(1.48)	(–2.03)		
L.Deficit_ta	–4.9800**	–4.5200**	–4.940**	–2.850	
	(–2.58)	(–2.50)	(–2.57)	(–1.43)	
L.Growth_ta	–0.0074	–0.0483	–0.097	–0.049	–0.048
	(–0.13)	(–0.39)	(–0.70)	(–0.63)	(–0.610)
ZScore_em	–0.1080	–0.0554			
	(–0.58)	(–0.32)			
D_group	1.4800**	1.310**	1.490**	1.790***	1.800***
	(2.19)	(2.03)	(2.22)	(2.64)	(2.670)
Tangibility		2.6800			
		(1.460)			
L.KZindex			–0.193**	–0.102	–0.091
			(–2.16)	(–1.16)	(–1.030)
L.Leverage_ta				–9.650***	–10.200***
				(–5.31)	(–5.776)
Growth_internal_funds					0.9430***
					(3.56)
Constant	–22.57***	–22.53***	–23.34***	–22.12***	–22.03***
	(–11.73)	(–11.68)	(–14.82)	(–13.98)	(–13.96)

(Contd)

(*Contd*)

	Model 1	Model 2	Model 3	Model 4	Model 5
Observations	7,276	6,264	7,287	7,287	7,281
Number of comp	1,401	1,334	1,403	1,403	1,402

Note: This table presents the results of Tobit regression on BE and firm-specific factors. The dependent variable is BE estimated using the negative index of credit allocative efficiency (ICAE) when the firm has a Q ratio lower than the industry and receives a higher proportion of loans compared to its peers. Independent variables include lagged and contemporaneous firm characteristics as described in the text. t-statistics are reported in parentheses. ***, **, and * represent statistical significance at 1, 5 and 10 per-cent levels. L. indicates one period lag. All the coefficients are raised by a factor of 10^5 for better interpretation of results.

We try alternative specifications to test standalone as well as interactive effects of corporate governance and credit growth on BE. However, to save space, we report only the most parsimonious Models 1–6 in Table 5.5.

The significant positive coefficient on *n_psb* in Model 1 suggests that firms with a higher number of government-controlled banks as lenders tend to engage in borrowing exuberance. This finding also corroborates the fact that PSBs contribute a major share of existing NPAs in India. Our finding suggests that this might be due to the lack of monitoring or ability to evaluate the risk involved in the projects they are funding. Further, Model 2 suggests that this adverse impact of the relationship with PSB is accentuated over the credit cycle growth. This might suggest that the buoyant economic environment encourages the PSBs to lend aggressively towards BE firms.

To gain a deeper insight into the bank–firm relationship and BE, we focus on the firm's relationship with the largest PSB in India, State Bank of India (Model 3). Consistent with the earlier findings on PSBs, we observe a positive but insignificant association between BE and firms associated with SBI, suggesting that the misallocation of bank credit is widely spread across the spectrum of PSBs in India.

Model 4 explores the impact of multiple banking relationships and BE. As argued earlier, existing literature suggests that multiple banking relationships may have incentives in emerging markets due to relatively restricted bank competition and the high cost of monitoring owing to poor disclosure practices. However, in the multi-bank relationship, we find that firms that had an association with more than one bank in the past typically overinvest. This could be driven by the fact that they obtain a loan from multiple banks and mismanage the investment opportunities.

Another aspect examined by this chapter analyses the ownership structure in determining BE. Model 5 shows that misallocation is higher among firms with

Table 5.5 Borrowing exuberance (BE) and corporate governance

Over investment	Model 1	Model 2	Model 3	Model 4	Model 5	Model 6
Credit growth	0.1150***	0.0734**	0.1140***	0.1760***	0.0959***	0.1020***
	(3.976)	(2.129)	(3.913)	(3.637)	(3.564)	(3.742)
L.Size_ta	0.5670**	0.5800**	1.0300***	0.8000*	1.5200***	1.6200***
	(2.216)	(2.272)	(4.351)	(1.807)	(7.864)	(7.841)
L.Age	−0.0354	−0.0354	−0.0566	−0.3890	−0.2980	−0.2120
	(−0.896)	(−0.900)	(−1.431)	(−0.600)	(−0.898)	(−0.629)
L.ICR_ dummy	0.2060	0.0229	0.0152	0.0655	−0.0058	−0.0054
	(0.768)	(0.857)	(0.558)	(0.856)	(−0.352)	(−0.333)
L.Deficit_ta	−4.6400**	−4.6600**	−4.5300**	−7.1000*	−5.3400***	−5.300***
	(−2.177)	(−2.191)	(−2.101)	(−1.843)	(−2.786)	(−2.763)
L.Growth_ta	0.3770	0.2660	0.3320	1.6400	−0.0019	−0.0021
	(0.394)	(0.277)	(0.346)	(0.946)	(−0.157)	(−0.173)
L.Zscore_em	−0.2430	−0.2470	−0.2880	0.1610	−0.0704	−0.0523
	(−1.281)	(−1.303)	(−1.497)	(0.414)	(−0.418)	(−0.310)
D_Group	1.1900*	1.1200	1.0700	−0.5550		
	(1.649)	(1.548)	(1.457)	(−0.494)		
N_PSB	0.7070***	0.2490				
	(4.451)	(0.957)				
Credit growth#n_PSB		0.0275**				
		(2.232)				
D_SBI			0.8150			
			(1.247)			
L.n_bank				0.5480***		
				(3.195)		
Sh_Banks_FI					0.1190	0.1180
					(1.382)	(1.378)
Sh_mutual_ funds					−0.2460***	−0.2560***
					(−3.031)	(−3.134)

(*Contd*)

(*Contd*)

Over investment	Model 1	Model 2	Model 3	Model 4	Model 5	Model 6
Sh_promoters					-0.0299*	-0.0282
					(-1.689)	(-1.593)
D_Bank_ Nominee					0.2700	0.5430
					(0.381)	(0.741)
Board_Size						-0.1230
						(-1.359)
Board_ independence						-0.0007
						(-0.0666)
Constant	-0.0002***	-0.0002***	-0.0002***	-0.0003***	-0.0002***	-0.0002***
	(-8.122)	(-7.753)	(-9.298)	(-6.277)	(-10.72)	(-10.71)
Observations	4,897	4,897	4,897	2,255	5,790	5,790
Number of firms	1,161	1,161	1,161	801	1,283	1,283

Note: This table presents the results of Tobit regression on BE and firm-specific corporate governance factors. The dependent variable is BE estimated using the negative index of credit allocative efficiency (ICAE) when the firm has a Q ratio lower than the industry and receives a higher proportion of loans than its peers. Independent variables include lagged and contemporaneous firm characteristics as described in the text. t-statistics are reported in parenthesis. ***, **, and * represent statistical significance at 1, 5 and 10 per-cent levels. L. indicates one period lag. All the coefficients are raised by a factor of 10^5 for better interpretation of results.

lower promoter shareholding. This result supports the alignment of interest hypothesis, which implies that higher promoter ownership aligns their interest with outside investors to monitor the management and reduce the misallocation. Further, we find that BE is negatively associated with mutual funds ownership. Due to their short-term focus on the management of outperforming portfolios, mutual funds often exhibit shareholder activism by removing the poorly governed firms from their portfolio.

Consequently, a firm with a lack of such activism seems to overinvest as they borrow more funds from banks than their actual requirement. We also control for the presence of banks or financial institutional shareholding and the presence of nominee directors. The positive coefficient of institutional investor ownership and the presence of nominee directors indicate the absence of monitoring by banks despite their block holding and board presence. However, the effect is statistically insignificant. This is not surprising as the passive nature of institutional investors and bank directors is often reported in the corporate governance literature.

The final model incorporates more board characteristics of the firms like board size and the proportion of independent directors. Though the results show that larger boards and a higher proportion of independent directors are associated with BE, the relationship is statistically insignificant. This raises concerns about the effectiveness of board governance in the context of bank credit allocation by firms. In addition, the lack of effective board governance in conditions such as weak creditor rights should be a concern in the accumulation of non-performing loans by the corporate sector in the country.

In sum, we observe corporate governance characteristics confirm the case for laxity from the side of banks as well as firms in borrowing exuberance of bank credit. Banks, specifically PSBs, are typically associated with higher BE and heighten the pro-cyclical behaviour of bank credit. Our findings further suggest that banks ignore the quality of the firms while allocating credit. Firms associated with multiple banks indulge more in overinvesting. Finally, the findings show that while promoter and mutual funds ownership are associated with a reduction in the BE, board governance and institutional investor monitoring do not seem to play a significant role.

Conclusion

This research explores the determinants of bank credit misallocation using micro level firm-specific data. Unlike a large body of literature addressing the misallocation of credit, which often considers it as an *ex-post* outcome and is often influenced by various external factors at a later period, we check for misallocation at the point of loan disbursal where the banks are supposed to use all available information about the prospects prudently. We study the firm-specific determinants of bank credit misallocation from three perspectives. The first one examines the creditworthiness of the firms receiving bank loans. Second, we examine if the firms borrow bank loans over and above their actual requirement. The third aspect of this research investigates the role of corporate governance structure in the misallocation of loans.

Our findings suggest that misallocation and BE are more prevalent among large as well as young firms. Further, misallocation is more common among the firms with a lower ICR and lower leverage, suggesting that the banks are not lending to non-creditworthy firms. However, banks allocate loans to firms with lower growth, lower deficit, lower financial constraints, and higher internal funds. This might suggest that Indian firms in need of funds are not receiving bank loans, while firms with less need of external funds continue to obtain more loans from banks. Finally, corporate governance is found to influence BE through ownership of promoters and mutual funds. The effect of board governance largely remains insignificant. The findings show that the PSBs are poor in allocating credit efficiently. Misallocation also tends to increase when the firms are associated with multiple banks.

In sum, while Indian banks are allocating credit to creditworthy firms, credit allocation seems disproportionate compared to the firms' financing requirements. Further, the governance structure of firms plays a significant role in credit misallocation.

Notes

1 For example, Banerjee and Duflo (2014) highlight that given the pervasive financial constraints in the Indian market, the firms tend to borrow whenever there is an availability of credit.

2 For comparison of bank-based systems under centralized and decentralized economies, see Dewatripont and Maskin (1995).

3 There is a large body of literature on the financial constraints faced by firms in obtaining external credit. For example, see Fazzari et al. (1988); Kaplan and Zingales (1997); Whited and Wu (2006); Hadlock and Pierce (2010).

4 KZindex= (–1.002 * ((total income – prior period and extraordinary income)/l_ total assets)) + (0.283 * Tobin's Q) + (3.139 * leverage) – (39.368 * (dividend/ lag total assets)) – (1.315 * ((cash and bank balance+ book value of marketable securities)/ lag total assets)).

5 Altman Z-score for emerging markets is defined as Zscore = 3.25+ (6.56 * (net working capital/total assets)) + (3.26 * (retained profits/losses/total assets)) + 6.72 * (pbdita/total assets)) + (1.05 * ((per share * shares outstanding)/total assets)).

6 Deficit = (dividend + net investment + change in net working capital – cash flow after interest and taxes).

7 However, the conflicting literature suggests that while bank monitoring improves the firm's corporate governance and ensures it takes efficient business actions, this better governance comes at the cost that banks have better information than other sources providing capital and gain advantages in terms of rent-seeking using firm's private information. Moreover, this informational monopoly over firms strengthens the bargaining position of the banks, which banks could use to cut off a firm's loan or even charge a high interest rate, decide on projects, impose compensating balances, and have the opportunity to refuse or relax covenants according to their credit rating.

6

Allocative Efficiency of Bank Credit and Firm Performance

The availability of investable funds at the disposal of firms has drawn considerable attention from business practitioners and researchers. Interestingly, the issue gets more complicated if the investable funds are not generated from firms' internal sources and instead raised from external sources like debt and equity. Any form of external capital comes with a set of expectations from the investors and creditors in terms of firms' ability to meet the obligations, generate better returns, and enhance future performance. Particularly, if the funds come in the form of bank credit, firms need to improve their performance downstream to service the debt obligation. In an efficient economic system, a firm is expected to borrow strictly according to its needs, and the funds are expected to flow from poor quality firms to good ones. However, it is often argued that if firms receive credit disproportionate to their needs, the possibility of firms mismanaging the funds amplifies, leading to future underperformance.

Therefore, an empirical exercise is undertaken in this chapter to explore the consequences of the allocation efficiency of bank credit on firm performance. Specifically, we seek answers to the following questions. First, does the misallocation of credit impact a firm's future performance? Second, more importantly, will misallocated bank credit reduce firms' performance downstream?

Literature throws some insights into the role of access to bank credit and the performance of firms. Several studies examine if access to credit, specifically bank debt, improves the productivity or performance of firms (Schiantarelli and Sembenelli, 1999; Gatti and Love, 2008; Rizov and Zhang, 2014). For example, Manaresi and Pierri (2018) provide evidence for the supply of banks' credit affecting the productivity of a large number of Italian firms. The study shows that credit supply boosts productivity growth, and this effect is persistent. Further, access to bank credit is also found to encourage the new firms to grow and innovate (Ayyagari, Beck, and Demirgüç-Kunt, 2007); Claessens and Laeven, 2005; Koeda and Dabla-Norris, 2008). Therefore, firms seem to have incentives in borrowing from the bank when access to other external sources of finance is difficult and the supply of bank credit is not constrained. However, Agarwal and Elston (2001) examine the impact of bank–firm relationship in the financing choices and performance for a sample of German firms and find that despite easier access to finance, there is no evidence to suggest that it translates into good firm performance.

While access to bank credit comes with many benefits, the efficiency in allocating bank credit remains a contentious area in financial literature. In one of the earlier works, Kane (1977) analyses the impact of government intervention in credit allocation and argues as follows:

> [A] decision to establish government credit allocation would kick off a long cycle of market and political interaction. For so ephemeral a good as credit, the period of time during which net social benefits are positive could be very short indeed. Credit rationing promises to make financial markets work less efficiently, to redistribute wealth in ways that could easily run counter to intentions, and to politicize further intersectoral economic conflict. In view of the difficulties of keeping selective credit controls effective in the face of borrowers' and lenders' energetic efforts to subvert them—both by relabelling loan contracts to disclose a priority purpose and by substituting unregulated (often regulation-induced) instruments, a far more promising way to improve sectoral access to loan funds is to eliminate ceilings on interest rates at deposit institutions. (Kane, 1977, p. 68)

Kaat (2016), using a comprehensive dataset that covers about 20,000 firm-year observations on the European capital flows and bank loans, finds that higher capital inflows are associated with more loans to less profitable firms, eventually leading to economic destruction. By focusing on firms with persistent problems in meeting their interest payments in the Organisation for Economic Co-operation and Development (OECD) countries, McGowan, Andrews, and Millot (2018) found that the presence and resources taken up by such firms constrain the growth of more productive firms. The study also argues that the share of industry capital sunk in zombie firms is associated with lower investment and employment growth of the healthy firms, leading to less productivity-enhancing capital reallocation. In a recent study, Andrews and Petroulakis (2019) explore the connection between zombie firms and banks and its consequences for aggregate productivity in 11 European countries. The study reveals that zombie firms are more likely to be connected to weak banks, and the increased survival of zombie firms congests the markets and constrains the growth of more productive firms.

In another strand of literature, the impact of credit misallocation has received significant attention, particularly among the European countries affected in the aftermath of the global financial crisis (GFC). For instance, di Mauro, Hassan, and Ottaviano (2018) report that credit allocation is more efficient in France and Germany when compared to Italy, as there exists a significant negative elasticity of credit to current productivity and significant positive elasticity of credit to the future productivity of firms. Another evidence on the misallocation is provided by Gopinath et al. (2017), which reported that capital inflows are misallocated towards firms with higher net worth but not necessarily more productive. Such misallocation resulted in a decline in the total factor productivity for the Spanish manufacturing sector. This phenomenon is also observed in Italy and Portugal, which faced economic turmoil after the 2007 GFC. Dias, Marques, and Richmond (2016) use firm-level data from Portugal to examine if the changes in resource misallocation lead to poor economic performance in recent years. The study shows that deteriorating allocative efficiency had erased close to 1.3 percentage points of the annual gross domestic product (GDP) during 1996–2011. More evidence on the allocative inefficiency in Portugal is presented in the work of Reis (2013), who identified that capital inflows which funded unproductive firms in the non-tradable sector were the leading cause for country-wide fall of productivity. Similar findings on the impact of misallocation are reported by Benkovskis (2015) for Latvia and Meza, Pratap, and Urrutia (2019) for Mexico, respectively.

Apart from Europe-centric studies, a few studies have examined the bank credit allocation efficiency and firm performance in a few other economies. For example, Benjamin and Meza (2009) analyse the real effects of Korea's 1997 crisis and report that a reallocation of resources towards low productivity sectors during the crisis period results in a falling total factor productivity (TFP). Using firm-specific borrowing costs, Gilchrist, Sim, and Zakrajšek (2013) find that resource loss for a subset of US manufacturing firms is relatively small due to such misallocation. Similarly, Midrigan and Xu (2014) and Hopenhayn (2011) argue that financial market frictions are unlikely to imply significant efficiency losses in an economy with relatively efficient capital markets. On the other hand, Song and Wu (2015) report lower productivity among Chinese firms when the resources are misallocated. Further, Ahearne and Shinada (2005) show that the banks continue to provide financial support for highly inefficient, debt-ridden Japanese firms. Such poor banking practices, in turn, prevent more productive companies from gaining market share, strangling a potentially important source of productivity gains for the overall economy.

It is also important to note that most of these studies use firms' productivity to measure the impact of misallocation of credit (Hsieh and Klenow, 2009, Restuccia and Rogerson, 2013). In contrast, very few studies examine the outcome of bank credit misallocation outside this framework. Moreover, apart from productivity, accounting-based performance measures like profitability and return on equity are often used to analyse the performance of firms. Therefore, we propose to fill the gap in the literature by explicitly examining the effects of credit (misallocation) on firms' profitability and other accounting-based performance measures from an emerging market perspective where banks are the single largest source of capital.

Contrary to the existing literature, which uses the factor productivity of firms, we use a unique framework that incorporates the index of credit allocative efficiency (ICAE) measure based on the Q theory. As discussed in Chapter 3, by construct, the ICAE is designed to distinguish between firms that receive an efficient allocation of bank credit and firms that obtain misallocated bank credit. Therefore, by classifying firms as misallocated or rightly allocated bank credit, we examine if the performance varies among these types of firms over time. We hypothesize that firms that received misallocated credit would perform poorly in the subsequent years as these firms are unable to deploy the excess capital efficiently to improve their productivity. On the other hand, we argue that firms that are credit-worthy and receive efficiently allocated bank credit would improve their performance eventually. Therefore, this research aims to contribute consequential evidence of misallocation of bank credit, especially in the context of the rising non-performing asset (NPA) problems among Indian banks.

Our findings highlight the importance of allocating credit judiciously to deserving firms. We observe that firms that were provided with misallocated bank credit turned out to be poor performers over time. On the other hand, the companies that received bank credit according to their quality eventually became good performers. This research further underscores the need for the bankers to look into the quality signals sent by firms while allocating credit. Particularly, ignoring the signals of poor quality could have detrimental effects on a firm's performance, and eventually, banks will have to bear the consequences when such misallocated loans turn out to be bad loans.

We carry out the investigation of impact of bank credit misallocation by using our main measure of allocative efficiency, the ICAE, and its components as ICAE positive and ICAE negative. A firm's performance is captured in terms of its accounting-based measures such as profitability of the firm, and in addition, to ensure robustness, we also use alternative measures like return on equity (ROE), return on capital employed (ROCE), and return on total assets (ROTA).

We hypothesize that misallocation of bank credit influences a firm's performance: firms with misallocated credit display poor future performance, while the efficient allocation of credit leads to improvement in a firm's performance. However, it is essential to note that the impact of misallocation might not get reflected on the firm's performance immediately. Hence, in order to capture this effect, we include up to four consecutive lag terms of the misallocation measure in the model.

Therefore, to estimate the impact of misallocation, first, we model the profitability of the firm, which is an indicator of firm performance as a function of negative ICAE (ICAE⁻) and its lagged terms. Next, the baseline specification is described in equation 6.1.

$$Y_{it} = \alpha_i + \beta_1 Y_{it-1} + \sum_{j=1}^{p} \beta_2 ICAE_{i,t-j}^{-} + \beta_3 X_{it-1} + \varepsilon_{it} \tag{6.1}$$

Here, Y_{it} is an accounting-based firm performance measure, which in our case is the profitability of the firm. Profitability is defined as a ratio of profits before depreciation, tax, and amortization (PBDITA) to total assets. $ICAE^{-}_{it-j}$ is our primary variable of interest that captures misallocation in bank credit. Up to four years lag in $ICAE^{-}_{it-j}$ are also used in the model. represents the random error. X_{it-1} is a vector of the previous year's firm-specific control variables such as firm size (*size_ta*: natural log of total assets), business group affiliation (*d_group*: dummy variable equal to 1 if firm belongs to a business group), growth (*growth_ta*: growth of total assets), and leverage (*leverage_ta*: ratio of long term debt to total assets) respectively[1].

Our second specification deals with efficient allocation and its impact on profitability. Efficient allocation is captured by the positive values of ICAE (ICAE⁺), and similar to the previous model, we use the following specification.

$$Y_{it} = \alpha_i + \beta_1 Y_{it-1} + \sum_{j=1}^{p} \beta_2 ICAE_{i,t-j}^{+} + \beta_3 X_{it-1} + \varepsilon_{it} \tag{6.2}$$

$ICAE^{+}$ is the proxy for efficient allocation of bank credit among sample firms. Similar to Model 1, lag terms up to four years and firm-specific control variables are included in this specification. Finally, as shown in equation 6.3, Model 3 incorporates both efficient and inefficient allocation at the firm level to understand the relative importance of each of these bank credit allocations.

$$Y_{it} = \alpha_i + \beta_1 Y_{it-1} + \sum_{j=1}^{p} \beta_2 ICAE_{i,t-j}^{-} + \sum_{j=1}^{p} \beta_2 ICAE_{i,t-j}^{+} + \beta_3 X_{it-1} + \varepsilon_{it} \tag{6.3}$$

Models 1–3 are estimated in a dynamic panel framework to address the expected persistency in the firm performance over time. Specifically, we use a generalized method of moments (GMM) estimator proposed by Arellano and Bond (1991), which includes lag terms of the dependent variable as covariates and addresses unobserved panel effects. Unlike static panel data models, the dynamic models include lagged levels of the dependent variable as regressors. However, including a lagged dependent variable as a regressor violates strict exogeneity because the lagged dependent variable is likely to correlate with the errors (Bhargava and Sargan, 1983). Therefore, in a typical Arellano–Bond method, the first difference of the regression equation is taken to eliminate the individual effects, and deeper lags of the dependent variable are used as instruments. To further improve the efficiency of our estimates, we use an alternative to the standard first difference GMM estimator. Following Blundell and Bond (1998), we use the GMM-SYS estimator, which contains both the levels and the first difference equations as instruments.

Relationship between Bank Credit Misallocation and Profitability

Our findings on the association between profitability and allocation efficiency of bank credit are presented in Table 6.1. Model 1 presents the effect of misallocation of bank credit on firm profitability. Consistent with our argument, we find that misallocation of bank credit affects the firm's performance negatively. It is also observed that the impact on profitability is not contemporaneous and appears with a lag. Notably, the impact of misallocation starts to appear with a lag of two years. The effect is found to be significant with a three-year lag as well. The findings also suggest that the excess credit might show some upward movement in a firm's performance in the initial periods after misallocation. However, this effect is short-lived, and the use of misallocated funds eventually adversely impacts the firm's profitability.

Next, we test the impact of efficient allocation on the firm's performance. The findings presented in Model 2 of Table 6.1 show that efficient allocation often leads to better performance of firms over a period of time as a significant positive association between ICAE⁺ and profitability is reported. This suggests that firms with positive values of ICAE are obtaining bank loans based on their market performance (relative to the industry) and the probability of such firms deploying the funds productively is higher. This positive impact is significant for all four lagged terms of ICAE⁺ as well.

Further, ICAE⁺ and ICAE⁻ firms are combined into one model, and the results are presented in Model 3 of Table 6.1. Again, our results remain robust as we find that the profitability of ICAE⁻ firms deteriorates in two years while ICAE⁺ firms' performance improves in a year itself.

Coefficients on control variables indicate that poor performance is associated with small, group-affiliated firms having a low growth rate and less leverage, irrespective of the specification used.

Finally, to check for the empirical validity of the models, we conduct a Sargan test to identify any over-identification problems and an Arellano–Bond test for serial correlation. The coefficients of these tests are reported in Table 6.1 for each specification. The insignificant Sargan test statistics for each of these models show an absence of over-identification problem. Further, the insignificant coefficient of second-order correlation in Arellano–Bond AR test reveals that models are free from any second-order residual auto-correlation.

Robustness Checks

In order to establish the robustness of our findings, we use alternate specifications of a firm's performance in our model based on different accounting measures.

Table 6.1 Bank credit misallocation and firm profitability

Variables	Model 1	Model 2	Model 3
L.Profitability	0.542***	0.527***	0.551***
	(66.19)	(65.39)	(44.21)
L.ICAE⁻	10.31		8.692
	(1.408)		(1.101)
L2.ICAE⁻	−76.20***		−53.15***
	(−40.82)		(−9.503)
L3.ICAE⁻	−37.81***		−16.29**
	(−11.47)		(−1.987)
L4.ICAE⁻	−3.506		1.724
	(−1.371)		(0.446)
L.Size_ta	−0.0243***	−0.0290***	−0.0278***
	(−41.92)	(−32.02)	(−27.19)
L.Leverage_ta	−0.0887***	−0.109***	−0.0790***
	(−9.865)	(−26.85)	(−9.374)
L.Growth_ta	−0.0138***	−0.0129***	−0.00246
	(−11.38)	(−25.98)	(−1.199)
d_group	0.0352***	0.0376***	
	(4.444)	(4.878)	

(Contd)

(*Contd*)

Variables	Model 1	Model 2	Model 3
L.ICAE⁺		30.49***	39.69***
		(5.719)	(3.146)
L2.ICAE⁺		64.70***	82.24***
		(20.14)	(4.789)
L3.ICAE⁺		87.63***	92.02***
		(36.92)	(17.33)
L4.ICAE⁺		38.07***	30.59***
		(8.690)	(4.963)
Constant	0.282***	0.324***	0.315***
	(38.08)	(29.46)	(27.77)
Sargan test	96.13352	99.83335	94.73253
	(1.000)	(1.0000)	(1.0000)
Second-order autocorrelation	–.47432	.02231	.01786
	(0.6353)	(0.9822)	(0.9857)

Note: This table presents the results of the Arellano–Bond dynamic panel data model estimates. The dependent variable is profitability, measured as a ratio of profits before depreciation, tax, and amortization (PBDITA) to total assets. L., L2., L3., and L4. indicate lag of orders 1, 2, 3, and 4 respectively. *t*-statistics are reported in parentheses. ***, **, and * indicate statistical significance at 1, 5, and 10 per-cent level.

Following the literature, the three most widely used accounting-based measures are employed in this research. These include ROE, ROCE, and ROTA.

First, we incorporate ROE as a measure of firm performance. ROE is defined as the ratio of net income to the shareholders' equity. The findings of this model are presented in Table 6.2. Similar to the earlier set of results, misallocated firms (that is, ICAE⁻ firms) perform poorly, while the efficiently allocated firms (that is, ICAE⁺ firms) improve their performance over time. This once again highlights the effect of allocating bank credit to the right set of firms.

The next set of robustness tests uses ROCE to measure firm performance. ROCE is an accounting-based firm performance measure that shows how efficiently a company can generate profits from its capital employed. Findings of the test using ROCE as a dependent variable are presented in Table 6.3. These findings confirm the earlier findings presented in this research. The ICAE⁻ firms are observed to perform poorly, and firms receiving an efficient allocation of credit perform well over time.

Table 6.2 Bank credit misallocation and return on equity (ROE)

Variables	Model 1	Model 2	Model 3
L.ROE	3.476***	3.360***	3.232***
	(100.3)	(88.91)	(141.8)
L.ICAE$^-$	−31,518***		−127,352***
	(−13.57)		(−44.92)
L2.ICAE$^-$	−132,411***		−162,715***
	(−18.08)		(−37.57)
L3.ICAE$^-$	15,572***		−1,347
	(4.941)		(−0.742)
L4.ICAE$^-$	−6,615		−31,304***
	(−1.598)		(−7.269)
L.Size_ta	−11.96***	−2.975***	−9.840***
	(−14.08)	(−3.682)	(−10.76)
L.Leverage_ta	−163.0***	−160.4***	−200.8***
	(−26.39)	(−38.03)	(−60.18)
L.Growth_ta	−72.13***	−54.74***	−73.74***
	(−37.85)	(−53.10)	(−49.19)
D_group	−63.57***	−88.83***	
	(−13.80)	(−19.58)	
L.ICAE$^+$		−175,231***	−161,572***
		(−64.74)	(−45.16)
L2.ICAE$^+$		48,855***	83,848***
		(25.34)	(25.50)
L3.ICAE$^+$		18,897***	21,784***
		(11.71)	(8.774)
L4.ICAE$^+$		−21,285***	−4,717**
		(−16.66)	(−2.014)
Constant	206.5***	139.6***	179.9***
	(25.56)	(17.57)	(23.99)
Sargan test	104.8433	105.9737	98.00178
	(0.9996)	(0.9995)	(1.0000)

(Contd)

(*Contd*)

Variables	Model 1	Model 2	Model 3
Second-order autocorrelation	–.96946	–.06214	–.04698
	(0.3323)	(0.9505)	(0.9625)

Note: This table presents the results of the Arellano–Bond dynamic panel data model estimates. The dependent variable is ROE measured as net income to shareholder's equity. L., L2., L3., and L4. indicate lag of orders 1, 2, 3, and 4 respectively. *t*-statistics are reported in parentheses. ***, **, and * indicate statistical significance at 1, 5, and 10 per-cent levels.

The next performance measure to check for robustness of our findings used in this research is ROTA. This ratio is measured as a product of the profit margin and the total asset turnover. The findings reported in Models 1–3 in Table 6.4 also remain invariant to the choice of the alternative measure of firm performance. We once again find that misallocation leads to poor firm performance.

Overall, all three robustness measures proposed in this research corroborate our main findings of Models 1–3 that misallocation of bank credit eventually leads to the poor performance of firms. On the contrary, when the allocation is efficient, the performance of firms improves.

Table 6.3   Bank credit misallocation and return on capital employed (ROCE)

Variables	Model 1	Model 2	Model 3
L.ROCE	0.504***	0.481***	0.517***
	(66.06)	(91.82)	(92.87)
L.ICAE–	–8,436***		–9,383***
	(–11.49)		(–6.895)
L2.ICAE–	–11,854***		–6,429***
	(–32.92)		(–11.05)
L3.ICAE–	–3,415***		1,057
	(–7.689)		(1.198)
L4.ICAE–	1,205**		2,696***
	(2.189)		(3.319)
L.Size_ta	–1.147***	–1.949***	–1.606***
	(–10.18)	(–21.74)	(–12.41)
L.Leverage_ta	–19.68***	–20.99***	–18.49***
	(–36.00)	(–61.84)	(–27.21)

(*Contd*)

(*Contd*)

Variables	Model 1	Model 2	Model 3
L.Growth_ta	–1.604***	–1.588***	–0.628***
	(–10.74)	(–11.92)	(–3.255)
Group Affiliation	9.162***	9.283***	
	(8.599)	(8.212)	
L.ICAE$^+$		8,355***	5,919***
		(41.76)	(12.86)
L2.ICAE$^+$		7,147***	5,175***
		(12.80)	(14.24)
L3.ICAE$^+$		10,996***	12,868***
		(23.97)	(26.23)
L4.ICAE$^+$		8,086***	10,135***
		(27.82)	(29.71)
Constant	15.22***	21.26***	22.23***
	(17.65)	(24.16)	(25.01)
Sargan test	99.311	98.610	98.273
	(1.0000)	(1.0000)	(1.0000)
Second-order autocorrelation	–1.3182	–1.1982	–1.2715
	(0.1875)	(0.2309)	(0.2035)

Note: This table presents the results of the Arellano–Bond dynamic panel data model estimates. The dependent variable is ROCE, measured as a ratio of net profits to capital employed. L., L2., L3., and L4. indicate lag of orders 1, 2, 3, and 4 respectively. *t*-statistics are reported in parentheses. ***, **, and * indicate statistical significance at 1, 5, and 10 per-cent levels.

Table 6.4 Bank credit misallocation and return on total assets (ROTA)

Variables	Model 1	Model 2	Model 3
L.ROTA	0.527***	0.555***	0.569***
	(111.7)	(88.14)	(76.53)
L.ICAE$^-$	–7,235***		–6,209***
	(–13.45)		(–4.723)
L2.ICAE$^-$	–7,975***		–6,382***
	(–20.20)		(–13.78)
L3.ICAE$^-$	–4,441***		–2,113***

(*Contd*)

(*Contd*)

Variables	Model 1	Model 2	Model 3
	(−8.291)		(−2.586)
L4.ICAE⁻	692.8**		1,919**
	(2.312)		(2.522)
L.Size_ta	−1.487***	−1.876***	−1.660***
	(−13.15)	(−43.61)	(−20.14)
L.Leverage_ta	−13.31***	−12.21***	−11.86***
	(−28.21)	(−73.46)	(−17.61)
L.Growth_ta	−1.571***	−1.641***	−1.360***
	(−7.667)	(−27.16)	(−10.41)
D_group	5.917***	5.159***	
	(5.809)	(5.436)	
L.ICAE⁺		6,808***	4,874***
		(59.70)	(13.44)
L2.ICAE⁺		3,266***	3,156***
		(8.278)	(6.442)
L3.ICAE⁺		2,697***	6,901***
		(13.92)	(22.83)
L4.ICAE⁺		6,523***	7,930***
		(99.36)	(34.57)
Constant	16.66***	18.88***	19.88***
	(15.55)	(25.81)	(27.94)
Sargan test	100.2513	100.4266	104.3791
	(1.0000)	(0.9999)	(0.9999)
Second-order autocorrelation	−1.2305	−1.3196	−1.3009
	(0.2185)	(0.1870)	(0.1933)

Note: This table presents the results of the Arellano–Bond dynamic panel data model estimates. The dependent variable is ROTA, measured as the product of profit margin and asset turnover. L., L2., L3., and L4. indicate lag of orders 1, 2, 3, and 4 respectively. *t*-statistics are reported in parentheses. ***, **, and * indicate statistical significance at 1, 5, and 10 per-cent levels.

Conclusion

This research investigates the impact of bank credit misallocation on firms' performance. The findings reported in this chapter highlight two important observations: first, allocative efficiency plays a crucial role in improving firms' performance in subsequent years. Second, misallocation of bank credit often leads to firms' poor performance as the poor quality firms mismanage the funds, which eventually destroys their value. The significant association between misallocation and a firm's future performance indicates that the Q-based approach proposed to measure the misallocation arising at the point of disbursement seems to be a good indicator of firm quality that the bankers and management can use while assessing the need for credit. The findings underscore the need to take note of the quality signals sent by firms while allocating credit.

Note

1   Note that we only report the most parsimonious models for all specifications after exploring various combinations of control variables (see Chapter 5 for the complete list).

7

Credit Reallocation by Indian Banks in the Aftermath of the Global Financial Crisis

The international economy was greatly impacted by the most severe financial crisis, which started in the United States in September 2008, with the collapse of Lehman Brothers. This marked the beginning of the global financial crisis (GFC) and evolved as the greatest crisis since the Great Depression in the 1930s. The GFC exposed the fundamental weakness of the financial systems, particularly in the banking sectors, across the economies. Amplification of the crisis was observed in terms of both scale and severity, affecting the key macroeconomic indicators and eventually leading one after another country towards recession. As the crisis progressed, the banking sector's fragilities were revealed. While examining the role of financial institutions contributing to the crisis, it became apparent that commercial banks disbursed substantial credit towards temporarily inflated asset values without paying much attention to the creditworthiness of the borrowers (Makin, 2019).

As a consequence of the crisis, the world's potential growth declined to –0.1 per cent in 2008–09, which was estimated to be 2.5 per cent before the crisis period (Felipe and Estrada, 2020). Among other indicators, the world unemployment rate increased from 4.9 per cent to 5.6 per cent from 2008 to 2009; inflation rate fell from 8.9 per cent to 2.9 per cent from 2008 to 2009, and industrial output declined from 18.9 trillion US dollars to 16 trillion US dollars from 2008 to 2009 (World Bank, 2019). Further, after the GFC, economies witnessed a sharp decline in the flow of credit, a fall in gross domestic product (GDP) growth rate, excessive budget deficits, inadequate investment, and sluggish wage growth (Makin, 2019). Though the crisis began in the industrialized countries, the emerging countries, which initially resisted the crisis, were also affected by the movements in the global market. While the developed countries introduced large fiscal stimulus packages by extending domestic and foreign borrowing to boost their economies, the emerging countries faced greater obstacles as the investors pulled out their capital where they perceived the slightest risk resulting in a low value of stocks and devaluation of the currency (International Labour Organization, 2011). As a result, actual growth for the developing and BRICS countries during 2008–09 was marked at 4.4 and 5.7 per cent, respectively, in contrast to the potential growth of 6.2 and 7.4 per cent, respectively, following the GFC (Felipe and Estrada, 2020).

Although the banking sector was affected by the GFC in different magnitudes for different economies, one common trend observed in the banking sector is a decline in the supply of bank credit following the crisis. For example, Chavaa and Purnanandam (2011) find that during the Russian crisis of 1998, US banks decreased lending and increased interest rates, leading to an adverse impact on the firms' output that relied heavily on banks' credit. The post-crisis period thus witnessed freezing of bank credit, a slump in real private investment, loss in investor confidence, and, finally, diminishing global savings and investment. Nevertheless, various studies show that the decline in the growth rate of bank credit was strikingly heterogeneous across the sectors within the economies, suggesting a significant change in the reallocation decisions of banks (Degryse and Ongena, 2007; Puri, Rocholl, and Steffen, 2011; Iyer et al., 2013; Ongena, Peydro, and van Horen, 2015; DeYoung et al., 2015; Liberti and Sturgess, 2018; Jonghe et al., 2020). The majority of banks started adopting strategic lending policies following the crisis and transmitted the negative funding shock to their borrowers through the reallocation of credit. For example, there was an unexpected freeze in the European interbank market during the post-crisis period. The Portuguese banks, which were relying more on interbank borrowing, reduced their credit supply more for small firms with weaker banking relationships (Iyer et al., 2013). Using the data on bank–firm relationships for Belgium, Jonghe et al. (2020) estimated that one standard-deviation increase in (*a*) sector market share, (*b*) sector specialization, or (*c*) firm soundness helps to reduce the transmission of the funding shock to credit supply by 22 per cent, 8 per cent, and 10 per cent, respectively.

Based on the aforementioned literature on bank credit and strategic lending, this chapter focuses on the growth of bank credit, the lending decision, and credit reallocation in India in the post-crisis period. Using a sample of 840 firm-level observations from the different sectors in the Indian economy, we examine the nature of bank credit allocation towards these firms after the GFC. Our research aims to investigate whether there is any evidence of strategic lending by the Indian banking sector as an optimum response to the GFC. Specifically, we consider (*a*) sector-specificity, (*b*) bank–firm relationship, and (*c*) risk management as a constituent of the optimum responses for credit reallocation decisions by banks in the post-crisis era. Comparing pre-crisis (2007) and post-crisis (2009 and 2010) firm-level data, we test the optimal response of banks in the following way:

1. Sector-specificity: Whether credit reallocation decisions by banks in the post-crisis period have been influenced by the sectoral share of the credit (share of bank credit to a particular sector to total bank credit disbursed to all sectors for that period) in the pre-crisis period.

2. Bank–firm relationship: Whether bank credit reallocation decision is related to the type of banking relation the firm holds – for example, single or multiple relations.

3. Risk management: Whether low-risk firms have received priority in credit allocation decisions by banks in the post-crisis period. We have used a battery of firm-specific characteristics such as leverage, profitability, distance to default, interest coverage ratio, long-term bank debt, age and size of the firm, and asset tangibility of the firm to measure a firm's financial viability.

The following sections of the chapter are organized by reviewing the literature on bank credit allocation using cross-country evidence, establishing the hypotheses, testing our hypothesis using summary statistics, and visualizing pre- and post-crisis period data. The chapter finally concludes by providing an overview of banks' optimal responses towards credit allocation in the aftermath of the GFC in India.

Banking Sector after the GFC

Following the GFC, banks of different countries responded to the crisis to varying degrees. A report by the Bank for International Settlements (BIS) on structural changes in banking summarizes that, in the post-crisis period, the banking sectors have broadly identified three key areas to ensure their stability (BIS, 2018). These are:

1. enhancing banks' resilience to future risks by accumulating substantial capital and liquidity buffers, improving risk management, and controlling internal practices;

2. implementing cost-cutting policies, understanding market sentiment to ensure future bank profitability; and

3. enhancing reforms to ensure system-wise stability.

Banks focused more on declining lending channels, shifting towards stable funding sources (deposits), and focusing on recovery frameworks.

Many banks received government capital injections in the US and Europe, and some were nationalized following the crisis (BIS, 2018). In the Spanish banking system, loan performance deteriorated, and savings-banks were worst hit by the crisis (BIS, 2018). Following the crisis, half of the top 20 emerging market economy (EME) banks lowered their loan to deposit ratios in 2009 owing to tighter liquidity conditions. For example, Antoniades (2014) shows that after categorizing banks into subsamples according to their asset size, the effect of liquidity risk on the credit supply was not uniform across banks. Smaller banks with an asset size of lesser than 500 million dollars witnessed less credit supply contraction due to their low exposures.

In contrast, banks with more than USD 10 billion contracted a larger part of their credit supply. Following the GFC, there was a severe downfall in the industrial production in Japan and negative terms of trade shock, which swept the capital base of the commercial banks in the country and became conservative in their lending decisions (Kawai and Takagi, 2009). Iyer et al. (2013) identify that the less solvent banks faced higher consequences of the illiquidity on the credit crunch compared to other banks in the country.

Further, a study on credit reallocation shows that the GFC negatively affected the Belgian financial system (Jonghe et al., 2020). The interbank funding of bank activities in Belgium dropped from EUR 500 billion in 2008 to around EUR 250 billion, 13 months after the declaration of bankruptcy by Lehman Brothers. In contrast, for the Latin American countries, the banking sector witnessed a heterogeneous response to the crisis; larger banks with higher capital, better and stable funding sources, and low-risk indicators were less hit by the financial shock and consequently supplied more credit, whereas banks with volatile funding sources and high-risk indicators supplied less credit as a response to the financial shock (Cantú, Claessens, and Gambacorta, 2019). As a policy response to the GFC, the financial sector in China went under severe change and moved its focus on bank lending towards a more dynamic sector with fewer regulatory mechanisms (Haasbroek and Gottwald, 2017). Credit supply by banks was also indirectly affected by the changes in the market power of banks. In a cross-country study during the period 2003–12, Demirgüç-Kunt et al. (2020) reveal that increased market power of banks affected the supply of loans for countries with poor restrictions on banking activities and supervisory power. Kato (2009) finds that for developing countries, as access to capital after the financial crisis was limited, efficient credit allocation by banks was necessary to promote economic growth in the post-crisis period. Overall, the changes in the banking sectors in the post-crisis period can be summarized as (*a*) reforms in banking market capacity and structure, (*b*) shifts in bank business models, and (*c*) changes in bank performance (BIS, 2018).

To capture the changes in the lending decision by banks in the post-crisis period, Figure 7.1 outlines the overall decline in bank credit supply to private non-financial sectors in the post-crisis period for various groups of countries.

Figure 7.1 indicates that bank credit towards private non-financial sectors significantly declined following the GFC and more prominently for the advanced economies and Euro areas. For the advanced economies, the credit growth rate towards private non-financial sectors declined from 10.1 per cent to –1.9 per cent, while for the Euro area, it was much worse with a decrease from 15.9 per cent to –2.8 per cent, comparing 2008 and 2009 values. Comparing with the advanced or Euro economies, though the Group of Twenty (G20) and emerging countries followed the same trend, the fall in credit growth was relatively moderate (20.1 per cent in 2008 to 13.7 in 2009).

The Indian economy was not without exception and faced a similar credit supply shock in various sectors. Ghosh and Chandrasekhar (2009) observe that the Indian banking industry is characterized by liquidity constraints in the post-crisis period. On the demand side, potential borrowers became unwilling to borrow due to slowdown and uncertainties, while on the supply side banks became more risk-averse.

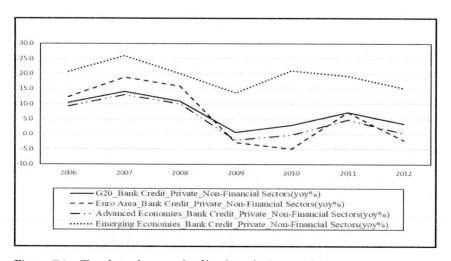

Figure 7.1 Trends in the growth of bank credit (per cent) in private non-financial sectors across the globe

Source: Federal Reserve Economic Data (FRED), https://fred.stlouisfed.org/.

Thus, accessing bank credit became increasingly difficult for enterprises requiring working capital due to stringent bank policies. As a result, as shown in Figure 7.2, bank credit growth (all scheduled commercial banks) in the country significantly declined from 22.3 per cent to 16.9 per cent after the GFC. A similar decline in credit growth to non-financial and private non-financial sectors is visible in Figures 7.3 and 7.4.

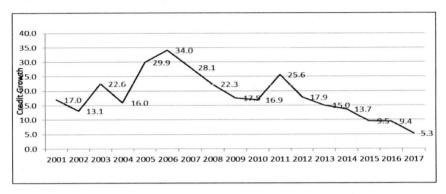

Figure 7.2   Credit growth of all scheduled commercial banks (SCBs) in India (YoY per cent)

Source: Reserve Bank of India, *Handbook of Statistics on Indian Economy*.

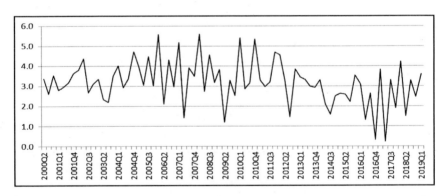

Figure 7.3   Bank credit growth for non-financial sectors in India (YoY per cent)

Source: Reserve Bank of India, *Handbook of Statistics on Indian Economy*.

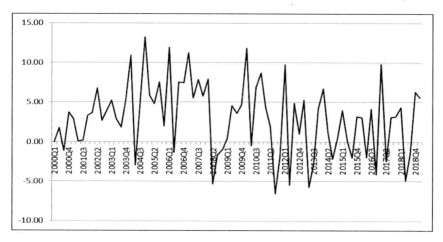

Figure 7.4 Bank credit growth for the private non-financial sector in India (YoY per cent)

Source: Reserve Bank of India, *Handbook of Statistics on Indian Economy*.

In the case of India, we find that reallocation of credit in the post-crisis period widely varied across the sectors in the economy. For example, Figures 7.5–7.9 show declining growth in bank credit across five major sectors of the Indian economy – namely construction, textile, power, iron and steel, and telecommunication.

Figure 7.5 shows a gradual decline in the credit growth in the construction sector from 39.7 per cent in 2008 to 37.8 per cent in 2009, further 14.8 per cent in 2010, and –1.8 per cent in 2011. In the textile sector, credit growth has declined from 28.8 per cent in 2008 to 6.5 per cent in 2009 following a slight improvement of 10.8 per cent in 2010.

From Figure 7.7, we observe a reduction in credit growth in the iron and steel sector from 30 per cent in 2008 to 20 per cent in 2009. The credit growth has fallen significantly from 95 per cent in 2008 to 31 per cent in 2009 in the telecommunication sector following the GFC. Interestingly, the credit growth in the power sector showed improvement in credit supply for the next two years (1.2 per cent increase in 2009 and more than 20 per cent increase in 2010) immediately after the crisis but started declining sharply (9 per cent decline in 2011 and 17 per cent decline in 2012) after the initial lag of two years as a response to the GFC.

From the plots on sectoral credit allocation by banks given thus far, we can draw two distinct observations: first, we witness strong evidence of a sharp reduction in the credit supply by banks immediately in the post-crisis period for construction,

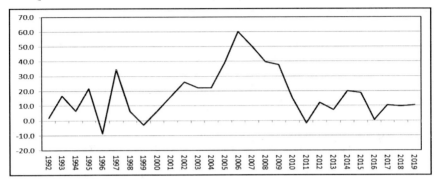

Figure 7.5 Bank credit growth in the construction sector in India (YoY per cent)

Source: Institute of Management Accountants (IMA) database.

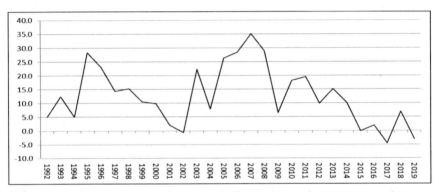

Figure 7.6 Bank credit growth in the textile sector in India (YoY per cent)

Source: Institute of Management Accountants (IMA) database.

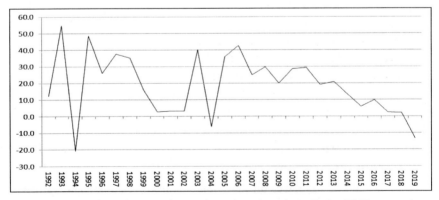

Figure 7.7 Bank credit growth in iron and steel sector in India (YoY per cent)

Source: Institute of Management Accountants (IMA) database.

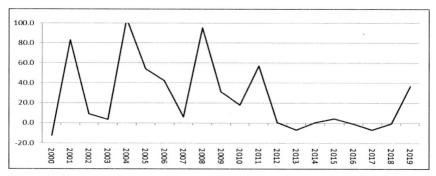

Figure 7.8   Bank credit growth in the telecommunication sector in India (YoY per cent)

Source: Institute of Management Accountants (IMA) database.

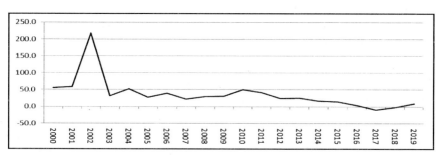

Figure 7.9   Bank credit growth in the power sector in India (YoY per cent)

Source: Institute of Management Accountants (IMA) database.

iron and steel, textile, and telecommunication sectors and with some lag in the power sector. Second, heterogeneity in the allocation of credit (variation in the proportion of credit cutback) across sectors after the global crisis suggests that all the sectors have not been equally affected by the negative credit shock.

Research Hypotheses

Using firm-level data from a range of 24 industrial sectors of the Indian economy, we test three specific hypotheses to capture the indicators associated with the reallocation of bank credit as an optimum response to the GFC. These are (*a*) sector-specificity, (*b*) bank–firm relationship, and (*c*) riskiness of firms.

Hypothesis 1: Sector Specificity

Based on a growing body of empirical literature relating to banks' market share, market power, and credit (Degryse et al., 2009), we hypothesize that banks reallocate credit according to their market power. Existing literature argues that bank borrowing of firms with higher market shares in their respective sectors is less exposed to credit supply shocks under severe funding shocks. Moreover, the argument that banks reallocate credit according to sector specialization further connects the bank funding shock transmission with the bank lending concentration (Acharya, Iftekhar, and Saunders, 2006; Degryse and Ongena, 2007; Tabak, Fazio, and Cajueiro, 2011; Jahn, Memmel, and Pfingsten, 2016; Beck, Jonghe, and Mulier, 2017). Through specific sector specialization, banks have a higher set of borrower's information and expect a higher recovery rate than other sectors with lower information. Therefore, we argue that there will be a general inclination of banks to continue lending to these specific sectors where they have specialized before the crisis. In other words, banks divert more financial resources to such sectors compared to other sectors. Therefore, we propose that firms borrowing from the specialized banks are less affected by a funding shock, indicating the potential downside to bank diversification (Laeven and Levine, 2007). We present our first hypothesis on sector specificity as follows.

Box 7.1 Hypothesis 1

In the post-crisis period, banks will reallocate higher credit towards those specific sectors where the share of long-term bank borrowing (LTBB) to total long-term bank borrowing for the sectors is higher in the pre-crisis period.

Hypothesis 2: Bank–Firm Relationship

It is well documented that following the GFC, banks became more resilient in considering their lender's portfolio and relied more on those firms which have maintained a dedicated long-term relation. On banks' side, this reduces the cost of monitoring and helps them to assess the repayment probabilities, recovery rate, and default rate. Following seminal work by Diamond (1984), long-term lending relationship occupies an area of significant importance in credit deployment. As argued by Diamond (1984), a strong bank–firm relationship strengthens the bank's monitoring capacity, mitigates the moral hazard problem, improves the firm's creditworthiness, and enhances the firm's reputation. Strong borrower–lender relation also benefits a firm's corporate governance and induces better monitoring (Dass and Massa, 2011).

Furthermore, long-term exclusive banking relationships allow banks to seek good investment opportunities among firms using the informational monopoly they have over a firm (Sharpe, 1990). The empirical literature argues that firms' single banking relationship is prioritized over multiple banking relations to establish the strength of the lending relationship. In addition, single banking relations are often less costly and lowers borrowing costs compared to multiple borrowing relations (Petersen and Rajan, 1994). The number of banks can be used as a proxy for a firm's quality, where low-quality firms which are denied credit support from a single or first bank may seek credit accessibility from the second bank at a higher rate of interest. We propose our second hypothesis on banking relationships maintained by a firm as follows.

Box 7.2   Hypothesis 2

Banks reallocate their credit towards firms that hold single banking relation rather than multiple banking relation in the post-crisis period.

Hypothesis 3: Risk Management

The third and final hypothesis is built from a strand of literature that relates firm characteristics to credit constraints. Existing literature suggests various firm-specific characteristics to identify financial constraints faced by a firm. These are firm size, age (Beck, Demirgüç-Kunt, and Levine, 2006; Hadlock and Pierce, 2010), asset tangibility (Almeida and Campello, 2007), leverage, and cash flows (Lamont, Polk, and Kaa-Requej, 2001; Whited and Wu, 2006). We complement this body of literature by testing whether firm-specific attributes like tangibility, leverage, distance to default, profitability, and interest coverage matter for credit supply when the banking sector is under stress.

Overall, our objective is to check whether firm-specific characteristics, which provide a holistic view to the lenders in terms of information, firm's riskiness, bank's monitoring cost, and the possibility of loan recovery, are essential in banks' lending decisions in the post-crisis period. Therefore, we propose the third hypothesis as follows.

Box 7.3   Hypothesis 3

Banks supply more credit to the low-risk firms in the post-crisis period.

Test of Research Hypotheses

We draw a firm-level sample of 840 firm-year observations from the Centre for Monitoring Indian Economy (CMIE) Prowess database for two years – 2007 and 2009. The sample included 413 and 427 observations, respectively, for each year. In addition, we use data in the year 2010 to perform a robustness check of our findings.

Sector Specificity 1: Industries

We segregate our sample firms into 24 broad categories based on the National Informatics Centre (NIC) codes for industries (Government of India, 2008). The share of long-term bank borrowing (LTBB) in each sector is computed for the pre-crisis (2007) and post-crisis (2009) periods. Figure 7.10 shows the distribution of the share of LTBB across various industrial sectors for pre- and post-crisis periods. We observe that in 2007, out of these 24 sectors, six key sectors, namely food products, textiles, coke and refined petroleum products, chemical and chemical products, and basic metal, contribute to nearly 87 per cent of the total long-term bank borrowing. Though the total share of long-term bank borrowing in these six sectors remains the same in the post-crisis period, the composition changes largely. For example, for the *food and food products* sector, the LTBB share has declined from 11.4 per cent in 2007 to 2.8 per cent in 2009. Similarly, the LTBB share has reduced for the *textiles* (21.5 per cent in 2007 to 4.9 per cent in 2009), *chemical and chemical products* (7.1 per cent in 2007 to 4.7 per cent in 2009), and *basic metal* sectors (32.2 per cent in 2007 to 12.6 per cent in 2009) in the post-crisis period. The LTBB share for *other non-metallic mineral products* sector remains unchanged (8.3 per cent) for both pre- and post-crisis periods.

On the contrary, the LTBB share for the *coke and refined petroleum products* sector improved significantly from 6.7 per cent in 2007 to 53.7 per cent in 2009. This implies that specific sectors with a high proportion of long-term bank borrowing in the pre-crisis period are essentially not those sectors that have acquired a higher portion of long-term bank borrowing in the post-crisis period. In other words, we can see strong heterogeneity in the bank credit supply during the post-crisis period across different sectors. Thus, sector specificity, or sector specialization, does not seem to be considered as an evaluating parameter for credit reallocation by Indian banks in the post-crisis period. Our observation contrasts with Jonghe et al. (2020), suggesting that the potential benefit of bank borrowing concentration within a sector may not be accurate in the case of India.

Sector Specificity 2: Market Power in Long-term Bank Borrowings

We further test the sector specificity of bank lending by examining the change concentration of long-term bank credit across firms after the financial crisis. In contrast to our earlier findings, Figure 7.11 shows that long-term bank debt seems to play a role in banks' credit reallocation decision in 2009. The LTBB

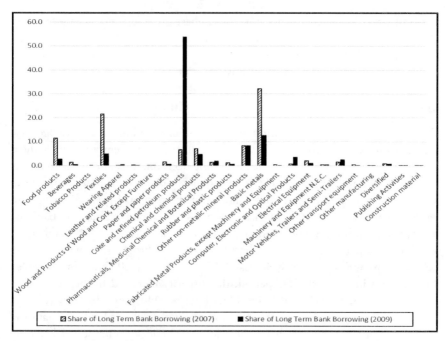

Figure 7.10   Share of long-term bank borrowing across sectors
Source: Authors' estimation.

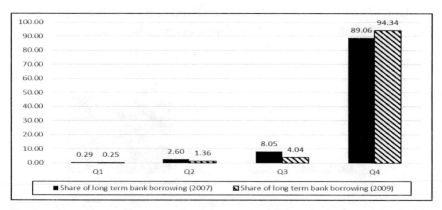

Figure 7.11   Share of long-term bank borrowing of firms by long-term bank debt
Source: Authors' estimation.

share of firms increased for firms in the highest quartile (Q4) in 2009 with a 94.3 per cent share. However, for the third quartile, we do not see a similar trend. It probably indicates that banks might have partially used market power in determining credit allocation in the post-crisis period.

Bank–Firm Relationship: Single versus Multiple

As discussed earlier, banks acquire a higher set of information and knowledge on a particular sector or a firm through specialization and thus attempt to reduce their monitoring cost, affecting their future lending decision. Thus, firms maintaining single banking relations are likely to have higher chances of availing bank credit than firms with multiple banking relations in the post-crisis period. Using our sample, we calculate the share of LTBB for firms with single and multiple banking relationships in both the pre- and post-crisis periods. Figure 7.12 shows that, in the pre-crisis period (2007), the share of LTBB for firms with single banking relationships was significantly low at 9.71 per cent in 2007 for our sample. Surprisingly, in the post-GFC period, the disparity increased further where the share of LTBB reduced by three times (2.19 per cent) for single banking relation firms, and the greater share was allotted to firms with multiple banking relations. This information indicates that banks do not consider a number of banking relationships as an indicator while considering their credit allocation decision in the post-crisis period.

Risk Management

Based on the existing literature, we argue that banks tend to reallocate their credit towards low-risk firms as a part of their optimum response to the GFC. To verify

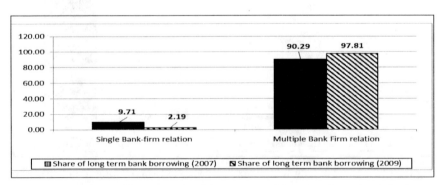

Figure 7.12 Share of long-term bank borrowing of firms with single-multiple banking relations

Source: Authors' estimation.

that, we consider a set of prominent firm-specific characteristics that capture financial viability and their ability to service the debt and check if these features provide any indication that banks reallocate their credit in the post-crisis period. These firm-specific attributes are the size and age of the firm, distance-to-default ratio, profitability, leverage ratio, interest coverage ratio, and tangibility ratio.

Firm size is measured as the natural log of total assets. We hypothesize that larger firms attract more credit because of their higher collateral value. Age is defined as the number of years since a firm's incorporation. Older firms may have already succeeded in building their reputation and hence might be better positioned to avail the credit in the post-crisis period than the younger firms with limited credit history. Therefore, older firms are likely to receive more bank loans based on their long presence in the market. To capture the likelihood of default, we employ distance to default,[1] a widely used proxy for corporate distress, which contrasts the standard deviation of a firm's asset value with its debt obligation (Chou, 2005). The higher distance to default implies a less expected default probability of a firm, while the lower value predicts the converse. We also consider firm profitability defined as PBITA (profit before interest, taxes, and amortization) to total assets to evaluate the financial health of a firm. Profitability captures the ability of a company to generate income relative to its operating cost and therefore indicates the firm's competency to utilize its asset in generating profit. A greater profitability ratio indicates a lower risk of default.

Further, we consider financial leverage as an indicator to understand the solvency of a firm. We use two alternative proxies of the leverage ratio: debt to total assets and debt-to-equity ratio. All the ratios interpret a high leverage ratio as a higher level of risk associated with a firm. A firm's ability to service debt payments is an important criterion to define financial viability. To proxy the firm's creditworthiness, we define interest coverage ratio (ICR) as the ratio of PBDITA to total interest expenses. Using the standard accounting conventions, we categorize firms into three categories based on ICR: being less than 1, between 1 and 2, and more than 2. A lower ICR value (less than one) indicates a higher risk associated with a firm where the same fails to cover its interest expenses by its earnings.

Similarly, higher ICR shows a firm is in a low-risk category wherein it is self-sufficient to cover the interest expenses. Finally, two alternate proxies of the tangibility ratio are defined. First is the ratio of the net fixed asset to total assets, and second is the ratio of plant and machinery to net fixed asset. Higher the tangibility lower, higher is the financial risk associated with the firm.

Taking all these indicators together, we categorize the firms as low risk if they are associated with higher profitability, interest coverage ratio, tangibility, and distance to default on the one hand and with lower leverage ratio on the other hand. Going by the conventional wisdom, we also conjecture that the older and bigger the firm, the lower is the risk associated with it. We divide the values of all the attributes into four quartiles (Q1<Q2<Q3<Q4) for 2007 and 2009 and calculate the share of long-term bank borrowing within each quartile to see the variation in the long-term borrowing between pre-and post-crisis period. Using these firm-level risk attributes, we evaluate banks' decision to reallocating credit towards low-risk firms as a response to the crisis. These are presented in Figures 7.13–7.21.

Firm Age

To test whether firm age is associated with banks' lending decision in the post-crisis period, we examine if the older firms have received more bank loans in the post-crisis period than the younger firms with limited credit history.

Figure 7.13 shows that older firms receive more bank loans (42.1 per cent in 2007 and 69 per cent in 2009) than the firms which are new entrants in the market. So, the age of a firm was considered in banks' lending decision in the post-crisis period.

Firm Size

Similarly, we have used firm size to examine whether big firms were prioritized over the small firms in credit allocation by banks in the post-crisis period. Again, as depicted in Figure 7.14, bigger firms received higher shares of bank credit when compared to smaller firms with lower asset values.

As expected, firms belonging to the highest size quartile (Q4) received the highest share of bank credit in the pre and post-crisis period (87.5 per cent in 2007

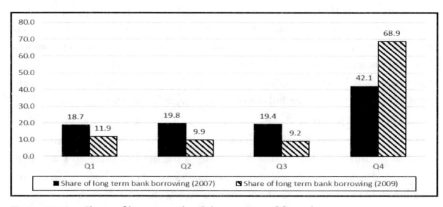

Figure 7.13   Share of long-term bank borrowing of firms by age
Source: Authors' estimation.

and 93.08 per cent in 2009). When we compare the change in the proportion compared to other size quartiles, we conclude that banks increased the credit to large firms as a part of the lending decision to mitigate the risk in the post-crisis period. Therefore, to manage the risk, banks seem to have deprived the smaller and younger firms, which are likely to be more financially constrained, and hence might have prolonged the effect of the crisis.

Firm's Profitability

Considering the share of bank borrowing across various profitability quartiles, Figure 7.15. shows that higher bank credit was extended towards the firms in the third quartile of the profitability distribution compared with the pre-crisis period data. Additionally, there has been a sharp decline (more than five times) in the share of bank credit for firms in the highest quartile in 2009. Therefore, firms' profitability was not considered an unambiguous factor in bank lending decisions in the post-crisis period.

Interest Coverage Ratio

Figure 7.16 shows that the share of bank borrowing for firms with higher ICR (more than 2) reduced in 2009 compared to 2007, while it increased significantly for firms with low ICR (for example, the share for Q1 increased from 3.63 per cent to 9.48 per cent), that is, risky firms. This indicates that credit reallocation in the post-crisis period did not seem influenced by the ICR, contrary to the

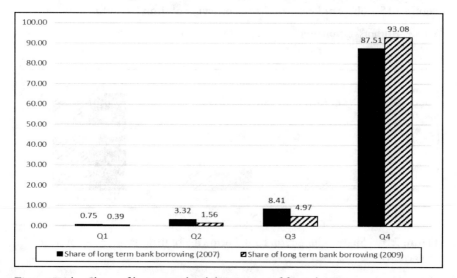

Figure 7.14 Share of long-term bank borrowing of firms by size

Source: Authors' estimation.

expectation. This is often cited as one of the adverse evidence of the Indian banking sector's failure to manage credit risk as a response to the crisis.

Tangibility Ratio

Figures 7.17 and 7.18 present two proxies of tangibility ratios that measure the collateral value. Comparing tangibility, irrespective of the definition used, in the pre-crisis (2007) period, both Figures 7.17 and 7.18 suggest that the share of bank credit of firms with a higher tangibility ratio (Q4) has reduced more than two times in the post-crisis period.

In contrast, high-risk firms belonging to Q1, with a lower tangibility ratio, were provided with more credit in the post-crisis period. There is thus no clear

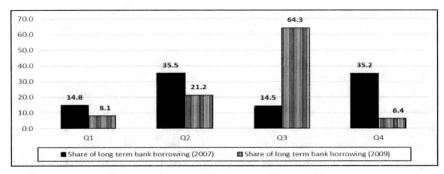

Figure 7.15 Share of long-term bank borrowing of firms by profitability ratio

Source: Authors' estimation.

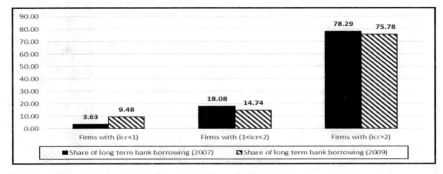

Figure 7.16 Share of long-term bank borrowing of firms by interest coverage ratio (ICR)

Source: Authors' estimation.

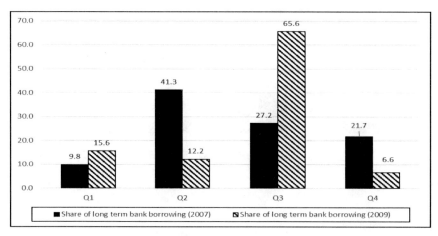

Figure 7.17   Share of long-term bank borrowing of firms by tangibility ratio (net fixed asset)

Source: Authors' estimation.

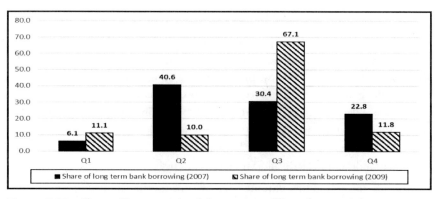

Figure 7.18   Share of long-term bank borrowing of firms by tangibility ratio (plant and machinery)

Source: Authors' estimation.

indication that the tangibility is effectively included in the bank's credit reallocation decision after the crisis.

Distance-to-Default Ratio

Figure 7.19 shows that the share of long-term bank borrowing for firms with higher distance to default (Q4) has increased from 47.5 per cent to 64 per cent)

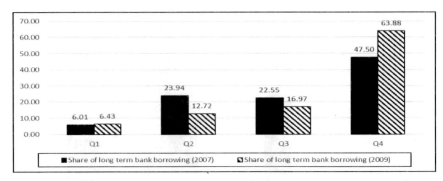

Figure 7.19 Share of long-term bank borrowing of firms by distance-to-default ratio

Source: Authors' estimation.

from 2007 to 2009. This indicates that banks considered the distance-to-default ratio as an important indicator and have reallocated their credit more towards the lower-risk firms (Q1, Q2) in 2009.

Firm Leverage

Lower the leverage, better the debt service capacity, and hence lower is the riskiness of a firm. Similar to the distance to default, Figures 7.20 and 7.21 highlight the share of long-term bank borrowing of firms based on their leverage ratio show more bank credit has been allocated to the set of firms with lower risk.

There is a decrease in the long-term bank borrowing of firms with high risk, that is, the firms in the higher quartiles of leverage ratio (Q3 and Q4) in the post-crisis period. Thus we conclude that leverage ratio might have been considered as a prominent indicator in credit allocation decisions by banks in the post-crisis period.

Considering the aforementioned set of firm-specific indicators and banks' response to credit allocation immediately after the GFC, we summarize our findings as follows:

1. The firm's age, size, leverage, and distance-to-default ratio are the four firm-specific attributes that seem to be considered in lending decisions by banks in the post-crisis period.

2. However, other critical risk management attributes such as profitability, tangibility, and interest coverage ratio show no uniform sign of being prudently utilized by banks in their credit reallocation decision in the post-GFC period.

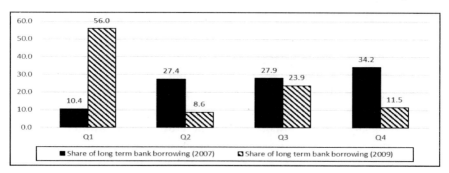

Figure 7.20 Share of long-term bank borrowing of firms by leverage ratio (debt to total asset)

Source: Authors' estimation.

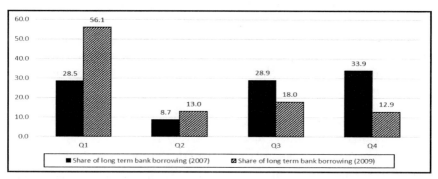

Figure 7.21 Share of long-term bank borrowing of firms by leverage ratio (debt to equity)

Source: Authors' estimation.

Robustness Checks

Considering the possibility of the slow response of bank credit allocation based on firm-specific characteristics, we further extend our research and perform a robustness check of the findings using the 2010 observations. We followed the same exercises, calculated the share of long-term bank borrowing for sample firms for 2010, and examined whether our findings are robust.

The robustness exercise using one additional year after GFC shows that while firm-specific attributes like age, size, profitability ratio, and ICR show similar results as in 2009, the role of other attributes and the bank–firm relationship is found to be ambiguous in banks' lending decision during 2010, following the GFC.

Conclusion

The chapter explores the changes in bank credit allocation in the post-GFC period for the Indian economy. Specifically, we examine whether the Indian banks followed any strategic lending pattern and optimally responded to their credit allocation decision based on sector-specificity, bank–firm relationship, and risk management as a response to the GFC. Our results highlight a decline in the bank credit supply towards non-financial firms coupled with reallocation across firms in the post-crisis period. However, no consistent pattern has been observed on the strategic lending decision by banks in the credit reallocation process to improve the stability and performance of the banking sector in India in the post-crisis period. Comparing the distribution of credit for the pre-crisis period (2007) and the post-crisis period (2009), our findings can be concluded as follows. First, the bank's credit allocation had been heterogeneous across sectors in the post-crisis period, suggesting that the sectors availing a higher share of bank credit before the crisis period were particularly not those that continued receiving higher credit share in the post-crisis period. In other words, in the post-crisis period, credit was reallocated towards some sectors with low credit concentration during 2007. Thus, reallocation of bank credit based on market power or higher share concentration in long-term bank debt of a few industrial sectors is not observed in the Indian context. Second, banking relations do not show unambiguous signs of gaining consideration in the bank's credit allocation decision post-crisis period.

In contrast to the conventional wisdom, the single bank–firm relationship as an indicator of a bank's monitoring costs fails to gain more prominence in the bank's credit reallocation decision following the GFC than firms with multiple-banking relations. Finally, based on the firm-specific characteristics, we further observe that the bank's reallocation decision was not consistently influenced by factors that indicate the riskiness of a firm. While in order to manage the risks, banks tend to focus on large and mature firms with low leverage and distance to default, firms' ability to service these debts in the future is overlooked. This is further corroborated by the fact that firms with low profitability, low ICR, particularly less than one and, low tangibility have received more credit in the post-crisis period. Most importantly, these findings are also consistent with another growing debate concerning the 'evergreening of loans' and 'zombie lending' by the Indian banking sector, which we explore in the next chapter.

Overall, our findings fail to establish an unambiguous conclusion that the Indian banking sector has responded optimally to the GFC by allocating credit to firms with the higher ability to service their liability in the future, in a way to abate the adverse effect of the crisis. This is also consistent with the widespread perception that the weak banking sector can prolong the crisis by misallocating credit to the less deserving firms with poor financial health while restraining credit to healthy firms (Caballero, Hoshi, and Kashyap, 2008; Acharya and Ryan, 2016). However, while assessing the role of bank, one must also consider the fact that, particularly in the context of an emerging economy, the allocation of credit to the weaker firms in the face of a crisis may not be necessarily bad for the health of the economy. Extending credit to the weaker firms may save them from taking drastic actions such as full or partial closure leading to layoffs. This further can help to address the adverse aggregate demand externalities which often deepen the recession (Mian, Sufi, and Verner, 2017). Therefore, to what extent the Indian banking sector has been successful in maintaining this delicate balance between the optimum reallocation of credit and stimulating the ailing economy by supporting the weaker section of the firms needs further research. This has been particularly challenging in India due to the lack of loan-level data to draw reliable inferences. Notwithstanding these limitations, we try to shed light on some of these important issues in the next chapter.

Note

1 Distance to default represents the distance between the expected value of assets of the company and the default point, which indicates the face value of the debt. The term 'distance to default' was used in the KMV model introduced by Kealhofer, McQuown, and Vasicek in 1974 (Kliestik, Misankova, and Kocisova, 2015).

8

The Zombie Story
Credit Boom and the Rise of Zombie Firms in the Indian Economy

Introduction

This chapter explores the extent to which the pro-cyclic credit bubble in the early 2000s led to the misallocation through the extension of bank credit towards firms that are less likely to cover future debt servicing costs. Such a practice of extending loans to non-viable borrowers is known as 'zombie lending' or 'evergreening'. Using a sample of 7,871 firm observations for the period of 1990–2017, we try to address three important questions: first, using a long time-series data spanning across multiple business cycles, we try to trace the rise in the incidence of zombie lending in India. Notably, we ask whether the recent spurt in zombie lending (after 2010) can be attributed to significant credit booms and a financial disruption, or they mirror a more general business cycle trend. Second, using a heterogeneous sample of firms cutting across many industries, we try to find what types of firms have attracted more zombie lending than others. Finally, we explore the causes of the rise of zombie lending, particularly in the post-crisis period. Specifically, we try to relate to the strand of literature that suggests that weak banks tend to roll over loans to non-viable firms to avoid declaring them as NPAs (Storz et al., 2017; Schivardi, Sette, and Tabellini, 2017). We further this literature by exploiting a natural opportunity in India by examining whether the pro-cyclic credit bubble in the pre-crisis period coupled with the economic slowdown as an aftermath of the global financial crisis (GFC) led to a rise in the incidence of zombie lending.

Zombie lending and the consequent window-dressing of the banks' balance sheet to manage the extent of non-performing assets (NPAs) on their book have recently gained increasing attention amongst academics and regulators. There is a widespread perception in the policy circle that politicization and weak organizations impede the process of creative destruction, which further increases the chances of misallocation (Caballero and Hammour, 2001). With persistent misallocation, banks tend to undercapitalize and fail to support healthy credit growth in the economy. While focusing primarily on survival, these banks foster an environment suitable for unprofitable, or 'zombie' lending (Tan, Huang, and Woo, 2016).

Like in many other countries, the banking sector in India is no exception. Despite strict regulatory interventions by the Reserve Bank of India (RBI), there has been an increase in the stressed assets, which escalated NPAs in India. While there is a plethora of anecdotal evidence of large-scale zombie lending by Indian banks leading to management of the extent of NPAs in their books, research on the extent and causes of such zombie lending remains limited. Therefore, our work aims to fill this gap in the literature.

Although there has been limited research on the topic, the media was ripe with anecdotal evidence of the evergreening of loans in the Indian banking sector. Banks have been extending credit to debt-laden companies to help them pay their previous loans. In order to avoid declaring NPAs, it is a common practice for banks to extend loans to stressed assets. This leads to the accumulation of enormous debt as weak debtors cannot repay the loans, which eventually end up as bad loans. There have been numerous newspaper reports on the evergreening of loans in India. For example, as reported in print media (based on the testimony of a whistleblower), ICICI Bank, the second-largest private lending bank, was accused of evergreening and allegedly extending the letter of credit to 31 borrowers ignoring the internal auditors' warning.[1] The report further stated that the banks delayed declaring assets worth at least USD 3 billion as NPAs. The RBI's annual inspection report on State Bank of India (SBI) has revealed practices of evergreening of loans, absence of credit surveillance, lack of credit need assessment, and loan security.[2] The report also shows an increase in credit to problematic sectors like the power sector and points out SBI's efforts to cover its bad debt. There are similar inspection reports on private sector banks such as Axis Bank and HDFC Bank, in addition to SBI and ICICI Bank. More recently, Yes Bank has also been accused of evergreening of loans with the realty group Housing Development and Infrastructure Limited (HDIL).[3]

A study by Subramanian (2016) reports that potentially there is a higher incentive for private sector banks to evergreen loans to not report a dip in profitability. By comparing the private and public sector lending portfolios, the study observes that by December 2013, an alarming number of stressed assets were confirmed by public sector banks (PSBs) but not by the private sector banks. However, at the end of March 2014, ICICI Bank reported a dip of 76 per cent in its profitability, suggesting private sector banks have been hiding stressed assets through evergreening.

More recently, by conducting a case study on Yes Bank, Subramanian (2020) asks if the RBI's reconstruction actions are appropriate or too late to address the problem of stressed assets. The study points out that Yes Bank was having trouble since 2019. However, the RBI had announced its reconstruction in March 2020. Further, the bank was allegedly involved in evergreening loans, political lending, and credit mispricing without looking at the risks involved for many years. Therefore, the author comments on the RBI's role that had been very passive during 2019, and the decision to reconstruct might be a step too late and too small.

Bankers actively look forward to restructuring as it helps in governance slippages. However, the absence of strict bankruptcy laws leads to the non-recovery of the bad loans, which further incentivizes bankers to help debtors rather than declaring NPAs and receive nothing. For example, Pandey, Sapre, and Sinha (2019) note that the Central Bank of India restructured a loan worth USD 80 million to Electhroterm Ltd. However, within months, the bank had to downgrade the loan to an NPA, resulting in a quarter's net loss. A similar incident was reported by UCO Bank with the same company, and the loan turned out as an NPA. The study concludes that although the RBI denounces evergreening, it does not consider aggressive debt restructuring harmful.

Finally, the RBI has consistently advised banks against the evergreening of loans by disapproving the practice of extending a line of credit to companies that are in heavy debt. The RBI also stresses that the purpose of restructuring bad loans is to maintain the economic value and not to evergreen problematic debts.[4] The RBI's *Report of the Committee to Review Governance of Boards of Banks in India*, 2014, distinctively documents evergreening as an exercise of misgovernance by the bank's management. The bank also implemented stricter regulations for restructuring loans to ensure that restructuring does not equate with the evergreening of weak loans. Despite the recognition of evergreening by Central Banks worldwide, there is evidence suggesting that evergreening of bad loans leads to zombie lending and the misallocation of resources (Acharya, 2017).

Against this backdrop, the chapter examines the extent and cause of such evergreening or zombie lending in the Indian economy, particularly following the unprecedented credit boom in the early 2000s. The rest of the chapter includes reviewing the literature on zombie lending and evergreening of loans, followed by identifying zombie firms within our sample using firm-specific criteria. The third section identifies the period of a significant rise in zombie lending and the characteristics of recipient firms. Next, in the fourth section, we present and test our hypothesis that the unprecedented credit boom in the early 2000s coupled with the GFC in 2008 led to a rise in zombie lending in India. The final section concludes the chapter.

Zombie Lending around the World

The term 'zombie' was first used by Caballero, Hoshi, and Kashyap (2008) in the context of the restructuring of the Japanese economy:

> [F]allout from a conscious policy of Japanese banks to keep extending credit to firms even when the prospects for being repaid are limited. Below we describe the evidence suggesting that this phenomenon has become pervasive and explain why the regulatory environment gives banks an incentive to do it. This phenomenon helps to explain the ongoing profit problems of the banks and also to explain slow growth because it implies that many firms that would otherwise be exiting are essentially receiving a subsidy that allows them to continue to operate. (Caballero, Hoshi, and Kashyap, 2008)

The study also explores the consequences of these subsidies for macro-performance in Japan and finds that subsidies kept many money-losing 'zombie' firms in business and depressed the creation of new businesses in the sectors where the subsidized firms are most prevalent. Peek and Rosengren (2005) also emphasize that stricter bank regulations could have helped the Japanese bank crisis in the 1990s. While the mainstream literature follows the definition of Caballero, Hoshi, and Kashyap (2008), recent studies provide further refinement in the definition of a zombie. For example, McGowan, Andrews, and Millot (2018) define zombies as old firms having persistent interest payments with underperforming labour productivity issues. Banerjee and Hofmann (2018) define a firm zombie which cannot cover its interest expense from the current earnings for a prolonged period. Therefore, a firm is considered a zombie if there is a prolonged period of lack of profitability and therefore is not in a position to repay its debt. McGowan, Andrews, and Millot (2018) identify such firms with interest coverage ratio (ICR) of less than 1 for three consecutive years and is at least 10 years old. Unearthing zombie firms in the Indian corporate sector, Kulkarni and Mukherjee (2017) use the creditor's ability to service the debt and define zombie firms as those with ICR below 1, leverage ratio with more than 0.20, and interest rate below the prime lending rate.

While exploring the reason behind the rise in zombie firms, several hypotheses are suggested in the literature. For instance, Peek and Rosengren (2005) suggest evergreening as extending additional bank credit to enable weak firms to meet their interest and outstanding loan obligations. Evergreening is considered a step towards creating zombie firms to cover the bank's bad debt (Caballero, Hoshi, and Kashyap, 2008; Pandey, Sapre, and Sinha, 2019). Our research contributes to the growing literature that explores the emergence of zombie firms due to weak banks in the economy. Banks with impaired balance sheets tend to loan to non-viable firms instead of writing them off with interest to avoid delaying bankruptcy (Banerjee and Hofmann, 2018). This is evident in the case of India, where Ghosh (2017) notes that reallocation of credit to risky firms is often noticed among banks with higher non-performing loans. Corroborating the weak bank argument, Andrews and Petroulakis (2019) find that the zombie-firm problem in Europe partly stems from bank forbearance. The increasing survival of zombie firms congests markets and constrains the growth of more productive firms, which has a detrimental impact on aggregate productivity growth. Studies also link monetary policy and zombie congestion, showing that favourable policies increase banks' risk appetite by providing more credit to unhealthy firms (White, 2012). Such behaviour can amplify during periods of growth when banks tend to relax their lending standards. As observed by Keeton (1999), increase in credit supply during periods of credit growth is significantly associated with the accumulation of bad loans. Similarly, Borio (2018) showed that 'too low for too long' policies increase cheap loan availability and lower productivity.

It is often argued that bank capitalization strongly influences the bank loan supply, suggesting a systematic undercapitalization and inefficient new lending in the economy (Gambacorta and Shin, 2016). This problem of credit misallocation gets channelized towards 'zombie lending' or 'evergreening' of loans. On the one hand, the zombie loans give adequate liquidity to impaired debtors for their outstanding debt. On the other hand, banks also avoid a default on these loans in the short run and delay their announcement of outstanding loans turning into NPAs. Consequently, subsidized credit is given to unproductive firms, and the line of credit for more productive firms is reduced (Acharya, 2017). In a similar study, Okamura (2011) shows the relationship between bank capitalization and zombie firms and reports that weakly capitalized banks increase bad debt. Giannetti and Simonov (2013) also estimate that credit supply would have been 2.5 times higher for healthier firms if banks were recapitalized efficiently. By looking into the evergreening aspect of banks, Niinimaki (2007) shows that weaker auditing systems are more prone to high moral hazard, stressing the importance of strict banking regulations.

Further, in an empirical analysis with data for 33 advanced and emerging countries from 1970 to 2007, Hume and Sentance (2009) show that the global credit boom in early 2000 was strikingly different from that of during the early 1970s and mid-to-late 1980s that lasted for an average of three years. The pattern of the credit boom in 2000 exhibited an up-leg that continued for nearly seven years. Thus, the early 2000s were marked by a boom in housing prices and mortgage debt, leading to an expansion in credit supply with lower collateral requirements and lower deleveraging pressure (Justiniano, Primiceri, and Tambalotti, 2014). Though credit expansion policies are essential measures to cope with the financial crisis, it is also evident that credit expansions worsen firm-level misallocation (Dong, 2020). Furthermore, exploring the relationship between credit expansion and misallocation shows that too much liquidity leads to overheating the economy, enhances the crowding-out effect, limits market-based monetary policy, and distorts the credit market (Bleck and Liu, 2016).

Finally, a drop in interest rates in certain countries is also considered to be another factor for an increase in the share of zombie firms (Banerjee and Hofmann, 2018). The study argues that weak and underperforming firms benefit from lower interest rates and are less likely to exit or restructure. Therefore, such firms remain active in the economy as zombies for a more extended period.

While the prevalence of zombie firms and their significant rise in numbers are factors of concern for policymakers, focus on the relation between zombie firms and their economic consequence started gaining importance in the banking literature after the GFC. For example, Banerjee and Hofmann (2018) observe that the increase in the share of zombie firms from 1980 is linked with financial pressures and economic disruptions. As zombie firms exhibit lower productivity and poor economic performance, an increase in the number of zombie firms may disrupt the economy and distort competition. By reducing product prices, increasing wages, zombie-dominated industries display depressing job creation and destruction and lower productivity (Caballero, Hoshi, and Kashyap, 2008).

Finally, a large segment of literature discusses credit misallocation, zombie borrowing, and debt restructuring. For example, Peek and Rosengren (2005), Ahearne and Shinada (2005), Kwon, Narita, and Narita (2015), Imai (2016), and Acharya (2017) are among the large number of studies that capture the emergence, presence, and dominance of zombie firms in advanced emerging and developing nations.

The impact of zombie firms on healthy firms is widely analysed in the Japanese economy after its macroeconomic stagnation during the 1990s which led to the phenomenon of forbearance lending (Ahearne and Shinada, 2005; Caballero, Hoshi, and Kashyap, 2008; Kwon, Narita, and Narita, 2015). Compared to other developed countries, Japan has stronger banking relationships characterized by main bank relationships and lending banks being in the same business group. Additionally, Japanese banking decisions are motivated by a sense of national duty to help distressed firms rather than just focusing on profitability. Even though there are clear objectives associated with banking relationships, the Japanese economy witnessed significant evergreening behaviour in affiliated banks with close ties with corporations (Peek and Rosengren, 2005).

Other studies on advanced economies include Storz et al. (2017) on the Euro area. Using bank–firm data on small and medium-sized enterprises (SMEs) from five stressed and two non-stressed countries, the study shows that zombie firms continued to borrow during 2010–14. The study also shows that the relationship between zombie firms and weak banks increased banks' indebtedness and recommends deleveraging of both banks and firms for sustainable economic recovery. The dominance of zombie firms is witnessed as these firms remained in the zombie state for an extended period and showed no sign of recovery or exit through bankruptcy. Using firm-level data of listed firms in 14 different economies, Banerjee and Hofmann (2018) show that zombie firms' frequency has increased since the 1980s. The study reports that the probability of staying as a zombie increased significantly from 0.6 in the 1980s to 0.85 in 2016. This increase is linked to the economic disruptions in the early 1990s and early 2000s. Specifically, there is a significant slowdown in zombie firms' asset disposal compared to healthy firms. The study further reports that an increase in 1 per cent of zombies in the economy leads to a decrease of 0.3 per cent in productivity.

One of the reasons for the zombie firms continuing in the economies is weak banks. Caballero, Hoshi, and Kashyap (2008) suggest that banks prefer to evergreen or rollover loans to zombie firms instead of writing them off. Keeping these zombie firms alive, banks allow zombie distortions in the market in many forms, such as higher market wages, lower product prices, lower productivity, and increase in liability to the government, guaranteeing these zombie firms to sustain employment. Furthermore, this disrupts the entry of newer and more productive firms and causes no more good lending opportunities for solvent banks. Other studies report consistent empirical evidence with economic disruptions associated with zombie lending (McGowan, Andrews, and Millot, 2018; Banerjee and Hofmann, 2018). Using the data on Italian banks, Schivardi, Sette, and Tabellini (2017) observe that credit misallocation during the European Financial Crisis was followed by low-capital banks renewing their lines of credit to non-viable firms. McGowan, Andrews, and Millot (2018) look for zombie firms' existence in the Organization for Economic Co-operation and Development (OECD) countries and find that zombie firms linger in a precarious nature, thereby causing crowding out opportunities for healthy firms. Using panel data from SMEs in Japan during 1999–2008, Imai (2016) studies the prevalence of zombie firms due to the evergreening of loans. The study shows that the investments from the evergreening of loans hurt the productivity and profitability of non-zombie firms.

Thus, the dominance of zombie firms or the congestion created by zombie firms is undoubtedly harmful to the economy and is an area of concern for policymakers worldwide. Another primary concern linked with zombie firms is a reduction in aggregate productivity due to shrinking healthy firms' opportunities, especially in the industrial sectors dominated by the share of zombie firms (Ahearne and Shinada, 2005).

Among the bank-based studies, Watanabe (2010) investigates bank capitalization and evergreening in the Japanese real-estate sector. The study finds that a considerable loss in bank capital leads to misallocation of credit to zombie firms. For emerging economies, Tan, Huang, and Woo (2016) look into the impact of state-owned banks on the share of zombie firms in China, establishing that a higher number of state-owned banks lead to a favourable environment for zombie firms to sustain with significant productivity failure in the economy. Furthermore, the study argues that the exit of zombie firms from the market improves industrial growth and employment rate.

Therefore, the adverse effects of zombie firms in the economy are well-documented in the literature. Given this backdrop, this chapter explores the rising dominance of zombie firms, the role of banks, and the importance of the credit boom in the Indian economy.

Identification of Zombies

Following the existing literature and based on the availability of reliable data, we try to identify the zombie firms in this section. As mentioned earlier, most of the studies build on the concept proposed by Caballero, Hoshi, and Kashyap (2008), which account for the availability of subsidized credit, productivity, and profitability aspects.

To define zombie firms, we closely follow the definition proposed by Kulkarni and Mukherjee (2017), extending Caballero, Hoshi, and Kashyap (2008) by further incorporating the aspect of evergreening, credibility and, profitability. Specifically, we focus on the following set of criteria: ICR, leverage ratio, credit rating, the existence of a long-term loan, interest rate of the borrowed loan, and an Altman Z-score. After working out various permutations and combinations on sample firms, we zeroed on two alterative but similar definitions of zombie firms. The primary difference between these two definitions stems from the proxies used to capture the firm's financial viability. While one definition is based on the Altman Z-score, the other uses distance to default (DTD).[5] Therefore, we define a firm to be a zombie if it continues to borrow from the bank at a subsidized rate (interest rate lower than the prevailing prime lending rate of SBI)[6] while having an interest coverage ratio less than 1, leverage ratio (measured as total debt to assets ratio) greater than 0.2, and Altman Z-score of less than 1.8 (or DTD at a higher percentile). Therefore, we indicate these two measures in our research as *zombie1* and *zombie2*, respectively. However, since the primary trend in the prevalence of zombie firms using these two alternative definitions remains similar, we opt to report results based on *zombie1* for the rest of the chapter.

Applying this set of criteria, we identify the zombie firms within our sample of 7,871 firms spanning 27 years (1990–2017). To understand the compositions of zombie firms in the sample, we looked at such firms' share across various segments such as industries, group affiliation, banking relationships, and primary lending banks (public and private sector banks). Figure 8.1 exhibits an overall trend in the share of zombie firms in India, using *zombie1* for the entire sample period. The share of zombie firms is magnified in the post-crisis period, and the average share

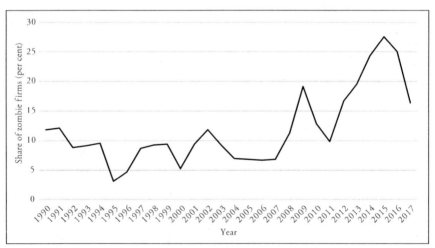

Figure 8.1 Share of zombie firms defined with Altman Z-score in 1990–2017

Source: Authors' estimation.

remains more than 15 per cent from 2010 to 2017, except during the year 2010–11. Therefore, understanding the cause of this phenomenal rise of zombie firms as an aftermath of the crisis period is one of the main objectives of our research.

Figure 8.2 compares the two alternative definitions of zombies, *zombie1* and *zombie 2*, based on Altman Z-score (*zombie1*) and DTD (*zombie2*), respectively, and reveals that they closely mirror each other. Note that due to the lack of reliable DTD estimates before 2000, we limit our comparison of two measures to after 2000.

Both the measures corroborate that the rise in zombies becomes more significant in the post-crisis period, particularly after 2010, starting at 10 per cent in 2011 and maintaining a uniformly positive pattern for the next few years. The share of zombies reached 28 per cent in 2015 and remained at an average of 18 per cent for an extended period of seven years (2010–17). Taking together all the years, we note a decline in zombies after 2000, possibly attributed to the Securitization and Reconstruction of Financial Assets and Enforcement of Security Interest (SARFAESI) Act, 2002, and a further decline after 2015 due to the RBI's growing recognition and active surveillance of zombie lendings through the implementation of the asset quality review (AQR) in July 2015.

In Figure 8.3, we look at the distribution of zombies across various industrial sectors. For this, we segregate our sample into nine broad sectors using a two-digit National Informatics Centre (NIC) code of industries (Government of India, 2008), namely chemical, construction, consumer goods, diversified, food and agro, machinery, metal, textile, and transport equipment. The figure shows that the

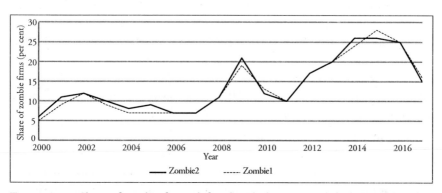

Figure 8.2 Share of zombie firms defined with distance to default (DTD) and Altman Z-score in 2000–17

Source: Authors' estimation.

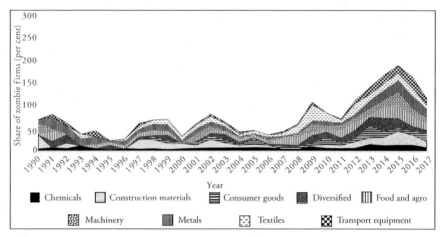

Figure 8.3 Share of zombie firms by industry classifications in 1990–2017

Source: Authors' estimation.

chemical, metal, and textile industries recorded a higher average share of zombies with 2.28, 2.23, and 2.33 per cent, respectively, compared to the average share of 1.32 per cent for all nine sectors. The share of zombie firms in the consumer goods sector has the least average value of 0.26, where zombification was absent for the initial period of seven years (1990–97) and started showing a larger share of zombie firms after 1997. The transport equipment sector followed a similar course with a consistently lower share of zombie firms (0.73 as all-year average).

Next, to highlight the significant rise in the share of zombie firms across specific sectors in the economy, we divide the entire sample period 1990–2017 into two sub-sample periods 1990–2009 and 2010–17. Table 8.1 shows that the rise in the share of zombie firms in each sector is attributed to the increase in zombification of firms during 2009–17. The average share of zombie firms across all sectors increased from 8.25 per cent to 19 per cent over 2009–17, more than double the sub-period 1990–2009. Additionally, the average share of zombies is significantly higher in the metal, transport, and textile sectors during 2009–17.

Next, in Figure 8.4, we present the share of zombie firms based on their affiliation to a business group. It is interesting to observe that in the early 1990s, the share of zombie firms was higher for group-affiliated firms. However, this trend changes as the share of standalone zombie firms rises significantly after 2010. For example, the share of zombie firms reached 10 per cent on an average (2010–17) for stand-alone (non-group affiliated in the figure) firms, which were 3.5 per cent (1990–2009). In contrast, it was 9 per cent for the group-affiliated firms (2010–17) compared to 5.5 per cent in 1990–2009. We thus observe a clear trend that the

Table 8.1 Share of zombie firms in sectors during the sub-periods 1990–2009 and 2009–17

Year/Industries		Chemicals	Construction	Consumer durables	Diversified	Food and agro	Machinery	Metals	Textiles	Transport	Overall
1990–09	Number of zombie firms	82	34	9	22	44	19	53	87	15	365
	Total number of firms	1054	272	179	296	451	422	513	830	408	4425
	Zombie (per cent)	7.78	12.5	5.03	7.43	9.76	4.5	10.33	10.48	3.68	8.25
2009–17	Number of zombie firms	107	24	17	65	72	55	121	43	41	655
	Total number of firms	810	174	123	270	365	277	551	603	273	3446
	Zombie (per cent)	13	20	14	24	20	20	22	24	15	19
1990–2017	Zombie (per cent)	10	15	9	15	14.	11	16	16	8	13

Source: Authors' estimation.

share of zombie firms started picking up regardless of ownership structure in the post-crisis period and more specifically after 2010.

Several researchers argue that a higher share of investments by public sector banks (PSBs) encourages an environment for zombie firms.[7] According to the nature of their banking relationships, we segregate the zombie firms to account for borrowing from PSBs and borrowings from all other sources. Figure 8.5 shows the share of zombie firms that borrow from PSBs in comparison with their counterparts that borrow from other sources from 2001 to 2017.[8] The figure indicates that the share of zombie firms borrowing from public sectors remained

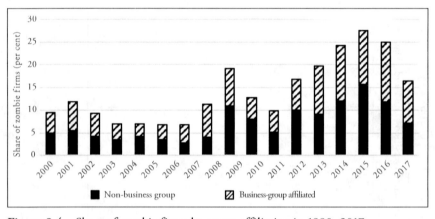

Figure 8.4 Share of zombie firms by group affiliation in 1990–2017

Source: Authors' estimation.

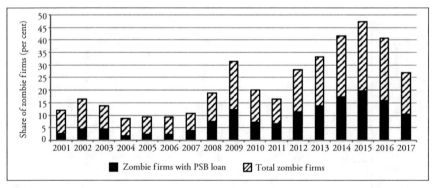

Figure 8.5 Share of zombie firms with public sector bank (PSB) borrowings in 2001–17

Source: Authors' estimation.

higher throughout the period while gaining further impetus in the pre-crisis period (after 2005). Therefore, we hypothesize that the increase in PSB lending before the crisis period and especially during the credit boom may have accelerated the rise of zombie firms in the Indian economy.

In Figure 8.6, we focus on a firm's banking relationship with SBI and its associates. SBI is the most prominent PSB, and the sample distribution shows that most zombie firms have SBI loans. Note that, due to the unavailability of continuous data for the banking relationships before 2000, we consider the period from 2000 to 2017 for this exercise. During 2000–09, the average share of zombie firms receiving the credit from SBI and its associates was 3.87 per cent, which increased threefold to 9.06 per cent for the years 2010–19.

Finally, Figure 8.7 presents the zombie firms' share based on the number of banking relationships held by a firm. For this, we categorize the sample firms into single banking relationships and multiple banking relationships, respectively.

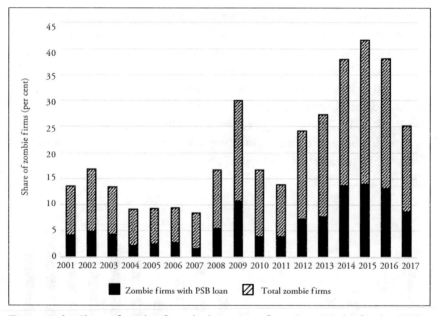

Figure 8.6 Share of zombie firms by borrowing from State Bank of India (SBI) and its associates in 2001–17

Source: Authors' estimation.

Figure 8.7 highlights two interesting facts. First, firms having multiple-bank relationships, on average, have a higher share of zombies, 8.10 per cent, compared to 2.47 per cent for firms having a single-bank relationship, for the period 2000–17. Second, the share of zombie firms with multiple-bank relations has further accentuated to 13.25 per cent for 2010–17. In contrast, the share of zombies has increased to 2.63 per cent for firms with single-bank relations in the post-GFC period.

Zombie Lending: Role of Credit Boom and the GFC

This section focuses on a plausible hypothesis of a significant rise in the share of zombie firms, particularly in the post-GFC period. We hypothesize that the availability of cheap and capacious credit growth in the period of a credit boom during the early 2000s and misallocation of such credits towards low-productive firms has caused the rise of zombie firms in the late 2000s, particularly after 2010 in India.

To test our hypothesis, we conduct a two-steps ocular approach: First, we observe the expansion of credit (credit growth rate and long-term bank borrowing [LTBB]) over the years 1990–2017, capturing the period of a significant rise in the supply of bank credit and test the trend in zombie intensification during that period. Second, in a more precise attempt, we examine whether there is any relation between borrowing exuberance (BE) and the rise of the zombie firms after 2010. As discussed in Chapter 3, we define BE as Tobin's Q-based measure of misallocation of resources due to inappropriate allocation of bank credit to firms with lower marginal returns to capital.[9]

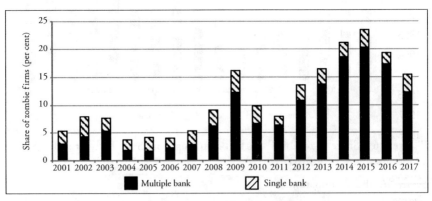

Figure 8.7 Share of zombie firms by banking relationships in 2001–17

Source: Authors' estimation.

Table 8.2 and Figure 8.8 provide the telltale support for our analysis's first step, suggesting a possible lagged association between bank credit growth and the share of zombie firms in the post-2004 credit boom. Table 8.2 calculates the average credit growth for three sub-periods: 1990–99, 2000–09, and 2010–17. The credit growth for the sub-period 2000–09 scores the highest average value with nearly 24 per cent compared to the entire period's (1990–2017) average of 17.4 per cent, the 1990–99 period's average of 15 per cent, and the 2010–17 period's average of 13 per cent, respectively.

Comparing credit growth, the share of zombie firms, and BE in Figure 8.8, we find that a significant spike in the zombie firms is seen in the years after procyclical credit growth in the economy. Moreover, this rise significantly increased since 2010, and we observe that the average for years 2010–17 is as high as 19 per cent compared to 9 per cent from 1990 to 2017.

In 2015, the share of zombie firms reached 28 per cent, the highest for the entire sample period, when credit growth followed a downward slope during that year. This indicates that the credit boom period in the early 2000s might have been responsible for the rise of zombie share in the years following 2010.

Table 8.2 Credit growth in the Indian economy for three sub-periods

Sub-period (1990–99)	Credit growth (per cent)	Sub-period (2000–09)	Credit growth (per cent)	Sub-period (2010–17)	Credit growth (per cent)
1990	18.49	2000	15.35	2010	16.84
1991	12.76	2001	14.40	2011	20.64
1992	6.89	2002	12.49	2012	16.97
1993	15.71	2003	28.44	2013	13.52
1994	3.96	2004	17.48	2014	13.55
1995	26.56	2005	37.25	2015	8.56
1996	20.23	2006	40.51	2016	9.06
1997	13.21	2007	28.22	2017	8.36
1998	14.48	2008	22.40		
1999	12.99	2009	18.01		
Average	**14.53**		**23.46**		**13.44**

Source: Authors' estimation.

To further substantiate our findings, we examine the average share of LTBB by zombie firms for the period 2000–17 in Figure 8.9. We find that the share of LTBB by zombie firms amplified by more than three times during 2010–17 compared to 2000–09, indicating that the zombie firms continued borrowings from banks during the post-2010 period.

Figure 8.10 further corroborates that the average LTBB by zombie firms in the post-2010 period was significantly higher than non-zombie firms. The value for the zombie firms rises more than twice compared to the set of non-zombie and all firms in the sample during this period.

Besides, we also looked at the persistence of zombie firms in our sample. To understand the probability of a zombie firm remaining a zombie, in the long run, we look at three different time windows – one, two, and three consecutive years. In Figure 8.11, we find that zombie firms' persistence to remain a zombie is substantially higher in the post-crisis period, particularly for the one and two years window.

Finally, we examine the hypothesis of a possible relationship between BE and the rise of the zombie firms after 2010. Figure 8.12 presents the BE of all sample firms and the firms that turned zombie after 2010.

The figure shows that, on average, over 45 per cent of total BE during the peak of the credit boom, that is, 2006–07, was captured by the firms that eventually turned zombies in the post-2010 period. Most importantly, these zombie firms

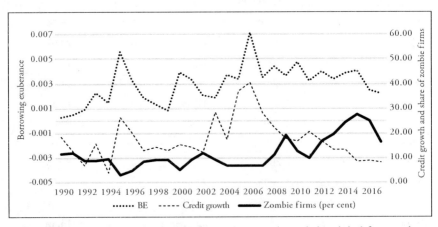

Figure 8.8 Trends in zombie lending, credit growth, and the global financial crisis (GFC) in 1990–2017

Source: Authors' estimation.

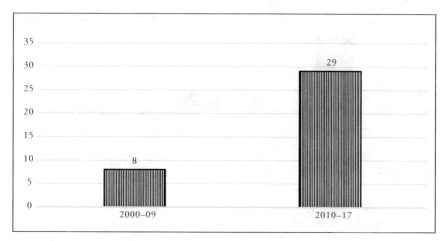

Figure 8.9 Average share of long-term bank borrowings (LTBBs) for zombie firms in 2000–17

Source: Authors' estimation.

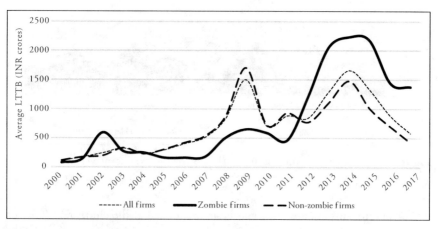

Figure 8.10 Average long-term bank borrowing (LTBB) for zombie and non-zombie firms in 2000–17

Source: Authors' estimation.

continued to attract a large proportion of the excess borrowing even after 2010. In contrast, before the credit boom in 2004, these zombies exhibited minimal aberration concerning BE. Therefore, there seems to exist strong evidence that the excessive flow of credit during the credit boom in early 2000 towards inefficient firms eventually led to the creation of zombie firms, which particularly accentuated after the GFC in 2010.

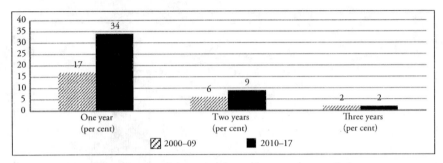

Figure 8.11   The persistence of zombie firms for one, two, and three years in 2000–17

Source: Authors' estimation.

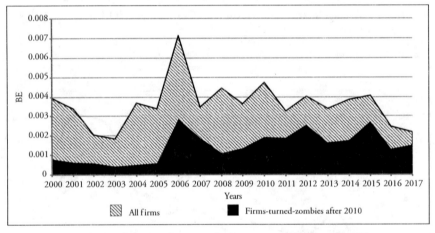

Figure 8.12   Share of zombie firms in the borrowing exuberance (BE)

Source: Authors' estimation.

Further, to substantiate our hypothesis, we looked at the churn rate (CR) of zombie firms following BE. We define CR as a rate at which a firm becomes a zombie following BE. We calculate the churn for all the three following years (CR1, CR2, and CR3) of an incident of BE by a firm. Figure 8.13 presents the CRs for four different time slots: 2000–03, 2004–08, 2009–13, and 2014–17, and it succinctly shows a significant increase in the CR after 2010, mainly the two- and three-year rates.

Further, Figure 8.13 also highlights that despite a steady decline in BE in the post-2010 period, there has been a significant increase in zombie firms, suggesting

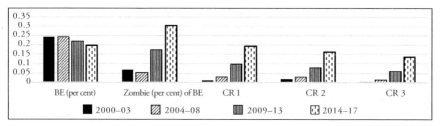

Figure 8.13 Effect of borrowing exuberance (BE) on the evolution of zombie firms in 2000–17

Source: Authors' estimation.

a possibility of evergreening bank loans following an inefficient credit allocation in the Indian economy. We thus find several telltale signs of sub-optimal credit allocation in the Indian economy, elucidating the emergence and evolution of a set of highly leveraged and financially non-viable zombie firms.

Relationship between Zombie Lending and BE

To validate exploratory analyses presented in the earlier section, we finally propose the following multivariate empirical models:

$$Zombie_{it} = \alpha_i + \sum_{j=1}^{J} \beta_j * BE\_dummy_{it-j} + \sum_{k=1}^{K} \gamma_k Z_{it} + \mu_{it} \tag{8.1}$$

$$Zombie_{it} = \alpha_i + \sum_{j=1}^{J} \beta_j * BE\_dummy_{it-j} + \sum_{j=1}^{J}$$

$$\beta_j \left(BE\_dummy_{it-j} * creditboom\_dummy \right) + \sum_{k=1}^{K} \gamma_k Z_{it} + \mu_{it} \tag{8.2}$$

By design, every firm i in our sample receives a bank loan in year t. To model the incidence of zombie lending, we define our dependent variable ($zombie_{it}$) as a binary variable that takes a value of 1 if a firm is classified as a zombie and 0 otherwise. The definition of a zombie firm follows the criteria described in the previous section. Equation 8.1 presents the baseline model with the independent variable as the past incidence of borrowing exuberance (BE_dummy_{it-j}) and firm-specific control variables (Z_{it}). The choice of our empirical model involves a class of limited dependent variable models. Following the literature and capturing the large time-invariant unobservable firm-specific factors, we select a panel logistic regression model estimated with random effects. The choice of random effect over the alternative of a fixed effect variant is primarily governed by the fact that our principal independent variable BE_dummy_{it-j} is also a dichotomous variable that takes the value 1 if the source of misallocation is through borrowing exuberance and 0 otherwise. To address the lagged effect of BE on the possibility of zombie borrowing, we explore several alternative lag structures and report the most parsimonious model using the appropriate selection criterion.[10]

To test our primary hypothesis that the BE by a firm originated mainly during the credit boom of 2004–08 and led to the existence of zombie firms in the future, we augment the baseline model in equation 8.2 by introducing an interaction term between *BE_dummy* and a time dummy (*Creditboom_dummy*) that takes the value of 1 during the 2004–08 and 0 otherwise. A positive significant coefficient on this variable would, therefore, validate our hypothesis. Finally, we introduce a set of control variables into our empirical models based on our exploratory analysis. Specifically, these include size and age of the firm, multiple bank–firm relationships, funding sources (presence of SBI loan), leverage (debt to total assets ratio), and business-group affiliation.

Further, since we observe a significant variation in zombie lending incidence, mainly after 2010, we also include time dummies for each year. Due to data availability, we estimate the model in equations 8.1 and 8.2 for the period 2001–17. Table 8.3 reports the estimation results for the dependent variable based on the two zombie definitions, namely *zombie1* and *zombie2*, respectively. Columns two and four in the table report the baseline model, and column three and five report the augmented model with interaction between BE and credit boom. The positive significant coefficient on the third lag of BE in all the specifications indicates the impact of past BE on the future incidence of zombie borrowing.

Further, the significant positive coefficient on the credit boom dummy suggests that BE originated, particularly during the boom period, contributing more to creating zombie firms in the future. Though not reported in the table due to space constraints, the coefficient of time dummies suggests a surge in the incidence of zombie lending after 2010. Finally, turning to the control variables, we observe that firm-specific attributes attract more zombie lending compared to others. For example, mature firms tend to receive more zombie lending, while this is also true for small firms. Therefore, it seems small and mature firms tend to receive more zombie lending compared to other firms. As defined, the zombie firms are likely to be more leveraged – a positive significant coefficient on leverage corroborates the same. The positive coefficients on the SBI dummy suggest that most of the zombie lendings are associated with SBI that holds the most significant share of India's NPAs.

Further, positive coefficients on the banking relation indicate that zombie lendings are associated with firms with multiple-bank relationships. However, none of these coefficients is statistically significant, suggesting a lack of robust causality. Finally, we observe that firms with business-group affiliation tend to capture a

Table 8.3 Empirical model – the effect of borrowing exuberance (BE) and zombie lending

Variables	Zombie1	Zombie1	Zombie2	Zombie2
BE_dummy (Lag2)	0.41	0.381	0.422	0.394
	(0.941)	(0.856)	(0.941)	(0.858)
BE_dummy (Lag3)	0.886**		0.834*	
	(2.013)		(1.858)	
Creditboom_dummy * BE_dummy (Lag3)		1.449**		1.368**
		2.462		2.243
Firm Age (Lag 1)	0.0219*	0.0224*	0.0126	0.0128
	(1.733)	(1.727)	(0.964)	0.947
Firm Size (Lag 1)	–0.500**	–0.510**	–0.383*	–0.394*
	(–2.359)	(–2.339)	(–1.770)	(–1.756)
Leverage (Lag 1)	11.46***	11.74***	14.38***	14.87***
	(5.747)	(5.695)	(5.486)	(5.33)
SBI dummy	0.144	0.137	0.265	0.251
	(0.279)	(0.261)	(0.508)	(0.468)
Multiple-banks relation dummy	0.924	0.926	0.563	0.567
	(1.369)	(1.343)	(0.832)	(0.813)
Group affiliation fummy	1.140*	1.166*	0.545	0.566
	(1.915)	(1.918)	(0.921)	(0.928)
Year effects	Yes	Yes	Yes	Yes
Constant	–10.47***	–10.45***	–11.37***	–11.5***
	(–4.392)	(–4.317)	(–4.256)	(–4.134)

Note: The table shows the results from estimation of equations 8.1 and 8.2 using panel logistic regression that controls for random effects in the error term. *t*-statistics are reported in parentheses. ***, **, * represent 1, 5, and 10 per-cent significance levels.

significant portion of zombie lending. This may not be a surprising result, given the large Indian business-group firms' notorious reputation to influence the banking sectors through their nexus with the political system and the ability to influence the credit decisions in their favour.

Conclusion

In this chapter, we highlight the existence of zombie firms in the Indian economy and investigate the cause of the rise in zombie firms in the post-2010 era. Using a sample of 7871 firms over the sample period of 1990–2017, we identify zombie firms in our sample using a set of firm-specific characteristics that include ICR, leverage, interest rate, and risk measures such as Altman Z-score or DTD. Our analysis highlights the following observations: first, there has been a significant increase in zombie firms' growth over the sample period 1990–2017, mainly after 2010. Further, the average share of LTBB for the zombie firms increased up to three times following 2010, highlighting that there has been a misallocation of credit towards non-viable firms in the economy. Finally, considering the zombie firms' persistence to remain a zombie for the next three consecutive years, we find that rate is much higher during 2010–17 compared to the pre-2010 period.

Second, we hypothesize that the pro-cyclic credit bubble in the early 2000s, coupled with the economic slowdown following the GFC, led to increased misallocation of credit through zombie lending. Our exploratory analysis shows that nearly 45 per cent of total BE that originated at the firm level during the credit boom period was attributed to firms that turned zombies in the post-2010 period. This is further substantiated because the three consecutive years' CR of a firm increases mainly after 2010, particularly for one and two years.

Third, the empirical model proposed in the study provides robust statistical evidence in favour of our hypothesis that past excessive borrowing, particularly during the early 2000 credit boom period, has significantly contributed to the surge of zombie lending in the post-2010 period.

Therefore, the study suggests that the excessive flow of credit towards inappropriate firms during early 2000 eventually led to the creation of zombie firms, particularly after 2010 as an aftermath of the GFC of 2008. Our findings are also in line with the existing literature, which argues that weak banks tend to roll over loans to non-viable firms to avoid declaring them as NPAs (Storz et al., 2017; Schivardi, Sette, and Tabellini 2017). In India, banks did not have a clear stressed assets resolution framework even as late as 2016. Thus, the absence of a proper legal framework led to a low recovery rate, further escalating into NPAs. Moreover, state-owned banks in India contributing to 70 per cent of NPAs indicate that the substantial involvement of public sectors distorted the markets (Malpass, 2019). Therefore, this chapter, to the best of our knowledge, for the first time systematically explores the rising dominance of zombie firms and examines the role of banks and the importance of the credit boom in the context of the emerging economy of India.

Notes

1 *Business Today*, 'Whistleblower Accuses ICICI Bank of Evergreening Loans: Report', 28 June 2018, https://www.businesstoday.in/industry/banks/story/icici-bank-evergreening-of-loans-defaults-148250-2018-06-28 (accessed on 21 March 2022).

2 See News18, 'RBI's Annual Inspection Report on SBI Reveals Deficiencies across Various Operations', 10 July 2019, https://www.news18.com/news/business/rbis-annual-inspection-report-on-sbi-reveals-deficiencies-across-various-operations-2224633.html (accessed on 21 March 2022); Moneycontrol, 'Evergreening of Loans, Cover-ups and More: Here's What RBI's Annual Inspection Report on SBI Reveals', 9 July 2019, https://www.moneycontrol.com/news/business/evergreening-of-loans-cover-ups-and-more-heres-what-rbis-annual-inspection-report-on-sbi-reveals-4184911.html (accessed on 21 March 2022).

3 See CNBC-TV18, 'Yes Bank, HDIL Accused of Moving Funds to Evergreen Loans in Mack Star, Says Report', 2 August 2019, https://www.cnbctv18.com/finance/yes-bank-hdil-accused-of-moving-funds-to-evergreen-loans-in-mack-star-says-report-4103301.htm (accessed on 21 March 2022).

4 For example, see 'Speech Delivered at National Institute of Bank Management, Pune on Fourteenth Convocation', N. S. Vishwanathan, Deputy Governor, Reserve Bank of India, 18 April 2018, https://www.rbi.org.in/Scripts/BS_SpeechesView.aspx?Id=1055 (accessed on 21 March 2022).

5 Firm-level estimates of DTD are obtained from the Risk Management Intelligence (RMI) database. In addition, computations and details of the empirical model can be accessed at Credit Research Initiative, National University of Singapore, https://nuscri.org.

6 It is important to note that the bank might lend healthy firms at less than the prime rate during the recession. Therefore, to avoid this mistreatment of any firm, which is otherwise healthy, as a zombie based on interest rate criteria, we have added aspects that capture a firm's financial health, such as Z-score, leverage, and ICR.

7 For example, see Tan, Huang, and Woo (2016) and the references therein.

8 Since banking relation data is available only after 2001, we report numbers only for 2001–17.

9 Please refer to Chapter 3 of our report for a detailed description and formulation. The term 'borrowing exuberance' can be considered 'excess borrowing' or 'prodigal borrowing'.

10 AIC stands for Akaike information criterion.

9

Epilogue

Financial Market essentially involves the allocation of resources. They can be thought of as the 'brain' of the entire economic system, the central locus of decision-making: if they fail, not only will the sector's profit be lower than they otherwise have been, but the performance of the entire economic system may be impaired.

—Joseph E. Stiglitz, 1993

In India, like in many emerging economies, banks continue as major financial intermediaries, facilitating the flow of external financing to the growing economy. Even in the post-liberalization period, the banking sector has remained the most prominent financial intermediary, contributing to nearly half of the total flow of funds to the Indian corporate sector.[1] As of November 2020, the Indian banking system consisted of 12 public sector banks (PSBs), 22 private sector banks, 46 foreign banks, and many rural banks. In India, PSB assets accounted for the largest share in the Indian banking market, with an asset base standing at the USD 1.52 trillion. As of January 2021, credit to non-food industries stood at USD 1.44 trillion.

Despite a growing body of literature on the role of banks in easing financial constraints in the economy through capital allocation, little evidence is available on the efficacy of such allocation.[2] Our work critically evaluates the role of the banking sector by investigating the nexus between bank credit and the efficiency of its allocation. Furthermore, by identifying the borrowing exuberance (BE) phenomenon during the credit boom period, we also provide the economic consequences of credit misallocation. In other words, we intend to examine one of the fundamental roles of the banks to efficiently allocate capital by delivering it to the most significant segment of the economy while withdrawing from underperforming ones. The topic gains particular relevance in the context of the recent crisis in the banking sector. Notably, one of the significant challenges faced by banks in recent times is the mounting burden of non-performing assets (NPAs).

There has been a continuous rise in the amount of NPAs over the decades in the Indian economy. The severity of the NPA problem is apparent as the ratio of NPAs to total advances in the economy increased from 2.5 per cent in 2010 to 11.5 per cent in March 2018, thereby eroding the capital base of the banks and drying up the credit availability in the market. The bad loans of Indian banks have amplified by five times from INR 1.43 trillion in 2011–12 to INR 8 trillion in the last few years with the compounded annual growth rate of 33 per cent. From the Reserve Bank of India (RBI) data, we observe that in September 2017, nearly 12.2 per cent of the total loans are stressed (NPA and restructured loans). Comparing with Asian, European, and US peers, the World Bank report shows that India's NPA stood significantly at a high rate of 9 per cent in recent years, against the acceptable bank NPA of 4 per cent (Paul, 2018). By March 2018, the total volume of gross NPAs in the economy shoots slightly above INR 10 lakh crores, of which the PSBs have contributed about 85 per cent. Mounting of NPAs of the PSBs was distinctly visible during 2015 when the PSBs' NPA amount exceeded the combined NPA of private and foreign banks in India. Data from the RBI show that the private sector share in PSBs' NPAs rose from 50.2 per cent in 2010 to 77.6 per cent in 2016, with a slight reduction to 72 per cent in 2017 (Ganatra, 2020).

More recently, the RBI, in its *Financial Stability Report* (July 2020), reports that the gross NPA ratio of Standard Chartered Banks (SCBs) marginally declined to 8.5 per cent in March 2020 as compared to 9.3 per cent in September 2019. However, it comes with a stark warning that in a 'very severe stressed scenario', the gross NPA ratio of the banking sector could rise to as high as 14.7 per cent of total loans by March 2021.[3] The core reasons behind the upsurge of NPA include low recovery rate, disproportionate NPA share levels by PSBs compared to the private banks, the enormous volume of loan disbursement without proper vigilance (Reserve Bank of India, 2019a). Therefore, the NPA crisis is one of the major components contributing to the country's ongoing banking sector crisis, in particular, and economic crisis, in general. It is also interesting to note that the banking sector crisis was preceded by a credit bubble period that has witnessed unprecedented growth, which is the highest in a quarter-century in India. Therefore, the origination of prodigal loans during the credit boom gained much media attention in the past couple of years. However, despite a plethora of anecdotal evidence pointing towards the BE, academic literature is silent about the systematic relationship between the credit bubble's pro-cyclical nature and the misallocation of credit. Using a micro-data of a large number of non-financial corporations from India, we propose a novel measure of bank credit misallocation at the point of disbursement and explore various facets of the current banking crisis. The following section summarizes the main findings of the study.

In Chapter 3, using a novel measure of allocative efficiency, that is, the index of credit allocative efficiency (ICAE), we evaluate the misallocation of credit towards lower Tobin's Q firms compared to firms with higher Q. As a preliminary insight, we observe that the bank's credit misallocation is higher among older and larger firms. In addition, misallocation is relatively higher for firms with a higher leverage ratio and higher ICR. In contrast to the expectation, we observe that firms with lower deficit levels are associated with high misallocation. Further, group affiliated firms have higher misallocation compared to standalone firms. Finally, metals, construction, and chemicals are some of the sectors which contribute to a considerable level of misallocation. Therefore, these initial insights provide the much-needed foundation for further development of empirical models in later chapters.

In Chapter 4, we explore the pro-cyclical nature of bank lending behaviour. Our results demonstrate a pro-cyclical association between the ICAE and credit growth, implying deteriorating efficiency in a bank's credit allocation and lending standards during the credit boom period. Moreover, the misallocation also gets amplified with the BE with banks extending credit towards low-quality firms.

In Chapter 5, while delving into the firm-specific determinants of misallocation, we highlight three main factors: (*a*) creditworthiness, (*b*) the requirement of the external fund, and (*c*) the corporate governance structure of the firm. The empirical findings corroborate that business exuberance is prevalent among large firms with lower ICR, deficit, growth, debt ratio, KZ-index, Z-score, higher tangibility, and business-group affiliation compared to their counterparts. Furthermore, the BE is significant for young firms, firms generating higher internal funds, and firms with multiple banking relationships. Additionally, PSBs, lower insider ownership, and the absence of board governance also embolden BE, resulting in a credit misallocation. On the other hand, higher institutional shareholding by mutual funds and higher promoter ownership are associated with firms with lower misallocation. Therefore, our findings suggest that though bank credit allocation is not directed towards non-creditworthy firms, banks lack judgement in credit allocation, which is carried on disproportionately compared to firms' needs. As a consequence, this plays a significant role in credit misallocation.

Chapter 6 examines the consequence of credit misallocation on firms' performance. Our findings indicate that recipients of misallocated bank credit were poor performers as we report a negative association between the two. However, the impact of misallocation on firm profitability appears only after a two-year lag, which suggests that the accumulation of misallocated credit over a few years leads to a loss in value. Overall, our findings suggest that efficient bank credit allocation plays a crucial role in improving firm performance over time.

In contrast to earlier chapters that deal with credit booms and the efficacy of credit allocation in Chapter 7, we focus on banks' credit reallocation mechanism and test how far lending policies have been optimal following the crisis period. Considering the overall structure, sector-specificity, bank–firm relationship, and risk-management of a firm, our findings remain inconclusive, suggesting that these attributes have not been utilized in the post-crisis period in credit allocation decisions banks. This raises questions about factors that affect lending decision-making in the banking sector. While comparing credit distribution in the pre- and post-crisis periods, we find that in the post-crisis period, credit is reallocated to industries with a low-credit concentration in contrast to the conventional wisdom of reallocation towards sectors with high market power or credit share. Similarly, single-bank–firm relation as an indicator of a bank's strong vigilance and monitoring power was also not considered an essential indicator of reallocation decisions in the post-crisis period. Finally, comparing 2007 and 2009 data, our findings remain ambiguous as to whether a firm's riskiness has consistently received importance and been prudently utilized as a component of the strategic lending decision by banks after the global financial crisis (GFC).

On the one hand, banks have focused on large (size) and mature (age) firms with lower leverage and distance to default but have also provided more credit to firms with low interest coverage ratio (ICR), profitability, and tangibility. Overall, our results show that the Indian banking sector has responded to the crisis sub-optimally by not adopting a strategic lending policy in their credit allocation, which the other economies have considered, particularly in the post-crisis period. These findings are consistent with the perception that the weak banking sector prolongs the crisis by being rigid in its credit allocation, thereby exacerbating the crisis.

Chapter 8 contributes to the ongoing debate on 'evergreening of loans' and 'zombie lending' in the Indian banking sector. Defining the zombie firms following the standard literature, we find that the share of the zombie firms in our sample stands at an average of 13 per cent, which increased to 18 per cent in the sub-period (2010–17). Next, we examine whether 'excess borrowing', which started during the credit boom era, has resulted in more zombie borrowing in the post-2010 period. After controlling for firm-specific attributes like size, age, banking relation, funding source, leverage, and business-group affiliation, we find a positive impact of past 'excess borrowing' on future 'zombie lending'. Our results also highlight that small, matured, more leveraged firms, with more public sector lending and strong business-group affiliation, capture a significant portion of zombie lending. We find that nearly 45 per cent of total 'excess borrowing' firms during the credit-boom period turned to 'zombies' in the post-2010 period. Overall, our findings corroborate that the pro-cyclicality of the Indian banking sector towards credit misallocation by providing excess credit to poor-quality firms during the credit boom period has eventually led to the creation of zombie firms in the post-crisis period in the Indian economy.

Measures to Address the Problem of Stressed Assets or NPAs in India

Since the early 1990s, the RBI has recognized the need to address stressed assets in the Indian banking sector. The institutional framework and prudential norms can be specified as preventive and restorative measures, respectively. Preventive measures primarily included the structural framework to empower banks with information, credit assessment capabilities, and effective corporate governance mechanisms. These measures range from the Narasimham Committee in 1991 that laid out the recommendations to address the NPA problem to the recent implementation of the Indian Banking Code, 2016. Restorative measures are implemented to restructure defaulted assets that will allow banks to clean up their balance sheets. The restorative measures include setting up Debt Recovery Tribunals in 1993 and the initiative of the Resolution Plan (RP), June 2019, which is mandatory for all lenders to apply in case of default. Table 9.1 describes the measures, implementation year, and their objectives since liberalization. Following the sharp rise in NPA among PSBs in recent years, since 2015, restorative measures have continuously evolved to control the NPA bubble in the Indian economy.

Maladies of the Indian Banking Sector

Our research attempts to provide a few insights into the current banking crisis in the Indian economy by decomposing the maladies into three different stages of prognosis: origination of the loan, servicing of loans, and recoveries of bad loans. We conjecture that the substantial proportion of NPA in India is an outcome of a process that starts at the point of disbursement of loan and gets further aggravated during the servicing through evergreening and finally leading to NPA. Therefore, we must understand the current crisis by shifting the focus of our contemporary discourse from an outcome-based measure such as NPA to a more dynamic

Table 9.1 Measures by the Reserve Bank of India (RBI) to address the non-performing asset (NPA) problem in the Indian economy

Measures	Objective and purpose	Year
Preventive measures		
Narasimham Committee	This was responsible for implementing strict prudential norms and improving managerial efficiency and avoiding practices like 'evergreening' or making fresh advances to settle interest dues and avoiding loan classification as NPAs.	1991
Credit Information Bureau	This was set up to support the bank's database with information on various categories of defaulters and facilitating an early warning system that prevents the banks from allocating loans to the defaulters.	2000
Asset reconstruction companies (ARCs)	The RBI registered 14 ARCs specializing in financial institutions that buy NPAs or bad loans from the banks to clean up the bank's balance sheet bypassing the lengthy court procedure. There are now 29 ARCs in total.	2002
Flexible structuring of long-term project loans to infrastructure and core industries	This facility opened up opportunities for periodic refinancing over existing loans for these sectors, supporting the debt repayment process, ensuring long-term viability, and generating cash flows during their production process.	2014
Central Repository of Information on Large Credits (CRILC)	This was set up to collect, store, and disseminate data on credit to the lenders.	2014
The Joint Lender's Forum (JLF) guidelines and a corrective action plan (CAP)	Guidelines are specified for early recognition of the stressed asset for all PSBs with stressed assets to avoid loans to the same individual from different banks. Under this, banks need to identify stressed assets into three subcategories under the special mention account (SMA) before a loan account turns into NPA.	2014
The Mission Indradhanush programme for PSBs by the Ministry of Finance	To revamp and transform the PSBs, seven-fold actions are suggested covering (*a*) appointments, (*b*) the Bank Board Bureau, (*c*) capitalization, (*d*) de-stressing, (*e*) empowerment, (*f*) framework for accountability, and (*g*) governance reform.	2015

(Contd)

(*Contd*)

Measures	Objective and purpose	Year
Preventive measures		
Asset quality review (AQR)	This was implemented for the early identification and classification of the assets before they become stressed.	2015
Insolvency and Bankruptcy Code (IBC)	This Code was enacted to strengthen creditors' rights by seizing defaulter's assets and lowering credit channelization towards insolvent borrowers. The IBC replaced all previously used insolvency systems. In addition, the law promoted credit access and entrepreneurship while resolving the insolvency issue within a stipulated time frame	2016
Restorative measures		
Debt Recovery Tribunals (DRTs)	Settlement of DRTs following the Recovery of Debts and Bankruptcy Act, 1993, was done to expedite the recovery of debts for banks and financial institutions.	1993
RBI one-time settlement Scheme	The RBI issued guidelines for one-time settlement schemes of the NPA cases.	2000
Lok Adalats	Lok Adalats were set up to recover small loans, limited up to five lakhs bypassing the long judiciary process.	2001
Compromise settlement	This comprised specific instructions on the recovery process of NPAs for advances below ten crores excluding the fraud cases and wilful defaulters.	2001
The Securitization and Reconstruction of Financial Assets and Enforcement of Security Interest (SARFAESI) Act	This Act takes action against wilful defaulters without court interference. Tribunals and banks were empowered to acquire and dispose of the secured assets in NPA accounts with one lakh or more outstanding.	2002
Corporate debt restructuring mechanism	This is a scheme enabling the lenders to oust the management of companies whose assets turned into NPAs.	2005
Strategic debt restructuring (SDR)	This is a scheme introduced to enable banks with corporate loans to convert a part of total outstanding and interest into shareholding equity in the borrower company.	2015

(*Contd*)

(*Contd*)

Measures	Objective and purpose	Year
Restorative measures		
Sustainable structuring of the stressed assets (S4A)	This involved identification and division of large stressed assets into debt and equity components to determine a sustainable debt level for the stressed borrower.	2016
Insolvency resolution process for corporate persons (CIRP) regulations	This allows for insolvency proceedings of corporates like private limited or limited company whereby any corporate debtor who commits a default would thereby allow a financial creditor, an operational creditor, or the corporate debtor itself to initiate insolvency resolution process.	2016
Prompt corrective framework (PCA)	This is a framework under which banks with weak financial metrics are put under watch by the RBI.	2017
Public Sector Asset Rehabilitation Agency (PARA)	This dedicated government-run asset reconstruction agency replaces existing ARCs to deal effectively with the bad assets of the PSBs.	2017
Circular on the resolution of stressed assets, RBI	RBI announced a harmonized and simplified generic framework on 12 February 2018 to resolve stressed assets substituting all the existing guidelines. The circular was contested in the Supreme Court and was revised.	2018
Resolution plan (RP)	The February 12 circular was revised and emphasized to initiate a resolution plan (RP) ahead of actual default and made it mandatory for all lenders to apply in case of default.	June 2019

approach by critically examining the process underlying the life cycle of the credit decision and identifying the inefficiencies at different stages of this cycle. The study provides a framework to decompose the inefficiencies at different stages of the credit cycle, thereby allowing the policymakers to develop more precise strategies to address these maladies. A similar, though not exact, dynamics was referred to in the Economic Survey, 2016–17, as a 'twin balance sheet problem' and attributed as a source of bad loans in banks' books. The 'twin balance sheet problem' implies that the deteriorating balance sheet of the corporate sector resulting from the decline in capacity utilization rate and dwindling profits has, in turn, worsened the bank's balance sheet.

Using a novel measure of credit misallocation, we argue that it is possible to identify inefficiencies at the point of credit generation. Such a measure is beneficial to the bankers and stakeholders of the firms as an early warning indicator of the ensuing crisis. Further, our ability to decompose the inefficiency into *borrowing exuberance* and *borrowing constraint* allows policymakers to develop differentiated strategies for each of these groups of firms rather than deploying a blanket approach. Moreover, as revealed by our research, these inefficiencies are pro-cyclical and are highly detrimental to the economy. Therefore, it calls for pro-cyclical surveillance, suggesting that policymakers need to be extra cautious during the expansionary phases of the economy.

It is important to note that NPAs can emerge from two broad factors – internal and external. While the banks and corporates might have little control over these external factors, we note that internal factors involving managerial efficiency in the credit approval system reflect banks' governance. Similarly, the firm's inability to service loans generated through BE shows weak governance at the firm level. Therefore, as a policy recommendation, we focus on the role of two key agencies – the lender (banks) and the borrower (borrowing entity, the corporate sector in this case) – to develop our recommendation to address the problem. While it may be difficult to single out any specific reason underlying the banking crisis, detailing different aspects of the generation of NPA suggests a set of factors that might play an essential role in resolving the crisis.

Governance: The Bank

As measured by our research and reported by many authors, including Raghuram Rajan, ex-governor of the RBI, the substantial inefficiencies generated at the first stage of the credit cycle, particularly during the period of credit growth, are due to the inadequate credit approval framework involving credit assessment, evaluation of credit risk, and the risk management capability of the banks. A large number of firms operating under BE or financial constraints demonstrate that banks fail to evaluate the prospect of the firms or their projects. Further, this reckless behaviour aggravates during the period of strong growth, mainly when the odds of making misjudgements are much higher. Moreover, many of these banks do not have the reliable, independent ability to undertake due diligence on their own. They tend to depend heavily on external agencies such as State Bank of India (SBI) caps or Industrial Development Bank of India (IDBI). The loan consortium has further encouraged herding behaviour, particularly among weak and smaller banks, to follow loan decisions undertaken by prominent players without doing their due diligence. However, to be fair to the managers, it is also important to note that the advent of universal banking in India, notwithstanding its potential benefits, has forced the bankers to make decisions involving technical aspects of the project without having adequate training or technical background leading to inefficient credit allocation. This is corroborated by the other studies based on the primary data (Das and Rawat, 2018):

> The focused discussion with bank executives' reveals that though there are a credit appraisal committee and project approval system in place, they often fail to attain the stated objective due to lack of required technical capabilities of the committee members. It is also found that often technical officers are placed or assigned some other responsibilities. The bank executives felt that there was a need for building up technical capabilities to ensure that the projects are properly appraised. (Das and Rawat, 2018, p. 22)

Therefore, as succinctly pointed out by Raghuram Rajan in his report to the parliamentary committee:

> [R]isk management processes still need substantial improvement in PSBs. Compliance is still not adequate, and cyber risk needs greater attention. Significantly more in-house expertise can be brought to project evaluation, including understanding demand projections for the project's output, likely competition, and the expertise and reliability of the promoter. Bankers will have to develop industry knowledge in key areas since consultants can be biased.[4]

Further, another related challenge with the NPA crisis in India has been the emergence of large willful defaults leading to diversion or misuse of funds other than initially intended by the borrower. Though still small relative to the overall volume of NPAs, as per the Credit Information Bureau (India) Limited (CIBIL) data, in recent years, the size of willful default on bank loans has increased substantially and stood at INR 2,79,191 crores as of 31 December 2017. Out of this, willful default of loans of PSBs stood at INR 2,22,570 crores, which is about 80 per cent of the total willful default. The policymakers need to delineate NPA from a willful default in which loss is due to patently illegal action by either the borrower or the banker. Although it may be hard to differentiate between banker exuberance, incompetence, and corruption, treating these under a similar bracket could entail a much bigger crisis. Policymakers should recognize that managers are supposed to take business risks as part of their duty, and some of these decisions may cause NPA downstream. However, treating all their wrong decisions with suspicions can lead to serious behavioural issues making the banker too risk-averse, refraining from taking any credit decision leading to an artificial under-investment for the economy. Therefore, the appropriate set of policies to address stressed assets should mitigate the exuberance based on little due diligence, particularly during the period of strong growth. The manager should be equipped with technical knowledge coupled with sophisticated predictive underwriting capabilities (either in-house or external) to make well-informed decisions leveraging all the possible information available at the time of approval. Setting up bodies like development financial institutions (DFIs) (particularly for the infrastructure projects) to help the bank to carry out due diligence using their subject-matter skill may go a long way to mitigate the NPA crisis. In this context, banks, particularly the PSBs, should follow the best practices involving credit approvals and underwritings from the booming private sector banks.

We also recognize that the credit policy and resulting loan quality of a bank have a strong association with the board, mirrored in the members' competence and independence. The boardroom dynamics could be complex, particularly for the PSBs, depending on the personalities, political dispensation, and skills of the respective heads, degree of trust among the directors, nature of the institute's strategic role, prevailing market conditions, and many more. As appropriately pointed out by the P. J. Nayak Committee, 2014, the board, particularly for the PSBs, needs to play a more proactive role in defining the business strategy and identifying risk. It is alarming that out of the total number of issues deliberated by the board, a mere 14 per cent pertained to business strategy and risk mitigation in the PSBs (Reserve Bank of India, 2014b). This can only be achieved if there is a significant improvement in the governance structure of the PSBs through an extensive overhaul and by limiting the interference from the government. In this context, an observation made by the P. J. Nayak Committee (Reserve Bank of India, 2014b, recommendation 3.1) is critical:

> [A]s the quality of board deliberation across firms are sensitive to the skills and independence of board members, it is imperative to upgrade the skills in boards of public banks by reconfiguring the entire appointments process for boards. Otherwise, it is unlikely that these boards will be empowered and effective.

Therefore, appointments of the directors and the chief executive officer (CEO) must be delegated to an independent body beyond the influence of the government to bring in the much-needed domain knowledge and professionalism, along with independence, to revamp the quality of the operation. The bank should also utilize outside talent in a limited way into management, particularly for the PSBs due to the severe talent deficit faced by them for various reasons. Finally, the board should be empowered to make independent strategic decisions while being held responsible.

Unfortunately, even at the later stages of the credit life-cycle after the initial loan approval stage, bankers' performance is equally dismal. Banks have failed miserably to perform their much-needed monitoring duties failing to mitigate the risk of the inflated cost of capital equipment through over-invoicing. As we have noted, bankers had further aggravated the crisis of bad decisions during 2004–06 by continuing financing promoters even when the initial project was under considerable stress through evergreening of loans, culminating in a much larger NPA. Ideally, this issue could be mitigated by setting up an effective monitoring mechanism (with a robust system of project monitoring and appraisal by the bank or introducing an appropriate contractual agreement by discouraging fraudulent behaviour). The bank should ideally leverage the massive data of their past transactions to develop an artificial intelligence-based early warning system to flag fraudulent activities by the promoters, including suspicious transactions, reflecting over-invoicing, and related party transactions (RPTs).

Further, a similar system can also be utilized for real-time monitoring of projects in terms of timelines, cost, and credibility of the promoter based on the newsfeeds (for example, web scraping). Often the cost of direct monitoring could be prohibitory, and banks might use innovative contractual agreements to mitigate such risk. As pointed out by Raghuram Rajan:

> Real risks have to be mitigated where possible and shared were not. Real risk mitigation requires ensuring that key permissions for land acquisition and construction are in place upfront, while key inputs and customers are tied up through purchase agreements. Where these risks cannot be mitigated, they should be shared contractually between the promoter and financiers or a transparent arbitration system agreed upon. So, for instance, if demand falls below projections, perhaps an agreement among promoters and financiers can indicate when new equity will be brought in and by whom.

Further, he argued:

> [A]n appropriately flexible capital structure should be in place. The capital structure has to be related to the residual risks of the project. The more the risks, the more the equity component should be (genuine promoter equity, not borrowed equity, of course), and the greater the flexibility in the debt structure. Promoters should be incentivized to deliver, with significant rewards for on-time execution and debt repayment. Where possible, corporate debt markets, either through direct issues or securitized project loan portfolios, should be used to absorb some of the initial project risks.

Finally, the bankers need to do an excellent job of recovering when the project fails. The heart of this process is the asset quality review (AQR), which should identify the bad loans and force banks to revive stalled projects without delays.

Once identified, bankers should speedily resolve the restructuring process either through out-of-court settlement process without being prosecuted or, in a worse case, through the new Bankruptcy Code. While commenting on the efficacy of the Bankruptcy Code, Raghuram Rajan noted:[5]

> The Bankruptcy Code is being tested by the large promoters, with continuous and sometimes frivolous appeals. The integrity of the process must be maintained, and bankruptcy resolution is speedy, without the promoter inserting a bid by an associate at the auction and acquiring the firm at a bargain-basement price. Given our conditions, the promoter should have every chance of concluding a deal before the firm goes to auction, but not after. Higher courts must resist the temptation to intervene routinely in these cases, and appeals must be limited once points of law are settled.
>
> That said, the judicial process is simply not equipped to handle every NPA through a bankruptcy process. Banks and promoters have to strike deals outside of bankruptcy, or if promoters prove uncooperative, bankers should have the ability to proceed without them.
>
> Bankruptcy Court should be a final threat, and much loan renegotiation should be done under the shadow of the Bankruptcy Court, not in it.

Governance: The Corporates

One of the pictures that emerge from the recent trends in the NPA crisis in the Indian banking sector is the strategic default by large corporations. One of the causes of strategic default is the economic slowdown[6] when the decline in economic activity causes the non-repayment of loans by corporations. Another cause is the exploitation of the financing system and especially the lack of effective loan monitoring and recovery system. It is well documented in the corporate governance literature that shareholders may expropriate wealth from bondholders by undertaking risky new projects that will allow them to reap most of the gains, whereas bondholders bear most of the cost (Klock, Mansi, and Maxwell, 2005). While a large body of empirical research links shareholder–bondholder conflict in widely held corporations, which are common in developed countries, such conflict becomes critical in corporations where ownership is concentrated in the hands of controlling shareholders.

The ownership structure of Indian corporates is concentrated in the hands of promoters who are members of the founding family and their relatives. Such concentration of control in the hands of insiders is associated with the expropriation of corporate resources by controlling owners allowing them to extract private benefits of control in various forms. Hence, disciplining the dominant promoters is at the heart of the corporate governance problem in India (Varma, 1998).

A significant proportion of the bad loans or written-off loans in the Indian banking sector are money lent to willful defaulters or promoters who can pay back to banks but would not do so willingly. According to the All India Bank Employees Association (AIBEA), as of September 2019, 17 PSBs have a total of INR 1.5 lakh crores aggregated as willful defaults contributed by a total of 2,426 loan accounts. Most of these cases include promoter entrenchment as these are accounts where borrowers are not willing to pay despite having the repayment capacity.

As per Raguram Rajan's speech on 'saving credit' in November 2014:[7]

> ... the flow of credit relies on the sanctity of the debt contract. In much of the globe, when a large borrower defaults, he is contrite and desperate to show that the lender should continue to trust him with the management of the enterprise. In India, too many large borrowers insist on their divine right to stay in control despite their unwillingness to put in new money.

He further adds that the sanctity of the debt contract has been 'continuously eroded in India in recent years, not by the small borrower but by the large borrower'.

Further, until recent times (that is, before 2017), to avoid unprofitable restructuring, coupled with an inability to force additional equity from unwilling promoters, the evergreening of loans became a natural choice for the PSBs, which allow the promoters to avoid default by paying only the interest and save banks from bringing bad loans onto the books.

On the issue of lack of incentives of promoters and bankers towards the stalling projects, it was pointed out by Raghuram Rajan that promoters had no interest in adding more equity:[8]

> Writing down the debt was then simply a gift to promoters, and no banker wanted to take the risk of doing so and inviting the attention of the investigative agencies. Stalled projects continued as 'zombie' projects, neither dead nor alive.

Further, he argues that inefficient restructuring and debt recovery systems allowed promoters to have more power, and they could hold on to their equity in both good times and in bad times.

Specifically:

> The inefficient loan recovery system gave promoters tremendous power over lenders. Not only could they play one lender off against another by

threatening to divert payments to the favoured bank, but they could also refuse to pay unless the lender brought in more money, especially if the lender feared the loan becoming an NPA. Sometimes promoters offered low one-time settlements (OTS) knowing that the system would allow the banks to collect even secured loans only after years.

Additionally, the lack of effective bankruptcy code for a long time and erstwhile Board for Industrial and Financial Reconstruction (BIFR) allowed promoters to regain control through proxy bidding at a much lower price.

However, the situation has improved since 2017, as the RBI constituted an internal advisory committee to determine cases to be referred under the Insolvency and Bankruptcy Code (IBC), a platform for the time-bound recovery of bad loans. According to the recent Cooperative for Assistance and Relief Everywhere (CARE) report, a total of 4,139 cases were admitted into the corporate insolvency resolution process (CIRP) at the end of December 2020, of which 41 per cent of the cases continue to remain in the resolution process and 27 per cent end in liquidation (with over two-thirds of these cases in BIFR). Around 22 per cent of cases have been closed on appeal or reviewed or settled, while another 9 per cent of the cases have been withdrawn under Section 12A. Only 8 per cent of the total cases have received approval of resolution plans. Compared to the low rate of recovery of 26 per cent in the pre-IBC period, the overall recovery rate, to date, in India has improved to 39.8 per cent. Finally, of the total claims which were settled via liquidation with an admitted claim amount of INR 4,95,970 crores till the end of 2020, the realizable value was only INR 1,97,364 crores (around 39 per cent of the admitted claim amount).[9]

In the context of the famous 12 big corporate defaults, where the RBI had initiated resolution proceedings, nine companies have been approved, while liquidation orders were issued against two companies. As summarized in Table 9.2, these 12 companies had outstanding claims of INR 3.45 lakh crores compared to a liquidation value of INR 73,220 crores. By the end of 2020, on average, the realization and valuation against liquidation stand at 49 per cent and 204 per cent, respectively.

Therefore, despite the delays, limited recovery, and litigations it caused, the IBC seems to have partially fulfilled its objective of facilitating the process of creative destruction by reallocating resources from unviable and failed companies to a more productive usage in order to foster growth. However, it remains to be seen how the IBC becomes more effective over a period of time in terms of both recovery rate and time to resolution.

Finally, even though the corporate governance regulations evolving since 2001 have focused on transparency in corporate disclosure and adopting independent boards, disciplining the entrenched promoters has been a challenge due to a lack of enforcement mechanisms. Besides, most of the board governance is adopted from the developed countries and lacks meaningful implementation against the dominance of promoters. While the new Companies Act, 2013, and the Securities and Exchange Board of India (SEBI) have instituted necessary corporate disclosure and board governance regulations, it still lacks a strong mechanism to enforce external corporate governance. These external mechanisms primarily include the market for corporate control and empowering lenders to monitor the management of the borrowing firm. While the Takeover Act of 1997 is a move towards developing an external market for corporate control, provisions like creeping acquisitions allow promoters to gain control without a tender offer. Such opportunities subsequently allow promoters to concentrate their shareholdings and thwart the potential takeover threat of debt-ridden companies.

Under the Companies Act, 2013, the appointment of a nominee director is made under Section 161(3):

Table 9.2 Summary of 12 large corporate default accounts

Corporate debtor	Amount admitted	Amount realized	Realization as % of claims	Realization as % of liquidation value	Resolution applicant
Electrosteel Steel	13,175	5,320	40	183	Vedanta Ltd
Bhushan Steel Ltd	56,022	35,571	64	253	Bamnipal Steel Ltd (Tata Steel)
Monnet Ispat and Energy Ltd	11,015	2,892	26	123	JSW and Aion
Essar Steel India	49,473	41,018	83	267	Arcelor Mittal
Alok Industries Ltd	29,523	5,052	17	115	Reliance Ltd, JM ARC

(*Contd*)

(Contd)

Corporate debtor	Amount admitted	Amount realized	Realization as % of claims	Realization as % of liquidation value	Resolution applicant
Jaypee Infratech Ltd	23,176	23,223	100	131	NBCC (India) Ltd
Jyoti Structures Ltd	7,365	3,691	50	387	Sharad Sanghi Group
Bhushan Power and Steel Ltd	47,158	19,350	41	209	JSW Steel Ltd
Amtek Auto Ltd	12,641	2,615	21	170	Deccan Value Investors LP and DVI PE Ltd
Era Infra Eng Ltd	Under CIRP				
Lanco Infratech Ltd	Liquidation				
ABG Shipyard Ltd	Liquidation				

Source: Cooperative for Assistance and Relief Everywhere (CARE)–Insolvency and Bankruptcy Code (IBC) update, 10 April 2021, banking, financial services, and insurance (BFSI) research.

> (3) Subject to the articles of a company, the board may appoint any person as a director nominated by any institution in pursuance of the provisions of any law for the time being in force or of any agreement or by the Central Government or the State Government by virtue of its shareholding in a Government company.

Notably, there are several ambiguities regarding the appointment of the nominee directors by the financial institutions. While one of the ambiguities of using such an appointment by the companies to fill out independent directors' positions is recently clarified in the Companies Act, 2013, the role and responsibilities of these directors are still unclear. For example, the voting power of a nominee director in matters of the lending company is restricted. This defies the very principle of appointment of a nominee director, which is to protect the lending institution's interest.

Given the objective of the corporate governance code in India as being a stakeholder approach (SEBI, 1998), the presence of nominee directors, if empowered by law to exercise their fiduciary duty, could be a step towards the effective board protecting the interest of stakeholders. This would be significant, particularly in the case of firms with higher promoter-controlled boards. At present, the appointment of nominee director is through substantial shareholding by the nominating institution or under special situations such as a clause in the loan agreement. Even though nominee directors are appointed to protect the interest of the nominating institution, their role extends beyond carrying out the fiduciary duty of the company board, and therefore, such appointments create a conflict of interest. If such conflicting scenarios are addressed in the law *a priori*, the responsibilities of the board will not be compromised.

Finally, among the factors in ensuring effective board governance, 'board diversity' has been recognized widely. Diversity is typically achieved by having a good mix of executive, non-executive, independent, women directors. In addition, the appointment of nominee directors could also add to the diversity of corporate boards, provided these directors bring in unique knowledge and experience from the finance and banking sector.

Summary of Policy Recommendations

Our research highlights that the major contribution towards NPAs starts at an early stage of the life-cycle of loans, particularly at the point of selection of the project. Therefore, in contrast to the conventional reactive approach of NPA management, we emphasize the proactive approach to identify the source of NPAs by drawing the following recommendations.

1. As argued in our research, misallocation of bank credit happens due to inadequate assessment of project quality at the beginning of the allocation. To address this critical aspect of credit allocation, banks need to significantly revamp their existing project-assessment process ensuring scrupulous, rigorous, and efficient assessment of loans at the point of disbursement. Among other things, we recommend two approaches to complement and increase the efficiency of the existing credit allocation process. First is by incorporating subject matter experts (SMEs), sourced externally or internally, and empowering them to oversee the project assessment and approval. Second, banks

should leverage advanced analytical tools using artificial intelligence and machine learning algorithms to augment the project assessment.

2. The skills of the existing loan-approving staff should be upgraded regularly by providing adequate training in modern tools to analyse the information. This will further ensure the retention of specialized talent and their improved judgement to evaluate the loan applications.

3. It is often argued that banks, particularly the small and weaker banks, tend to herd towards the lead bank in the consortia. Such behaviour results in correlated lending decisions without adequate due diligence by the banks. This should be monitored and discouraged using an effective corporate governance mechanism at the bank level.

4. While it is observed that the universal banking system has several advantages, there is an issue of an asset–liability mismatch for banks undertaking projects with significantly long gestation periods, such as the ones in infrastructure, energy, and real estate. To avoid such a mismatch, the government should establish specialized institutions such as DFIs to fund longer-term projects.

5. As identified in our research, a large proportion of misallocated funds are sustained through zombie financing due to evergreening practices at the bank level. While regulatory concerns are raised to curb such tendencies, we recommend setting up an early warning system to capture evergreening incidences.

6. As argued in our research, bank monitoring can be an effective mechanism to curb the misallocation of credit. However, our research does not find any significant effect of bank monitoring in India, particularly for nominee directors. Therefore, we recommend strengthening the corporate governance practices by banks, specifically involving nominee directors' roles.

7. Although our research does not investigate the role of RPTs, we argue that RPTs can be a potential source of bank credit misallocation. Firms, where related parties have limited access to bank credit lines, can engage in practices like tunnelling for outright misuse and expropriation of bank credit. Therefore, the existing risk management process should be further strengthened by incorporating the disclosure requirements and evaluation of RPTs of the borrowing firms.

While we emphasize the aforementioned recommendations that are proactive in nature, it is noteworthy that several reactive measures are instituted in the country to manage the NPAs. Among these measures, the IBC was set up in 2016 to expedite the recovery and restructuring of stressed assets. However, as discussed earlier, while the IBC facilitated faster recovery than other regulations of the Debt Recovery Tribunals (DRTs) and the Securitization and Reconstruction of Financial Assets and Enforcement of Security Interest (SARFAESI) Act, the resolution of bad debts remained limited even for substantial debt portfolios. Also, most of the debt claims ended in liquidation with a significant loss of economic value. Therefore, the major challenge in the IBC has been the imperfect realization of debt claims. Further, many asset reconstruction companies (ARCs) have been established to buy bad loans from commercial banks. However, in 2016–17, ARCs recovered only about 5 per cent of total NPAs (Government of India, 2016–17). Despite having the expertise to manage the NPAs, there are two problems with the existing ARC model. First, most of these ARCs are privately run and lack sufficient capital to buy large amounts of bad loans from banks. Second, banks find it difficult to accept the low prices offered by ARCs and do not actively participate in the restructuring.

Most recently, the Union Budget of 2021–22 proposed setting up a bad bank system with an ARC, asset management company (AMC), and alternative investment funds (AIF) as part of the same entity. The bad bank model is proposed to overcome the limitations of the existing IBC–ARC model by addressing both the speed of recovery and stressed assets' pricing. It is important to note that as the proposed bad bank is the related party to the bank, strengthening banks' corporate governance becomes a critical aspect of the efficacy of the reform process.

The corporate governance code for banks should specify disclosure and the framework of monitoring, approve RPTs, and ensure the independence of the bad bank board and appointment of bad bank management. We also recommend developing a framework for bad banks' corporate governance, disclosure of information, and transparency of transactions between bad bank and parent bank.

Finally, it is important to note, all the measures suggested cannot fructify unless the more profound structural flaws involving the government's overarching control of the banking sector through PSBs and the average size of the Indian banks are addressed at the fundamental level. As of March 2019, the bad loans of Indian banks amounted to more than INR 9 lakh crores, of which the PSB itself contributed 81 per cent. Despite several waves of free-market reforms, the government continues to maintain excessive control over PSBs. While, on average, state banks control 32 per cent of all banking assets in the emerging nation, India holds a striking share of 75 per cent. However, the landscape of the Indian banking sector has changed over the last few years, with PSBs steadily losing market share to private sector banks. As per the RBI's report *Trends and Progress of Banking in India*, 2018–19, from a high of 74 per cent in 2010, PSBs' share of banking assets has steadily declined to 61 per cent in 2019, which is still significantly higher than the average number of emerging markets. Many committees in the past and other experts have constantly argued for lesser government intervention in the banking sector as it distorts credit allocation. In fact, the second Narasimham Committee of 1998 suggested more than three decades ago that a government should dilute its stake in PSBs to 33 per cent. The recent P. J. Nayak Committee reflects the same suggestion of lesser government and more governance in PSBs. However, as noted by Y. V Reddy, 'the dominant role of banks in financial intermediation in emerging economies and particularly in India, will continue in the medium-term; and the banks will continue to be "special" for a long time'.

Further, another structural challenge with the banking sector is the average size of the Indian bank. It is widely acknowledged that large banks can support higher credit growth while maintaining a strong balance sheet and better lending practices by driving synergies using their scales.[10] According to the Banker Database (2020):

> … out of the top 1000 banks globally, over 200 are located in the USA, just above 100 in Japan, over 80 in Germany, over 40 in Spain and around 40 in the UK. Even China has as many as 16 banks within the top 1000, out of which as many as 14 are in the top 500. India, on the other hand, had 20 banks within the top 1000, out of which only 6 were within the top 500 banks. This is perhaps reflective of differences in the size of economies and of the financial sectors. (Banker Database, 2020)

More recent data show SBI, the largest bank of India with assets of USD 0.6 trillion, is the only Indian bank in the top 50 banks globally with an asset size of about a sixth of the world's largest bank, the Industrial and Commercial Bank of China.

This structural challenge was highlighted three decades ago by the Narasimham Committee report, 1991, recommending that India needs to have three large banks with a global presence and ten banks with a national presence. Therefore, the recent bank consolidation is a definite move towards creating banks of a global scale. The latest round of bank consolidation has brought down the total PSBs to 12, intending to create larger, stronger banks with enhanced capacity for credit. It is further noted in the Banker Database (2020):

> Asia-Pacific countries by Tier 1 capital, 2000–19, by rank, shows China and Japan swapping places, with China going top and Japan falling to second, after the global financial crisis. The other significant move is that

of India from the ninth position in 2000 to either fourth or fifth position since 2009, reflecting how this huge emerging market is beginning to develop a banking sector worthy of its economic size and influence. (Banker Database, 2020)

Conclusion

Using a large sample analysis, our research provides empirical evidence on the existence of bank credit misallocation at the point of disbursement. The main contribution of the study is to develop a novel measure of misallocation, which allows us to identify the source of NPA and analyse the consequences of such misallocation during the life-cycle of the credit. Nevertheless, the study has some notable limitations, primarily due to the lack of availability of appropriate data. We note that although the results presented in the study are consistent with the current narrative of the misallocation of bank credit leading to unsustainable levels of NPA in India, the findings are primarily correlational. Therefore, any future study establishing the causalities more firmly will add significant value to the extant literature. While revealing this complex nature of misallocation using the disaggregated borrower-level information is of significant interest, the availability of information on loan contracts and the loan's purpose is hard to come by in India due to its confidentiality. Such data can provide an opportunity to identify the exact nature of misallocation and identify the possibility of evergreening of loans far more robustly.

There are a few natural extensions of this study for future research. For example, one interesting area of research could be to understand the nexus between bank credit misallocation and inefficient RPTs undertaken by the firms.

To conclude, as Winston Churchill was working to form the United Nations after the Second World War, he famously said, 'Never let a good crisis go to waste'. Therefore, Churchill's insight that there is an opportunity to learn in the heart of any crisis motivates us to explore various aspects of the current banking crisis, and the study is an attempt in that direction. Based on our findings, we recommend that the government utilizes the natural opportunity provided by the current crisis for aggressive banking reforms. The reforms should focus on the following aspects. First, the government's stake in the banking sector should be reduced. Second, ailing PSBs should be effectively merged to create large, technically advanced, efficient, and healthy banks with strong balance sheets. Third, by improving the efficacies of IBC, constructive destruction using a faster resolution of the bad loans can be facilitated. Finally, well-governed private banks should be encouraged to participate in capital formation to foster economic growth in the country.

Notes

1   This is as of March 2018.

2   The existing literature widely recognizes the role of bank credit in influencing corporate strategy and performance through several facets that include monitoring by banks (Grossman and Hart, 1982; Diamond, 1984; Stiglitz and Weiss, 1983), screening of creditworthy firms (Diamond 1989, 1991), and reduction of information costs incurred by firms (Fama, 1985; Yosha, 1995). Further, the empirical literature also finds evidence on banks' uniqueness as financial intermediaries allow countries with a well-developed banking system to grow faster than underdeveloped ones (Bernanke and Gertler, 1990; Levine and Zervos, 1998; Claessens and Laeven, 2005).

3   Very recently, the RBI's *Financial Stability Report* released in July 2021 indicates that the gross NPA ratio of SCBs in March 2021 stood at 7.48 per cent, which may further increase up to 9.80 per cent by March 2022 under the baseline scenario and to 11.2 per cent under a severe stress scenario.

4   The excerpts are quoted from the note prepared by Professor Raghuram G. Rajan on 6 September 2018, at the request of Dr Murli Manohar Joshi, MP and Chairman of the Parliament Estimates Committee. The note can be downloaded from *Hindu Business Line*, 'Note to Parliamentary Estimates Committee on Bank NPAs', https://www.thehindubusinessline.com/money-and-banking/article24924543.ece/binary/Raghuram%20Rajan%20Parliamentary%20note%20on%20NPAs (accessed in January 2021).

5   *Economic Times*, 'Big Promoters Using IBC to File Frivolous Appeals: Raghuram Rajan', 12 September 2018, https://economictimes.indiatimes.com/industry/banking/finance/banking/big-promoters-using-ibc-to-file-frivolous-appeals-raghuram-rajan/articleshow/65776796.cms?from=mdr (accessed in January 2021).

6   See Guiso, Sapienza, and Zingales (2013) and the references therein.

7   'Saving Credit', talk by Dr Raghuram G. Rajan, Governor, RBI at the Third Dr Verghese Kurian Memorial Lecture at IRMA, Anand on 25 November 2014, https://m.rbi.org.in/scripts/BS_SpeechesView.aspx?Id=929 (accessed in January 2021).

8   The excerpts are quoted from the note prepared by Professor Raghuram G. Rajan on 6 September 2018, at the request of Dr Murli Manohar Joshi, MP and Chairman of the Parliament Estimates Committee. The note can be downloaded from *Hindu Business Line*, 'Note to Parliamentary Estimates Committee on Bank NPAs', https://www.thehindubusinessline.com/money-and-banking/article24924543.ece/binary/Raghuram%20Rajan%20Parliamentary%20note%20on%20NPAs (accessed in January 2021).

9   CARE, 'IBC Update: Cases admitted in Q3FY21 at 20 per cent of cases admitted in Q3FY20', 10 April 2021, BFSI Research.

10 At a country level, China's banks made USD 321 billion in 2017, which is 10 per cent up on 2016 and represents nearly 29 per cent of global profits. On the other

hand, India's banks lost USD 9 billion, accounting for 79 per cent of total top 1000 losses. Moreover, China's banks grew their tier 1 capital by 20 per cent, or USD 336 billion, in 2017. This is just slightly more than the tier 1 capital of Industrial and Commercial Bank of China (ICBC), which is both China's and the world's largest bank and which, in turn, grew its capital by USD 43 billion, the equivalent of adding a Standard Chartered or a Union Bank of Switzerland (UBS) (Banker Database, 2020).

Bibliography

Abiad, A., D. Leigh, and A. Mody (2007). 'International Finance and Income Convergence: Europe is Different'. IMF Working Paper, 1–36, International Monetary Fund, Washington, DC.

Abaid, A., N. Oomes, and K. Ueda (2008). 'The Quality Effect: Does Financial Liberalization Improve the Allocation of Capital?' *Journal of Development Economics* 87(2): 270–82.

Acharya, V. V. (2017). 'The Unfinished Agenda: Restoring Public Sector Bank Health in India', 7 September, R. K. Talwar Memorial Lecture, Indian Institute of Banking and Finance, Mumbai.

Acharya, V., H. Iftekhar, and A. Saunders (2006). 'Should Banks Be Diversified? Evidence from Individual Bank Loan Portfolios'. *Journal of Business* 79(3): 1355–1412.

Acharya, V., and R. Rajan (2020). 'Indian Banks: A Time to Reform?' Downloaded from https://faculty.chicagobooth.edu/-/media/faculty/raghuram-rajan/research/papers/paper-on-banking-sector-reforms-rr-va-final.pdf. Accessed on 8 March 2021.

Acharya, V., and S. Ryan (2016). 'Banks' Financial Reporting and Financial System Stability'. *Journal of Accounting Research* 54(2): 277–340.

Adams, R. B., and D. Ferreira (2007). 'A Theory of Friendly Boards'. *Journal of Finance* 62(1): 217–50.

Adrian, T., and H. S. Shin (2010). 'The Changing Nature of Financial Intermediation and the Financial Crisis of 2007–2009'. *Annual Review of Economics* 2(1): 603–18.

Agarwal, R., and J. A. Elston (2001). 'Bank–Firm Relationships, Financing and Firm Performance in Germany'. *Economics Letters* 72(2): 225–32.

Ahearne, A. G., and N. Shinada (2005). 'Zombie Firms and Economic Stagnation in Japan'. *International Economics and Economic Policy* 2(4): 363–81.

Aikman, D., A. G. Haldane, and B. D. Nelson (2015). 'Curbing the Credit Cycle'. *Economic Journal* 125(585): 1072–1109.

Albertazzi, U., and D. Marchetti (2010). 'Lending Supply and Unnatural Selection: An Analysis of Bank–Firm Relationships in Italy after Lehman'. Working Paper Series No. 756, Bank of Italy, Rome.

Almeida, H., and M. Campello (2007). 'Financial Constraints, Asset Tangibility, and Corporate Investment'. *Review of Financial Studies* 20(5): 1429–60.

Alonso, P. D. A., F. J. L. Iturriaga, J. A. R. Sanz, and E. V. González (2005). 'Determinants of Bank Debt in a Continental Financial System: Evidence from Spanish Companies'. *Financial Review* 40(3): 305–33.

Andrews, D., and F. Petroulakis (2019). 'Breaking the Shackles: Zombie Firms, Weak Banks and Depressed Restructuring in Europe'. ECB Working Paper No. 2240, European Central Bank, Frankfurt.

Ang, J. B. (2008). 'What Are the Mechanisms Linking Financial Development and Economic Growth In Malaysia?' *Economic Modelling* 25(1): 38–53.

Antoniades, A. (2014). 'Liquidity Risk and the Credit Crunch of 2007–2008: Evidence from Micro-level Data on Mortgage Loan Applications'. BIS Working Paper No. 473, Bank for International Settlements, Basel.

Arellano, M., and O. Bover (1995). 'Another Look at the Instrumental Variable Estimation of Error-components Models'. *Journal of Econometrics* 68(1): 29–51.

Arellano, M., and S. Bond (1991). 'Some Tests of Specification for Panel Data: Monte Carlo Evidence and an Application to Employment Equations'. *Review of Economic Studies* 58(2): 277–97.

Arena, M., and B. Julio (2015). 'The Effects of Securities Class Action Litigation on Corporate Liquidity and Investment Policy'. *Journal of Financial and Quantitative Analysis* 50(1–2): 251–75.

Arpa, M., I. Giulini, A. Ittner, and F. Pauer (2001). 'The Influence of Macroeconomic Developments on Austrian Banks: Implications for Banking Supervision'. In 'Marrying the Macro- and Micro-prudential Dimensions of Financial Stability', vol. 1 (BIS Papers), edited by Bank for International Settlements, 91–116. Bank for International Settlements, Basel.

Asimakopoulos, I., and P. P. Athanasoglou (2013). 'Revisiting the Merger and Acquisition Performance of European Banks'. *International Review of Financial Analysis* 29(C): 237–49.

Athanasogloua, P., B. I. Daniilidis, and M. Delis (2014). 'Bank Procyclicality and Output: Issues and Policies'. *Journal of Economics and Business* 72 (March–April): 58–83.

Ayyagari, M., T. Beck, and A. Demirgüç-Kunt (2007). 'Small and Medium Enterprises across the Globe'. *Small Business Economics* 29(4): 415–34.

Baboucek, I., and M. Jancar (2005). 'Effects of Macroeconomic Shocks to the Quality of the Aggregate Loan Portfolio'. Czech National Bank Working Papers 2005/01, Czech National Bank, Prague.

Bandiera, O. G. (2000). 'Does Financial Reform Raise or Reduce Saving?' *Review of Economics and Statistics* 82(2): 239–63.

Banerjee, A. (1997). 'A Theory of Misgovernance'. *Quarterly Journal of Economics* 112(4): 1289–1332.

Banerjee, A., and E. Duflo (2005). 'Growth Theory through the Lens of Development'. In *The Handbook of Economic Growth*, vol. 1(A), edited by P. Aghion and S. Durlauf, 473–552. North Holland: Elsevier.

——— (2014). 'Do Firms Want to Borrow More? Testing Credit Constraints Using a Directed Lending Program'. *Review of Economic Studies* 81(2): 572–607.

Banerjee, R., and B. Hofmann (2018). 'The Rise of Zombie Firms: Causes and Consequences'. *BIS Quarterly Review* (September). https://www.bis.org/publ/qtrpdf/r_qt1809g.pdf. Accessed in January 2021.

Banker Database (2020). 'Explore the Database'. https://www.thebankerdatabase.com/index.cfm/rankings/. Accessed in January 2021.

Barth, M., R. Kasznik, and M. McNichols (2001). 'Analyst Coverage and Intangible Assets'. *Journal of Accounting Research* 39(1): 1–34.

Bawa, J., V. Goyal, S. Mitra, and S. Basu (2019). 'An Analysis of NPAs of Indian Banks: Using a Comprehensive Framework of 31 Financial Ratios'. *Indian Institute of Management Bangalore (IIMB) Management Review* 31(1): 51–62.

Beck, T., A. S. L. I. Demirgüç-Kunt, L. Laeven, and R. Levine (2008). 'Finance, Firm Size, and Growth'. *Journal of Money Credit and Banking* 40(7): 1379–1405.

Beck, T., A. Demirgüç-Kunt, and R. Levine (2006). 'Bank Concentration, Competition, and Crises: First Results'. *Journal of Banking and Finance* 30(5): 1581–1603.

Beck, T., O. Jonghe, and K. Mulier (2017). Bank Sectoral Concentration and (Systemic) Risk: Evidence from a Worldwide Sample of Banks. CEPR Discussion Papers, No. 12009, Centre for Economic Policy Research, London.

Beck, T., R. Levine, and N. Loayza (2000). 'Finance and the Sources of Growth'. *Journal of Financial Economics* 58(1–2): 261–300.

Benjamin, D., and F. Meza (2009). 'Total Factor Productivity and Labor Reallocation: The Case of the Korean 1997 Crisis'. *BE Journal of Macroeconomics* 9(1): 1–41.

Benkovskis, K. (2015). 'Misallocation of Resources in Latvia: Did Anything Change after the Crisis?' Working Paper 5/2015, Bank of Latvia, Riga.

Berger, A. N., and G. F. Udell (1995). 'Universal Banking and the Future of Small Business Lending'. Center for Financial Institutions Working Papers 95-17, Wharton School Center for Financial Institutions, University of Pennsylvania, Philadelphia.

——— (2002). 'Small Business Credit Availability and Relationship Lending: The Importance of Bank Organisational Structure'. *Economic Journal* 112(477): F32–F53.

——— (2004). 'The Institutional Memory Hypothesis and the Procyclicality of Bank Lending Behavior'. *Journal of Financial Intermediation* 13(4): 458–95.

Berger, A. N., L. F. Klapper, M. S. M. Peria, and R. Zaidi (2008). 'Bank Ownership Type and Banking Relationships'. *Journal of Financial Intermediation* 17(1): 37–62.

Berglöf, E., and E. Perotti (1994). 'The Governance Structure of the Japanese Financial Keiretsu'. *Journal of Financial Economics* 36(2): 259–84.

Bernanke, B. S., and M. Gertler (1990). 'Financial Fragility and Economic Performance'. *Quarterly Journal of Economics* 105(1): 87–114.

——— (1995). 'Inside the Black Box: The Credit Channel of Monetary Policy Transmission'. *Journal of Economic Perspectives* 9(4): 27–48.

Bertrand, M., P. Mehta, and S. Mullainathan (2002). 'Ferreting Out Tunneling: An Application to Indian Business Groups'. *Quarterly Journal of Economics* 117(1): 121–48.

Bhaduri, S. (2000). 'Liberalisation and Firms' Choice of Financial Structure in an Emerging Economy: The Indian Corporate Sector'. *Development Policy Review* 18(4): 413–34.

Bhaduri, S. N., and A. Kumar (2014). 'Allocation of Capital in the Post-liberalized Regime: A Case Study of the Indian Corporate Sector'. *Development Studies Research: An Open Access Journal* 1(1): 137–47.

Bhaduri, S., and G. K. Basudeb (2000). 'A Hallmark of India's New Economic Policy: Deregulation and Liberalization of the Financial Sector'. *Journal of Asian Economics* 11(3): 333–46.

Bhaduri, S., and A. Bhattacharya (2018). 'Financial Liberalization and Allocation of Capital: Dark Side of the Moon'. *Journal of Quantitative Economics* 16(1): 163–85.

Bhargava, A., and J. D. Sargan (1983). 'Estimating Dynamic Random Effects Models from Panel Data Covering Short Time Periods'. *Econometrica: Journal of the Econometric Society* 51(6): 1635–59.

Bhattacharyya, S., and A. Saxena (2009). 'Does the Firm Size Matter? An Empirical Enquiry into the Performance of Indian Manufacturing Firms'. *PES (People's Education Society) Business Review* 4(2): 87–98.

Bikker, J., and P. Metze (2005). 'Bank Provisioning Behaviour and Procyclicality'. *Journal of International Financial Markets, Institutions and Money* 15 (2): 141–57.

BIS (2010). *80th Annual Report*. BIS Annual Economic Report, 28 June, Bank for International Settlements, Basel.

——— (2018). 'Structural Changes in Banking after the Crisis'. BIS Working Paper, CGFS Papers, No. 60, Bank for International Settlements, Basel.

Bleck, A., and X. Liu (2017). 'Credit Expansion and Credit Misallocation'. *Journal of Monetary Economics* 94(C): 27–40.

Blundell, R., and S. Bond (1998). 'Initial Conditions and Moment Restrictions in Dynamic Panel Data Models'. *Journal of Econometrics* 87(1): 115–43.

Bofondi, M., and T. Ropele (2011). 'Macroeconomic Determinants of Bad Loans: Evidence from Italian Banks'. Occasional Papers, Economic Research and International Relations (89), Bank of Italy, Rome.

Bongini, P., G. Ferri, and H. Hahm (2000). 'Corporate Bankruptcy in Korea: Only the Strong Survive?' *Financial Review* 35(4): 31–50.

Boot, A. W., A. V. Thakor, and G. F. Udell (1991). 'Equilibrium Analysis, Policy Implications'. *Economic Journal* 101(406): 458–72.

Booth, L., V. Aivazian, A. Demirgüç-Kunt, and V. Maksimovic (2001). 'Capital Structures in Developing Countries'. *Journal of Finance* 56(1): 87–130.

Borensztein, E., and J. W. Lee (2005). Financial Reform and the Efficiency of Credit Allocation in Korea'. *Journal of Policy Reform* 8(1): 55–68.

Borio, C. (2018). 'A Blind Spot in Today's Macroeconomics'. Panel remarks at the BIS–IMF–OECD Joint Conference on 'Weak Productivity: The Role of Financial

Factors and Policies', Paris, 10–11 January 2018. https://www.bis.org/speeches/sp180110.pdf. Accessed in January 2021.

Borio, C., P. Disyatat, and M. Juselius (2014). 'A Parsimonious Approach to Incorporating Economic Information in Measures of Potential Output'. BIS Working Paper No. 442, Bank for International Settlements, Basel.

Borio, C., C. Furfine, and P. Lowe (2001). 'Procyclicality of the Financial System and Financial Stability: Issues and Policy Options'. BIS Papers, No. 1 (March), Bank for International Settlements, Basel, 1–57.

Bouvatier, V., A. López-Villavicencio, and V. Mignon (2012). 'Does the Banking Sector Structure Matter for Credit Procyclicality?' *Economic Modelling* 29(4): 1035–44.

Breuer, J. (2006). 'Problem Bank Loans, Conflicts of Interest, and Institutions'. *Journal of Financial Stability* 2(3): 266–85.

Caballero, R. J., and M. L. Hammour (2001). 'Creative Destruction and Development: Institutions, Crises, and Restructuring'. NBER Working Paper No. 7849, National Bureau of Economic Research, Cambridge, MA, 213–41.

Caballero, R. J., T. Hoshi, and A. K. Kashyap (2008). 'Zombie Lending and Depressed Restructuring in Japan'. *American Economic Review* 98(5): 1943–77.

Cantú, C., S. Claessens, and L. Gambacorta (2019). 'How Do Bank-specific Characteristics Affect Lending? New Evidence Based on Credit Registry Data from Latin America'. BIS Working Paper No. 798, Bank for International Settlements, Basel.

Caporale, G. M., S. D. Colli, and J. S. Lopez (2014). 'Bank Lending Procyclicality and Credit Quality During Financial Crises'. *Economic Modelling* 43 (December): 142–57.

Caporale, G., J. Hunter, and F. Ali (2014). On the Linkages Between Stock Prices and Exchange Rates: Evidence from the Banking Crisis of 2007–2010;. *International Review of Financial Analysis* 33 (May): 87–103.

Care Ratings (2018). 'Report on NPAs of Banks', 15 May 2018. https://www.careratings.com/uploads/newsfiles/NPA%20Update%20March%202018.pdf. Accessed on 8 March 2021.

———— (2021). 'Analysis of Movement in Stressed Advances', 13 February 2021. https://www.careratings.com/uploads/newsfiles/13022021110239_Analysis_of_Movement_in_Stressed_Advances.pdf. Accessed on 8 March 2021.

Carlin, W., and C. Mayer (2003). 'Finance, Investment, and Growth'. *Journal of Financial Economics* 69(1), 191–226.

Carvalho, D. (2014). 'The Real Effects of Government-Owned Banks: Evidence from an Emerging Market'. *Journal of Finance* 69(2): 577–609.

Chadha, A., and R. Oriani (2010). 'R and D Market Value under Weak Intellectual Property Rights Protection: The Case of India'. *Scientometrics* 82(1): 59–74.

Chan, S. G., E. Koha, F. Zainir, and C. C. Yong (2015). 'Market Structure, Institutional Framework and Bank Efficiency in ASEAN 5'. *Journal of Economics and Business* 82 (November–December): 84–112.

Chandrasekhar, C. P., and P. Pal (2006). 'Financial Liberalisation in India: An Assessment of Its Nature and Outcomes'. *Economic and Political Weekly*: 975–88.

Chari, A., and P. Henry (2002). 'Capital Account Liberalization: Allocative Efficiency or Animal Spirits?' NBER Working Paper No. w8908, National Bureau of Economic Research, Cambridge, MA.

Chavaa, S., and A. Purnanandam (2011). 'The Effect of Banking Crisis on Bank-dependent Borrowers'. *Journal of Financial Economics* 99(1): 116–35.

Chavan, P., and L. Gambacorta (2019). 'Bank Lending and Loan Quality: An Emerging Economy Perspective'. *Empirical Economics* 57(1): 1–29.

Chen, C. M., M. Ariff, T. Hassan, and S. Mohamad (2014). 'Does a Firm's Political Connection to Government Have Economic Value?' *Journal of the Asia Pacific Economy* 19(1): 1–24.

Chen, X., M. Skully, and B. Kym (2005). 'Banking Efficiency in China: Application of DEA to Pre- and Post-deregulation Eras: 1993–2000'. *China Economic Review* 16(3): 229–45.

Cho, Y. (1988). 'The Effect of Financial Liberalization on the Efficiency of Credit Allocation: Some Evidence for Korea'. *Journal of Development Economics* 29(1): 101–10.

Chou, H.-C. (2005). 'Expected Default Probability, Credit Spreads and Distance-from-Default'. *Journal of American Academy of Business* 7(1): 144–52.

Claessens, S., and L. Laeven (2005). 'Financial Dependence, Banking Sector Competition, and Economic Growth'. *Journal of the European Economic Association* 3(1): 179–207.

Clement, P. (2010). 'The Term "Macroprudential": Origins and Evolution'. *BIS Quarterly Review* (March). https://www.bis.org/publ/qtrpdf/r_qt1003h.pdf. Accessed in January 2021.

Cole, R., and R. Turk (2007). 'Legal Origin, Creditor Protection and Bank Lending: Evidence from Emerging Markets'. MPRA Paper 4713, University Library of Munich, Germany.

Cole, S. (2009). 'Fixing Market Failures or Fixing Elections? Agricultural Credit in India'. *American Economic Journal: Applied Economics* 1(1): 219–50.

Cong, L. W., H. Gao, J. Ponticelli, and X. Yang (2019). 'Credit Allocation under Economic Stimulus: Evidence from China'. *Review of Financial Studies* 32(9): 3412–60.

Coricelli, G., M. Joffily, C. Montmarquette, and M. C. Villeval (2010). 'Cheating, Emotions, and Rationality: An Experiment on Tax Evasion'. *Experimental Economics* 13(2): 226–47.

Cucinelli, D. (2015). 'The Impact of Non-performing Loans on Bank Lending Behavior: Evidence from the Italian Banking Sector'. *Eurasian Journal of Business and Economics* 8(16): 59–71.

Cull, R., W. Li, B. Sun, and L. C. Xu (2015). 'Government Connections and Financial Constraints: Evidence from a Large Representative Sample of Chinese Firms'. *Journal of Corporate Finance* 32 (June): 271–94.

Das, S. K., and P. S. Rawat (2018). 'Dimensions of NPAs in Indian Schedules Commercial Banks'. ISID Working Paper No. 200, Institute for Studies in Industrial Development, New Delhi.

Dass, N., and M. Massa (2011). 'The Impact of a Strong Bank–Firm Relationship on the Borrowing Firm'. *Review of Financial Studies* 24(4): 1204–60.

De Bock, R., and A. Demyanets (2012). 'Bank Asset Quality in Emerging Markets: Determinants and Spillovers'. IMF Working Paper WP/12/71, International Monetary Fund, Washington, DC.

Degryse, H., and S. Ongena (2007). 'The Impact of Competition on Bank Orientation'. *Journal of Financial Intermediation* 16(3): 399–424.

Degryse, H., O. Havrylchyk, E. M. Jurzyk, and S. Kozak (2009). 'Foreign Bank Entry and Credit Allocation in Emerging Markets'. EBC Discussion Paper No. 23, European Banking Center, Tilburg University, Nethlerlands.

Degryse, H., M. Kim, and S. Ongena (2009). *Microeconometrics of Banking Methods, Applications, and Results.* Oxford University Press.

Demirgüç-Kunt, A., and E. Detragiache (1998). 'The Determinants of Banking Crises in Developing and Developed Countries'. *Staff Papers* 45(1): 81–109.

Demirgüç-Kunt, A., M. Soledad, M. Periab, and T. Tresselc (2020). 'The Global Financial Crisis and the Capital Structure of Firms: Was the Impact More Severe among SMEs and Non-listed Firms?' *Journal of Corporate Finance* 60 (February). https://doi.org/10.1016/j.jcorpfin.2019.101514.

Demirgüç-Kunt, A., and V. Maksimovic (1998). 'Law, Finance, and Firm Growth'. *Journal of Finance* 53(6): 2107–37.

Denis, D. J., and V. T. Mihov (2003). 'The Choice among Bank Debt, Non-Bank Private Debt, and Public Debt: Evidence from New Corporate Borrowings'. *Journal of Financial Economics* 70(1): 3–28.

Devereux, M. B., and G. W. Smith (1994). 'International Risk Sharing and Economic Growth'. *International Economic Review* 35(3): 535–51.

Dewatripont, M., and E. Maskin (1995). 'Credit and Efficiency in Centralized and Decentralized Economies'. *Review of Economic Studies* 62(4): 541–55.

Dewatripont, M., and J. Tirole (1994). *The Prudential Regulation of Banks*, vol. 6. Cambridge, MA: MIT Press.

DeYoung, R., A. Gron, G. Torna, and A. Winton (2015). 'Risk Overhang and Loan Portfolio Decisions: Small Business Loan Supply before and during the Financial Crisis'. *Journal of Finance* 70(6): 2451–88.

Di Mauro, F., F. Hassan, and G. I. Ottaviano (2018). 'Financial Markets and the Allocation of Capital: The Role of Productivity'. CEP Discussion Paper No 1555, July, London School of Economics.

Diamond, D. W. (1984). 'Financial Intermediation and Delegated Monitoring'. *Review of Economic Studies* 51(3), 393–414.

——— (1991). 'Monitoring and Reputation: The Choice between Bank Loans and Directly Placed Debt'. *Journal of Political Economy* 99(4): 689–721.

Diamond, D. W. (1989). 'Reputation Acquisition in Debt Markets'. *Journal of Political Economy* 97(4): 828–63.

———. (1991). 'Monitoring and Reputation: The Choice between Bank Loans and Directly Placed Debt'. *Journal of Political Economy* 99(4): 689–721.

Dias, D. A., C. R. Marques, and C. Richmond (2016). 'Misallocation and Productivity in the Lead Up to the Eurozone Crisis. *Journal of Macroeconomics* 49: 6–70.

Dickey, D. and W. A. Fuller (1979). 'Distribution of the Estimators for Autoregressive Time Series with a Unit Root'. *Journal of the American Statistical Association* 74 (366): 427–31.

Dinç, I. S. (2005). 'Politicians and Banks: Political Influences on Government-owned Banks in Emerging Markets'. *Journal of Financial Economics* 77(2): 453–79.

Ding, D., and G. Ge (2005). 'Market Orientation, Competitive Strategy and Firm Performance: An Empirical Study of Chinese Firms'. *Journal of Global Marketing* 18(3–4): 115–42.

Dong, F., and Z. Xu (2020). 'Cycles of Credit Expansion and Misallocation: The Good, the Bad and the Ugly'. *Journal of Economic Theory* 186. https://doi.org/10.1016/j.jet.2020.104994.

Easterwood, J. C., and P. R. Kadapakkam (1991). 'The Role of Private and Public Debt in Corporate Capital Structures'. *Financial Management* 20(3): 49–57.

Ekpu, V. (2011). 'Small Business Lending by Large and Small Banks: A Survey of the Literature'. Presensted at the Scottish Graduate Programme in Economics (SGPE), PhD Annual Conference, Crieff, Scotland.

Fairfield, P., J. Whisenant, and T. Yohn (2003). 'Accrued Earnings and Growth: Implications for Future Profitability and Market Mispricing'. *Accounting Review* 78(1): 353–71.

Fama, E. F. (1980). 'Banking in the Theory of Finance'. *Journal of Monetary Economics* 6(1): 39–57.

———. (1985). 'What's Different about Banks?' *Journal of Monetary Economics* 15(1): 29–40.

Fazzari, S., R. G. Hubbard, and B. Petersen (1988). 'Investment, Financing Decisions, and Tax Policy'. *American Economic Review* 78(2): 200–05.

Felipe, J., and G. Estrada (2020). 'What Happened to the World's Potential Growth after the 2008–2009 Global Financial Crisis?' *Journal of the Japanese and International Economies* 56(C).

Ferreira, M. A., and P. Matos (2012). 'Universal Banks and Corporate Control: Evidence from The Global Syndicated Loan Market'. *Review of Financial Studies* 25(9): 2703–44.

Festic, M., A. Kavkler, and S. Repina (2011). 'The Macroeconomic Sources of Systemic Risk in the Banking Sectors of Five New EU Member States'. *Journal of Banking and Finance* 35(2): 310–22.

Filosa, R. (2007). 'Stress Testing of the Stability of the Italian Banking System: A VAR Approach'. Heterogeneity and Monetary Policy 0703, Dipartimento di Economia Politica, Universita di Modena e Reggio Emilia, Modena and Reggio Emilia.

Firth, M., C. Lin, P. Liu, and S. M. Wong (2009). 'Inside the Black Box: Bank Credit Allocation in China's Private Sector'. *Journal of Banking and Finance* 33(6): 1144–55.

Franco, G., O. K. Hope, and H. Lu (2017). 'Managerial Ability and Bank-Loan Pricing'. *Journal of Business Finance and Accounting* 44(9–10): 1315–37.

Galindo, A., A. Micco, G. Ordoñez, A. Bris, and A. Repetto (2002). 'Financial Liberalization: Does It Pay to Join the Party?' *Economia* 3(1): 231–61.

Galindo, A., F. Schiantarelli, and A. Weiss (2007). 'Does Financial Liberalization Improve the Allocation of Investment? Micro-evidence from Developing Countries'. *Journal of Development Economics* 83(2): 562–87.

Gambacorta, L., and H. S. Shin (2016). 'Why Bank Capital Matters for Monetary Policy'. *Journal of Financial Intermediation* 35(B): 17–29.

Gambera, M. (2000). 'Simple Forecasts of Bank Loan Quality in the Business Cycle'. Emerging Issues Series S&R-2000-3, Supervision and Regulation Department, Federal Reserve Bank of Chicago.

Ganatra, R. (2020). 'Indian Banks' High NPAs and Abysmally Low Recovery: Revamp or Perish'. *Business World*, 5 June.

Gangopadhyay, S., and R. Lensink (2001). 'Corporate Ownership as a Means to Solve Adverse Selection Problems in a Model of Asymmetric Information and Credit Rationing'. SOM Research Institute, Economics, Econometrics and Finance, University of Groningen, Netherlands.

Gangopadhyay, S., R. Lensink, and R. van der Molen (2001). 'Business Groups, Financing Constraints, and Investment: The Case of India'. *Journal of Development Studies* 40(2): 93–119.

Gatti, R., and I. Love (2008). 'Does Access to Credit Improve Productivity? Evidence from Bulgaria'. *Economics of Transition and Institutional Change* 16(3): 445–65.

Gavin, M., and R. Hausmann (1996). 'The Roots of Banking Crises: The Macroeconomic Context'. Research Department Publications, Research Department (4026), Inter-American Development Bank, Washington, DC.

Germain, L., N. Galy, and W. Lee (2014). 'Corporate Governance Reform in Malaysia: Board Size, Independence and Monitoring'. *Journal of Economics and Business* 75(C): 126–62.

Ghatak, M., and R. Kali (2001). 'Financially Interlinked Business Groups'. *Journal of Economics and Management Strategy* 10(4): 591–619.

Ghosh, J., and C. Chandrasekhar (2009). 'Costs of "Coupling": The Global Crisis and the Indian Economy'. *Cambridge Journal of Economics* 33(4): 725–39.

Ghosh, S. (2007). 'Bank Monitoring, Managerial Ownership and Tobin's Q: An Empirical Analysis for India'. *Managerial and Decision Economics* 28(2): 129–43.

Ghosh, S., and D. M. Nachane (2003). 'Are Basel Capital Standards Pro-cyclical? Some Empirical Evidence from India'. *Economic and Political Weekly* 38(8): 777–84.

Ghosh, S., D. M. Nachane, A. Narain, and S. Sahoo (2003). 'Capital Requirements And Bank Behaviour: An Empirical Analysis of Indian Public Sector Banks'. *Journal of International Development* 15(2): 145–56.

Giannetti, M. (2003). 'Do Better Institutions Mitigate Agency Problems? Evidence from Corporate Finance Choices'. *Journal of Financial and Quantitative Analysis* 38(1): 185–212.

Giannetti, M., and S. Ongena (2009). 'Financial Integration and Firm Performance: Evidence from Foreign Bank Entry in Emerging Markets'. *Review of Finance* 13(2): 181–223.

Giannetti, M., and A. Simonov (2013). 'On the Real Effects of Bank Bailouts: Micro Evidence from Japan'. *American Economic Journal: Macroeconomics* 5(1): 135–67.

Gilchrist, S., J. W. Sim, and E. Zakrajšek (2013). 'Misallocation and Financial Market Frictions: Some Direct Evidence from the Dispersion in Borrowing Costs'. *Review of Economic Dynamics* 16(1): 159–76.

Goldsmith, R.W. (1969). *Financial Structure and Development*. New Haven, CT: Yale University Press.

Gopinath, G., Ş. Kalemli-Özcan, L. Karabarbounis, and C. Villegas-Sanchez (2017). 'Capital Allocation and Productivity in South Europe'. *Quarterly Journal of Economics* 132(4): 1915–67.

Gormley, T. (2010). 'The Impact of Foreign Bank Entry in Emerging Markets: Evidence from India'. *Journal of Financial Intermediation* 19(1): 26–51.

Gorton, G., and A. Winton (2002). 'Bank Liquidity Provision and Capital Regulation in Transition Economics'. In *Designing Financial Systems in Transition Economies: Strategies for Reform in Central and Eastern Europe*, edited by A. Meyendorff and A. V. Thakor. Cambridge, MA: MIT Press.

Gourinchas, P. O., R. Valdes, and O. Landerretche (2001). 'Lending Booms: Latin America and the World'. *Economía Journal: The Latin American and Caribbean Economic Association (LACEA)* 0 (Spring 20): 47–100.

Government of India (2008). *India: Annual Survey of Industries, 2008–09*. New Delhi: Central Statistics Office (Industrial Statistics Wing), Ministry of Statistics and Programme Implementation.

——— (2017). *Economic Survey 2016–17*, vols. 1–2. New Delhi: Ministry of Finance, Department of Economic Affairs, Economic Division.

——— (2020). *Economic Survey 2019–20*, vols. 1–2. New Delhi: Ministry of Finance, Department of Economic Affairs, Economic Division.

Greenwald, B., and J. Stiglitz (1986). 'Externalities in Economies with Imperfect Information and Incomplete Markets'. *Quarterly Journal of Economics* 101(2): 229–64.

Grossman, S., and O. Hart (1982). 'Corporate Financial Structure and Managerial Incentives'. In John J. McCall, *Economics of Information and Uncertainty*, 107–40. Cambridge, MA: National Bureau of Economic Research.

Guha-Khasnobis, B., and S. N. Bhaduri (2000). 'A Hallmark of India's New Economic Policy: Deregulation and Liberalization of the Financial Sector'. *Journal of Asian Economics* 11(3): 333–46.

Guiso, L., P. Sapienza, and L. Zingales (2013). 'The Determinants of Attitudes Toward Strategic Default on Mortgages'. *Journal of Finance* 68(4): 1473–1515.

Guo, L., and R. W. Masulis (2015). 'Board Structure and Monitoring: New Evidence from CEO Turnovers'. *Review of Financial Studies* 28(10): 2770–2811.

Gup, B. E. (1998). *Bank Failures in the Major Trading Countries of the World: Causes and Remedies*. Westport, CT: Greenwood Publishing Group.

Gurley, J. G., and E. S. Shaw (1955). 'Financial Aspects of Economic Development'. *American Economic Review* 45(4): 515–38.

Guttentag, J., and R. Herring (1986). 'Disaster Myopia in International Banking'. Essays in International Finance No. 164 (September), Department of Economics, Princeton University, New Jersey.

Haasbroek, M., and J. C. Gottwald (2017). 'The Impact of the Global Financial Crisis on China's Banking Sector'. *Copenhagen Journal of Asian Studies* 35(1): 5–30.

Hadlock, C. J., and J. R. Pierce (2010). 'New Evidence on Measuring Financial Constraints: Moving Beyond the KZ Index'. *Review of Financial Studies* 23(5): 1909–40.

Hardy, D., and C. Pazarbaşioğlu (1999). 'Determinants and Leading Indicators of Banking Crises: Further Evidence'. *IMF Staff Papers* 46(3): 247–58.

Harris, J. R., F. Schiantarelli, and M. G. Siregar (1994). 'The Effect of Financial Liberalization on the Capital Structure and Investment Decisions of Indonesian Manufacturing Establishments'. *World Bank Economic Review* 8(1): 17–47.

Harris, M., and A. Raviv (1991). 'The Theory of Capital Structure'. *Journal of Finance* 46(1): 297–355.

Hart, O., A. Shleifer, and R. Vishny (1997). 'The Proper Scope of Government: Theory and and Application to Prisons'. *Quarterly Journal of Economics* 112(4): 1126–61.

Hellwig, M. (1991). 'Banking, Financial Intermediation and Corporate Finance'. In *European Financial Integration*, edited by A. Giovannini and C, pp. 35–63. Cambridge: Cambridge University Press.

Hicks, John R. (1969). *A Theory of Economic History*. Oxford: Oxford University Press.

Hodrick, R., and E. Prescott (1981). 'Post-war U.S. Business Cycles: An Empirical Investigation'. Discussion Papers 451, Center for Mathematical Studies in Economics and Management Science, Northwestern University, Evanston.

Hodrick, R., and E. Prescott (1997). 'Postwar U.S. Business Cycles: An Empirical Investigation'. *Journal of Money, Credit and Banking* 29(1): 1–16.

Hoggarth, G., A. Logan, and L. Zicchino (2005). 'Macro Stress Tests of UK Banks'. BIS Papers. In 'Investigating the Relationship between the Financial and Real Economy', vol. 22, edited by Bank for International Settlements, 392–408. Bank for International Settlements, Basel.

Hooks, L. M. (2003). 'The Impact of Firm Size on Bank Debt Use'. *Review of Financial Economics* 12(2): 173–89.

Hopenhayn, H. A. (2011). 'Firm Microstructure and Aggregate Productivity'. *Journal of Money, Credit and Banking* 43: 111–45.

Hoshi, T., A. Kashyap, and D. Scharfstein (1990). 'Bank Monitoring and Investment: Evidence from the Changing Structure of Japanese Corporate Banking Relationships'. In *Asymmetric Information, Corporate Finance, and Investment*, edited by R. G. Hubbard, 105–26. Chicago: University of Chicago Press.

Hovakimian, G. (2011). 'Financial Constraints and Investment Efficiency: Internal Capital Allocation across the Business Cycle'. *Journal of Financial Intermediation* 20(2): 264–83.

Hsieh, C. T., and P. J. Klenow (2009). Misallocation and manufacturing TFP in China and India. *Quarterly Journal of Economics* 124(4): 1403–48.

Hubbard, R. (1998). 'Capital-Market Imperfections and Investment'. *Journal of Economic Literature* 36(1): 193–225.

Hume, M., and A. Sentance (2009). 'The Global Credit Boom: Challenges for Macroeconomics and Policy'. *Journal of International Money and Finance* 28(8): 1426–61.

Illueca, M., N. Lars, and G. Udell (2012). 'Do Changes in the Timeliness of Loan Loss Recognition Affect Bank Risk Taking?' *SSRN Electronic Journal.* https://dx.doi.org/10.2139/ssrn.2022644.

Illueca, M., L. Norden, and G. F. Udell (2014). 'Liberalization and Risk-Taking: Evidence from Government-Controlled Banks'. *Review of Finance* 18(4): 1217–57.

International Labour Organization (2011). 'A Review of Global Fiscal Stimulus'. EC-IILS Joint Discussion Paper Series No. 5, Geneva.

Imai, K. (2016). 'A Panel Study of Zombie Smes In Japan: Identification, Borrowing and Investment Behavior'. *Journal of the Japanese and International Economies* 39(C): 91–107.

Iyer, R., S. Lopes, J. L. Peydro, and A. Schoar (2013). 'Interbank Liquidity Crunch and the Firm Credit Crunch: Evidence from the 2007–2009 Crisis'. *Review of Financial Studies* 27(1): 347–72.

Jahn, N., C. Memmel, and A. Pfingsten (2016). 'Banks' Specialization versus Diversification in the Loan Portfolio'. *Schmalenbach Business Review* 17(1–3): 25–48.

James, C. (1987). 'Some Evidence on the Uniqueness of Bank Loans'. *Journal of Financial Economics* 19(2), 217–35.

Jaramillo, F., F. Schiantarelli, and A. Weiss (1992). 'The Effect of Financial Liberalization on the Allocation of Credit: Evidence from a Panel of Ecuadorian Firms'. Working Paper 1092, World Bank, Washington, DC.

Jayaratne, J., and P. Strahan (1996). 'The Finance–Growth Nexus: Evidence from Bank Branch Deregulation'. *Quarterly Journal of Economics* 111(3): 639–70.

Jensen, M. C. (1986). 'Agency Costs of Free Cash Flow, Corporate Finance, and Takeovers'. *American Economic Review* 76(2): 323–29.

Jhingan, S., and N. Yadav (2018). 'India: Ever-Greening of Loans and Bad Debts: RBI's Stand and Its Implications'. Mondaq, 5 Novemeber. https://www.mondaq.com/india/financial-restructuring/751730/ever-greening-of-loans-and-bad-debts--rbi39s-stand-and-its-implications. Accessed on 21 March 2022.

Jimenez, G., V. Salas, and J. Saurina (2006). 'Determinants of Collateral'. *Journal of Financial Economics* 81(2): 255–81.

John, K., and S. Kedia (2000). 'Design of Corporate Governance: Role of Ownership Structure, Takeovers, Bank Debt and Large Shareholder Monitoring'. Working Paper FIN-00-048, Stern School of Business, New York University, 1–54.

Jonghe, O., H. Dewachter, K. Mulier, S. Ongena, and G. Schepens (2020). 'Some Borrowers Are More Equal than Others: Bank Funding Shocks and Credit Reallocation'. *Review of Finance* 24(1): 1–43.

Justiniano, A., G. E. Primiceri, and A. Tambalotti (2014). 'The Effects of the Saving and Banking Glut on the US Economy'. *Journal of International Economics* 92: S52–S67.

Kaat, D. M. (2016). 'International Capital Flows and the Allocation of Credit across Firms'. Annual Conference 2016 (Augsburg): Demographic Change, German Economic Association, Berlin.

Kane, E. J. (1977). 'Good Intentions and Unintended Evil: The Case against Selective Credit Allocation'. *Journal of Money, Credit and Banking* 9(1): 55–69.

Kaplan, S. N., and L. Zingales (1997). 'Do Investment-Cash flow Sensitivities Provide Useful Measures of Financing Constraints?' *Quarterly Journal of Economics* 112(1): 169–215.

Kato, T. (2009). 'Impact of the Global Financial Crisis and Its Implications for the East Asian Economy'. International Monetary Fund, Korea International Financial Association, First International Conference, Washington, DC.

Kawai, M., and S. Takagi (2009). 'Why Was Japan Hit So Hard by the Global Financial Crisis?' ADBI Working Paper Series, No. 153, Asian Development Bank Institute, Tokyo.

Keeton, W. R. (1999). 'Does Faster Loan Growth Lead to Higher Loan Losses?' Economic Review 84(Q2), pp. 57–75, Federal Reserve Bank of Kansas City.

Keeton, W., and C. Morris (1987). 'Why Do Banks' Loan Losses Differ?' *Economic Review* 72 (May): 3–21.

Ketkar, K., and S. Ketkar (1992). 'Bank Nationalization, Financial Savings, and Economic Development: A Case Study of India'. *Journal of Developing Areas* 27(1): 69–84.

Keynes, J. M. (1936). 'The Supply of Gold'. *Economic Journal* 46(183): 412–18.

Khwaja, A., and A. Mian (2005). 'Do Lenders Favor Politically Connected Firms? Rent Provision in an Emerging Financial Market'. *Quarterly Journal of Economics* 120(4): 1371–1411.

King, R. G., and R. Levine (1993). 'Finance, Entrepreneurship and Growth: Theory and Evidence'. *Journal of Monetary Economics* 32(3): 513–42.

Kiyotaki, N., and J. Moore (1997). 'Credit Cycles'. *Journal of Political Economy* 105(2): 211–48.

Kliestika, T., M. Misankova, and K. Kocisova (2015). 'Calculation of Distance to Default. *Procedia Economics and Finance* 23: 238–43.

Klock, M. S., S. A. Mansi, and W. F. Maxwell (2005). 'Does Corporate Governance Matter to Bondholders?' *Journal of Financial and Quantitative Analysis* 40(4): 693–719.

Koeda, J., and M. E. Dabla-Norris (2008). 'Informality and Bank Credit: Evidence from Firm-level Data'. IMF Working Paper No. 08 (94), International Monetary Fund, Washington, DC.

Kozak, S. (2016). 'Do Low Interest Rates Mean Low Earnings for Banks?' *Oeconomia* 15(1): 41–49.

Kulkarni, N., and A. Mukherjee (2017). 'Misallocation Due to Inefficient Exits: Evidence from India'. CAFRAL Working Paper, Research Department, Reserve Bank of India, Mumbai.

Kumar, N. (2020). 'Political Interference and Crowding Out in Bank Lending'. *Journal of Financial Intermediation* 43 (July): 100815.

Kumar, R., G. D. Krishna, and S. Bhardwaj (2016). 'Indradhanush: Banking Sector Reforms'. Working Paper (25 January), Centre For Policy Research, New Delhi.

Kwiatkowski, D. P. (1992). 'Testing the Null Hypothesis of Stationarity against the Alternative of a Unit Root: How Sure Are We that Economic Time Series Have a Unit Root'. *Journal of Econometrics* 54(1–3): 159–78.

Kwon, H. U., F. Narita, and M. Narita (2015). 'Resource Reallocation and Zombie Lending in Japan in the 1990s'. *Review of Economic Dynamics* 18(4): 709–32.

La Porta, R., F. Lopez-de-Silanes, and A. Shleifer (2002). 'Government Ownership of Banks'. *Journal of Finance* 57(1): 265–301.

——— (2006). 'What Works in Securities Laws?' *Journal of Finance* 61(1): 1–32.

Laeven, L. (2001). 'Insider Lending and Bank Ownership: The Case of Russia'. *Journal of Comparative Economics* 29(2): 207–29.

Laeven, L., and R. Levine (2007). Is There a Diversification Discount in Financial Conglomerates? *Journal of Financial Economics* 85(2): 331–67.

Laeven, L., and R. Levine (2009). 'Bank Governance, Regulation and Risk Taking'. *Journal of Financial Economics* 93(2): 259–75.

Lamont, O., C. Polk, and J. Kaa-Requej (2001). 'Financial Constraints and Stock Returns'. *Review of Financial Studies* 14(2): 529–54.

Leeth, J. D., and J. A. Scott (1989). 'The Incidence of Secured Debt: Evidence from the Small Business Community'. *Journal of Financial and Quantitative Analysis* 24(3): 379–94.

Lensink, R., R. van der Molen, and S. Gangopadhyay (2003). 'Business Groups, Financing Constraints and Investment: The Case of India'. *Journal of Development Studies* 40(2): 93–119.

Levine, R. (1997). 'Financial Development and Economic Growth: Views and Agenda'. *Journal of Economic Literature* 35(2): 688–726.

———. (2005). 'Finance and Growth: Theory and Evidence'. In *Handbook of Economic Growth*, vol. 1, part A, edited by P. Aghion and S. Durlauf, 865–934. Amsterdam: Elsevier.

Levine, R., and S. Zervos (1998). 'Stock Markets, Banks, and Economic Growth'. *American Economic Review* 88(3): 537–58.

Liberti, J., and J. Sturgess (2018). 'The Anatomy of a Credit Supply Shock: Evidence from an Internal Credit Market'. *Journal of Financial and Quantitative Analysis* 53(2): 547–79.

Lindenberg, E. B., and S. A. Ross (1981). 'Tobin's q Ratio and Industrial Organization'. *Journal of Business* 54(1): 1–32.

Lowe, P. (2002). 'Credit Risk Measurement and Procyclicality'. BIS Working Paper No. 116. Bank for International Settlements, Basel.

Makin, A. (2019). 'Lessons for Macroeconomic Policy from the Global Financial Crisis'. *Economic Analysis and Policy* 64: 13–25.

Malpass, D. (2019). 'A Strong Financial Sector for a Stronger India'. World Bank Speeches And Transcripts, NITI Transforming India Lecture, Vigyan Bhavan, New Delhi.

Manaresi, F., and M. N. Pierri (2018). 'Credit Supply and Productivity Growth'. BIS Working Paper No. 711, Bank for International Settlements, Basel.

Masulis, R. W., and S. Mobbs (2011). 'Are All Inside Directors the Same? Evidence from the External Directorship Market'. *Journal of Finance* 66(3): 823–72.

McGowan, A. M., D. Andrews, and V. Millot (2018). 'The Walking Dead? Zombie Firms and Productivity Performance in OECD Countries'. *Economic Policy* 33(96): 685–736.

McKinnon, R. I. (1974). 'Money and Capital in Economic Development'. *World Development* 2(3): 87–88.

Melitz, M. J. (2003). 'The Impact of Trade on Intra-Industry Reallocations and Aggregate Industry Productivity'. *Econometrica* 71(6): 1695–1725.

Mendoza, E. G., and M. E. Terrones (2008). 'An Anatomy of Credit Booms: Evidence from Macro Aggregates and Micro Data'. NBER Working Paper No. w14049. National Bureau of Economic Research, Cambridge, MA.

Mendoza, E. G., and M. E. Terrones (2012). 'An Anatomy of Credit Booms and Their Demise'. NBER Working Paper No. w18379. National Bureau of Economic Research, Cambridge, MA.

Messai, A., and F. Jouini (2013). 'Micro and Macro Determinants of Non-performing Loan'. *International Journal of Economics and Financial Issues* 3(4): 852–60.

Meza, F., S. Pratap, and C. Urrutia (2019). 'Credit, Misallocation and Productivity Growth: A Disaggregated Analysis'. *Review of Economic Dynamics* 34: 61–86.

Mian, A., A. Sufi, and E. Verner (2017). 'Household Debt and Business Cycles Worldwide'. *Quarterly Journal of Economics* 132(4): 1755–1817.

Midrigan, V., and D. Y. Xu (2014). 'Finance and Misallocation: Evidence from Plant-level Data'. *American Economic Review* 104(2): 422–58.

Mikkelson, W., and M. Partch (1986). 'Valuation Effects of Security Offerings and the Issuance Process'. *Journal of Financial Economics* 15(1–2): 31–60.

Minsky, H. P. (1992) 'The Financial Instability Hypothesis'. Working Paper 74, Jerome Levy Economics Institute, Annandale on Hudson, New York.

Misra, B., and S. Dhal (2010). 'Pro-cyclical Management of Banks' Non-Performing Loans by the Indian Public Sector Banks'. BIS Asian Research Paper 16, Bank for International Settlements, Basel.

Mohan, T. R. (2005). 'Bank Consolidation: Issues and Evidence'. *Economic and Political Weekly* 40(12): 1151–61.

Morck, R., B. Yeung, and W. Yu (2000). 'The Information Content of Stock Markets: Why Do Emerging Markets Have Synchronous Stock Price Movements?' *Journal of Financial Economics* 58(1–2): 215–60.

Nachane, D. M, S. Ghosh, and P. Ray (2005). 'Bank Nominee Directors and Corporate Performance: Micro-evidence for India'. *Economic and Political Weekly* 40(12): 1216–23.

Nachane, D., S. Ghosh, and P. Ray (2006). 'Basel II and Bank Lending Behaviour: Some Likely Implications for Monetary Policy'. *Economic and Political Weekly* 41(11): 1053–58.

Nagarajan, D., N. Sathyanarayan, and A. Ali (2013). Non-Performing Asset Is a Threat to India Banking Sector: A Comparative Study between Priority and Non-priority Sector Lending in Public Sector Banks'. *International Journal of Advanced Research in Management and Social Sciences* 2(11): 29–43.

Nam, S. W. (1996). 'The Principal Transactions Bank System in Korea and a Search for a New Bank–Business Relationship'. In *Financial Deregulation and Integration in East Asia*, National Bureau of Economic Research–East Asian Seminar on Economics, vol. 5, edited by T. Ito and A. O. Krueger, 277–306. Chicago: University of Chicago Press.

Niinimaki, J. P. (2007). 'Evergreening in Banking'. *Journal of Financial Stability* 3(4): 368–93.

Okamura, K. (2011). '"Zombie" Banks Make "Zombie" Firms'. Available at SSRN: https://ssrn.com/abstract=1786496.

Ongena, S., J. Peydro, and N. van Horen (2015). 'Shocks Abroad, Pain at Home? Bank–Firm Level Evidence on Financial Contagion during the Recent Financial Crisis'. *IMF Economic Review* 63(4): 698–750.

Pandey, R., A. Sapre, and P. Sinha (2019). 'Loans on Loans: The Ever-greening of Bank Loans in the Indian Corporate Sector'. Working Paper, National Institute of Public Finance and Policy, New Delhi. https://www.researchgate.net/profile/Pramod-Sinha/publication/337363530_Loans_on_Loans_The_ever-greening_of_bank_loans_in_the_Indian_corporate_sector/links/5dd4040e458515cd48abd527/Loans-on-Loans-The-ever-greening-of-bank-loans-in-the-Indian-corporate-sector.pdf. Accessed in January 2021.

Pandit, B., and N. Siddharthan (2003). 'MNEs and Market Valuation of Firms: A Cross-sectional Study of Indian Electrical and Electronic Goods Manufacturing Firms'. *Applied Economics* 35 (6): 675–81.

Paul, A. (2018). 'Examining the Rise of Non-Performing Assets in India'. PRS Legislative Research, New Delhi. https://www.prsindia.org/content/examining-rise-non-performingassets-india. Accessed in January 2021.

Peek, J., and E. Rosengren (2005). 'Unnatural Selection: Perverse Incentives and the Misallocation of Credit in Japan'. *American Economic Review* 95(4): 1144–66.

Petersen, M., and R. Rajan (1994). 'The Benefits of Lending Relationships: Evidence from Small Business Data'. *Journal of Finance* 49(1): 3–37.

Phillips, P., and P. Perron (1988). 'Testing for a Unit Root in Time Series Regression'. *Biometrika* 75(2): 335–46.

Puri, M., J. Rocholl, and S. Steffen (2011). 'Global Retail Lending in the Aftermath of the US Financial Crisis: Distinguishing between Supply and Demand Effects'. *Journal of Financial Economics* 100(3): 556–78.

Qian, M., and B. Y. Yeung (2015). 'Bank Financing and Corporate Governance'. *Journal Of Corporate Finance* 32(C): 258–70.

Raheja, C. G. (2005). 'Determinants of Board Size and Composition: A Theory of Corporate Boards'. *Journal of Financial and Quantitative Analysis* 40(2): 283–306.

Rajan, R. (1992). 'Insiders and Outsiders: The Choice between Informed and Arm's-Length Debt'. *Journal of Finance* 47(4): 1367–1400.

———. (1994). 'Why Bank Credit Policies Fluctuate: A Theory and Some Evidence'. *Quarterly Journal of Economics* 109(2): 399–441.

———. (2016). 'Interesting, Profitable, and Challenging: Banking in India Today', FICCI–IBA Annual Banking Conference, Mumbai.

Rajan, R., H. Servaes, and L. Zingales (2000). 'The Cost of Diversity: The Diversification Discount and Inefficient Investment'. *Journal of Finance* 55(1): 35–80.

Rajan, R., and L. Zingales (1998). 'Financial Dependence and Growth'. *American Economic Review* 88(3): 559–86.

——— (2001). 'Financial Systems, Industrial Structure, and Growth'. *Oxford Review of Economic Policy* 17(4): 467–82.

Reddy, Y. V. (2002). 'Public Sector Banks and the Governance Challenge: Indian Experience'. Paper presented at World Bank, International Monetary Fund, and Brookings Institution Conference on 'Financial Sector Governance: The Role of the Public and Private Sectors', 18 April, New York City.

Ree, J. (2011). 'Impact of the Global Crisis on Banking Sector Soundness in Asian Low-income Countries'. IMF Working Paper WP/11/115, International Monetary Fund, Wahington, DC.

Reis, R. (2013). 'The Portuguese Slump and Crash and the Euro Crisis'. *Brookings Papers on Economic Activity* (Spring): 143–93.

Reserve Bank of India (2001). Report on Banking Sectors Reform (Narasimhan Committee II,1998). http://rbidocs.rbi.org.in/rdocs/PublicationReport/Pdfs/24157.pdf. Accessed on 21 March 2022.

——— (2008). *Report on Currency and Finance: 2006–08*, vol. 1, 4 September. https://rbi.org.in/scripts/publicationsview.aspx?id=10487. Accessed in January 2021.

——— (2014a). 'Report of the Committee to Review Governance of Boards of Banks in India'. https://rbidocs.rbi.org.in/rdocs/PublicationReport/Pdfs/BCF090514FR.pdf. Accessed on 21 March 2022.

Reserve Bank of India (2014b) 'P. J. Nayak Committee: Report of the Committee to Review Governance of Boards of Banks in India'. Mumbai.

—— (2019a). *Financial Stability Report*, issue 19. Mumbai.

—— (2019b). *Report on Trends and Progress of Banking in India, 2018–19.* 24 December. Mumbai.

—— (2020). *RBI Bulletin*, vol. 74, issue 12, December. Mumbai.

Restuccia, D., and R. Rogerson (2008). 'Policy Distortions and Aggregate Productivity with Heterogeneous Establishments'. *Review of Economic Dynamics* 11(4): 707–20.

Restuccia, D., and R. Rogerson (2013). 'Misallocation and Productivity'. *Review of Economic Dynamics* 16(1): 1–10.

Richardson, S. (2006). 'Over-investment of Free Cash Flow'. *Review of Accounting Studies* 11(2): 159–89.

Rizov, M., and X. Zhang (2014). 'Regional Disparities and Productivity in China: Evidence from Manufacturing Micro Data'. *Papers in Regional Science* 93(2): 321–39.

Robinson, J. (1952). 'The Generalization of the General Theory'. In J. Robinson, *The Rate of Interest and Other Essays*, 67–142. London: Macmillan.

Salas, V., and J. Saurina (2002). 'Credit Risk in Two Institutional Regimes: Spanish Commercial and Savings Banks'. *Journal of Financial Services Research* 22(3): 203–24.

Samantaraya, A. (2009). 'An Index to Assess the Stance of Monetary Policy in India in the Post-reform Period'. *Economic and Political Weekly* 44(20): 46–50.

Samantaraya, A. (2016). 'Procyclical Credit Growth and Bank NPAs'. *Economic and Political Weekly* 51(12): 112–19.

Samantaraya, A., K. Seenaiah, and B. Rath (2015). 'Determinants of Bank Profitability in the Post-reform Period: Evidence from India'. *Global Business Review* 16(5_suppl): 82–92.

Sapienza, P. (2004). 'The Effects of Government Ownership on Bank Lending'. *Journal of Financial Economics* 72(2): 357–84.

Sarkar, J. and Sarkar, S. (2000). 'Large Shareholder Activism in Corporate Governance in Developing Countries: Evidence from India'. *International Review of Finance* 1(3): 161–94.

Saunders, A., E. Strock, and G. Nickolaos (1990). 'Ownership Structure, Deregulation, and Bank Risk Taking'. *Journal of Finance* 45(2): 643–54.

Schiantarelli, F., and A. Sembenelli (1999). 'The Maturity Structure of Debt: Determinants and Effects on Firms' Performance? Evidence from the United Kingdom and Italy'. World Bank Policy Research Working Paper Series 1699, World Bank, Washington, DC.

Schivardi, F., E. Sette, and G. Tabellini (2017). 'Credit Misallocation during the European Financial Crisis'. Bank of Italy Temi di Discussione (Working Paper) No. 1139, Bank of Italy, Rome.

Schumpeter, Joseph A. (1911). *The Theory of Economic Development*. Cambridge, MA: Harvard University Press.

Securities and Exchange Board of India (SEBI) (1998). 'Report by Committee on Corporate Governance under the Chairmanship of Shri Kumar Mangalam', January 2000. Mumbai.

Shah, A. (2015). 'The Anatomy of the Indian Credit Boom of 2004–2008'. Working Paper, NIPFP-DEA Research Program, National Institute of Public Finance and Policy, New Delhi.

Sharpe, S. (1990). 'Asymmetric Information, Bank Lending, and Implicit Contracts: A Stylized Model of Customer Relationships'. *Journal of Finance* 45(4): 1069–87.

Shaw, E. S. (1974). 'Financial Deepening in Economic Development'. *Journal of Finance* 29(4): 1345–48.

Shyam-Sunder, L., and S. C. Myers (1999). 'Testing Static Tradeoff against Pecking Order Models of Capital Structure'. *Journal of Financial Economics* 51(2): 219–44.

Sisli-Ciamarra, E. (2012). 'Monitoring by Affiliated Bankers on Board of Directors: Evidence from Corporate Financing Outcomes'. *Financial Management* 41(3): 665–702.

Škarica, B. (2013). 'Determinants of Non-performing Loans in Central and Eastern European Countries'. EFZG Working Papers Series, No. 1307, Faculty of Economics and Business, University of Zagreb.

Smith, J. K. (1987). 'Trade Credit and Informational Asymmetry'. *Journal of Finance* 42(4): 863–72.

Song, Z., and G. L. Wu (2015). 'Identifying Capital Misallocation'. Working Paper, University of Chicago, Chicago. https://personal.ntu.edu.sg/guiying.wu/SW_Misallocation_201501.pdf. Accessed in January 2021.

Srinivasan, A., and A. Thampy (2017). The Effect of Relationships with Government-owned Banks on Cash Flow Constraints: Evidence from India'. *Journal of Corporate Finance* 46(C): 361–73.

Stein, J. (2002). 'Information Production and Capital Allocation: Decentralized versus Hierarchical Firms'. *Journal of Finance* 57(5): 1891–1921.

Stiglitz, J. E. (1989). 'Imperfect Information in the Product Market'. In *Handbook of Industrial Organization*, vol. 1, edited by R. Schmalensee and R. Willig, 769–847. Amsterdam: Elsevier.

——— (1993) 'The Role of the State in Financial Markets'. *World Bank Econimc Review* 7(suppl_1): 19–52.

Stiglitz, J. E., and A. Weiss (1981). 'Credit Rationing in Markets with Imperfect Information'. *American Economic Review* 71(3): 393–410.

——— (1983). 'Incentive Effects of Terminations: Applications to the Credit and Labor Markets'. *American Economic Review* 73(5): 912–27.

Storz, M., M. Koetter, R. Setzer, and A. Westphal (2017). 'Do We Want These Two to Tango? On Zombie Firms and Stressed Banks in Europe'. ECB Working Paper 2104, European Central Bank, Frankfurt.

Subramanian, K. (2016). 'Evergreening by Private Sector Banks'. *Mint*, 18 May. https://www.livemint.com/Opinion/JzjnrWzyv1twWY0NrDAYHJ/Evergreening-by-private-sector-banks.html. Accessed in January 2021.

Subramanian, S. (2020). 'Opinion: Reserve Bank of India's Action Too Late, Too Little—or a Ray of Hope?' *Mint*, 8 March. https://www.livemint.com/opinion/columns/reserve-bank-of-india-s-action-too-late-too-little-or-a-ray-of-hope-11583688824665.html. Accessed in January 2021.

Sufian, F. (2011). 'Financial Depression and the Profitability of the Banking Sector of the Republic of Korea: Panel Evidence on Bank-specific and Macroeconomic Determinants'. *Asia-Pacific Journal of Rural Development* 17(2): 65–92.

Tabak, B., D. Fazio, and D. Cajueiro (2011). 'The Effects of Loan Portfolio Concentration on Brazilian Banks' Return and Risk'. *Journal of Banking and Finance* 35(11): 3065–76.

Taboada, A. G. (2011). 'The Impact of Changes in Bank Ownership Structure on the Allocation of Capital: International Evidence'. *Journal of Banking and Finance* 35(10): 2528–43.

Tan, Y., Y. Huang, and W. T. Woo (2016). 'Zombie Firms and the Crowding-out of Private Investment in China'. *Asian Economic Papers* 15(3): 32–55.

Taylor, L. (1983). *Structuralist Macroeconomics: Applicable Models for the Third World*. New York: Basic Books.

Thoraneenitiyan, N., and N. Avkiran (2009). 'Measuring the Impact of Restructuring and Country-specific Factors on the Efficiency of Post-crisis East Asian Banking Systems: Integrating DEA with SFA'. *Socio-Economic Planning Sciences* 43(4): 240–52.

Titman, S., K. Wei, and F. Xie (2004). 'Capital Investments and Stock Returns'. *Journal of Financial and Quantitative Analysis* 39(4): 677–700.

Tobin, J. (1965). 'Money and Economic Growth'. *Econometrica: Journal of the Econometric Society* 33(4): 671–84.

Ueda, K. (2006). 'Banks as Coordinators of Economic Growth'. IMF Working Paper 06/264, International Monetary Fund, Washington, DC.

Van Wijnbergen, S. (1982). 'Stagflationary Effects of Monetary Stabilization Policies: A Quantitative Analysis of South Korea'. *Journal of Development Economics* 10(2): 133–69.

———. (1983a) 'Credit Policy, Inflation and Growth in a Financially Repressed Economy'. *Journal of Development Economics* 13(1–2): 45–65.

———. (1983b). 'Interest Rate Management in LDC's'. *Journal of Monetary Economics* 12(3): 433–52.

Varma, J. R. (1998). 'Indian Financial Sector Reforms: A Corporate Perspective'. *Vikalpa* 23(1): 27–38.

Vishwanathan, N. S. (2016). 'Asset Quality of Indian Banks: Way Forward'. National Conference of ASSOCHAM on 'Risk Management: Key to Asset Quality', New Delhi. https://www.rbi.org.in/scripts/BS_SpeechesView.aspx?Id=1023. Accessed on 21 March 2022.

Watanabe, W. (2010). 'Does a Large Loss of Bank Capital Cause Evergreening? Evidence from Japan'. *Journal of the Japanese and International Economies* 24(1): 116–36.

White, W. R. (2012). 'Ultra-easy Monetary Policy and the Law of Unintended Consequences'. Working Paper No. 126, Globalization and Monetary Policy Institute, Federal Reserve Bank of Dallas.

Whited, T. M., and G. Wu (2006). 'Financial Constraints Risk'. *Review of Financial Studies* 19(2): 531–59.

Williams, J., and N. Nguyen (2005). 'Financial Liberalisation, Crisis, and Restructuring: A Comparative Study of Bank Performance and Bank Governance in South East Asia'. *Journal of Banking and Finance 29* (8–9): 2119–54.

World Bank (2019). 'World Bank Open Data'. Retrieved from https://data.worldbank.org/. Accessed in January 2021.

Wurgler, J. (2000). 'Financial Markets and the Allocation of Capital'. *Journal of Financial Economics* 58(1–2): 187–214.

Wurgler, J., M. Baker, and J. C. Stein (2003). 'When Does the Market Matter? Stock Prices and the Investment of Equity-dependent Firms'. *Quarterly Journal of Economics* 118(3): 969–1005.

Xie, B. (2016). 'Does Fair Value Accounting Exacerbate the Procyclicality of Bank Lending?' *Journal of Accounting Research* 54(1): 235–74.

Yeh, Y., P. Shu, and S. Chiu (2013). 'Political Connections, Corporate Governance and Preferential Bank Loans'. *Pacific Basin Finance Journal* 21(1): 1079–1101.

Yosha, O. (1995). 'Information Disclosure Costs and the Choice of Financing Source'. *Journal of Financial Intermediation* 4(1): 3–20.

Index